Frommer's®

SAN FRANCISCO Free & dirt cheap

1st Edition

by Matthew Richard Poole

Wiley Publishing, Inc.

Published by:

Wiley Publishing, Inc.

111 River St.
Hoboken, NJ 07030-5774

ISBN 978-0-470-39905-7

Editor: Kathleen Warnock
Production Editor: Eric T. Schroeder
Cartographer: Elizabeth Puhl with Guy Ruggiero
Production by Wiley Indianapolis Composition Services
Interior design by Lissa Auciello-Brogan
Photo on p. xii by Cathy Krendel; p. 4 by Aly Bowman; photo on p. 14 courtesy of Hotel des Arts; photos on p. 34, 76, 134, 180, 206, 232, 252, by Delynn Parker and Matthew Richard Poole

For information on our other products and services or to obtain technical support, please contact our Customer Care Department within the U.S. at 800/762-2974, outside the U.S. at 317/572-3993 or fax 317/572-4002.

Wiley also publishes its books in a variety of electronic formats. Some content that appears in print may not be available in electronic formats.

Manufactured in the United States of America

5 4 3 2 1

CONTENTS

LIST OF MAPS

About the Author

Matthew Richard Poole, a native Californian who lives in San Francisco, has authored more than two dozen travel guides to California, Hawaii, and abroad. Before becoming a full-time travel writer and photographer, he worked as an English tutor in Prague, ski instructor in the Swiss Alps, and scuba instructor in Maui and Thailand. His other Frommer's titles include *Frommer's California, Frommer's Los Angeles, Frommer's San Francisco,* the *Frommer's Irreverent Guide to San Francisco,* and *Frommer's Portable Disneyland.*

Acknowledgments

I'd like to give props to my fellow frugalites who helped me put this first edition of *Free & Dirt Cheap* together: Cate Dayrit, Kristin Luna, Amanda Perez, Dan Braun, Kristine Desrochers, and the most equanimitable editor a perpetually tardy writer could ever hope for, Kathleen Warnock.

—Matthew Poole

An Invitation to the Reader

In researching this book, we discovered many wonderful places—hotels, restaurants, shops, and more. We're sure you'll find others. Please tell us about them, so we can share the information with your fellow travelers in upcoming editions. If you were disappointed with a recommendation, we'd love to know that, too. Please write to:

Frommer's San Francisco Free & Dirt Cheap, 1st Edition
Wiley Publishing, Inc. • 111 River St. • Hoboken, NJ 07030-5774

An Additional Note

Please be advised that travel information is subject to change at any time—and this is especially true of prices. We therefore suggest that you write or call ahead for confirmation when making your travel plans. The authors, editors, and publisher cannot be held responsible for the experiences of readers while traveling. Your safety is important to us, however, so we encourage you to stay alert and be aware of your surroundings. Keep a close eye on cameras, purses, and wallets, all favorite targets of thieves and pickpockets.

Free & Dirt Cheap Icons & Abbreviations

We also use four feature icons that point you to the great deals, in-the-know advice, and unique experiences that separate urban adventurers from tourists. Throughout the book, look for:

FREE Events, attractions, or experiences that cost no more than your time and a swipe of your Metrocard.

FINE PRINT The unspoken conditions or necessary preparations to experience certain free and dirt cheap events.

★ The best free and dirt cheap events, dining, shopping, living, and exploring in the city.

Special events worth marking in your calendar.

Frommers.com

Now that you have this guidebook to help you plan a great trip, visit our website at **www.frommers.com** for additional travel information on more than 4,000 destinations. We update features regularly to give you instant access to the most current trip-planning information available. At Frommers.com, you'll find scoops on the best airfares, lodging rates, and car rental bargains. You can even book your travel online through our reliable travel booking partners. Other popular features include:

- Online updates of our most popular guidebooks
- Vacation sweepstakes and contest giveaways
- Newsletters highlighting the hottest travel trends
- Podcasts, interactive maps, and up-to-the-minute events listings
- Opinionated blog entries by Arthur Frommer himself
- Online travel message boards with featured travel discussions

Other Great Guides for Your Trip:

Frommer's San Francisco

Pauline Frommer's San Francisco

Frommer's San Francisco Day by Day

Frommer's 24 Great Walks in San Francisco

Frommer's San Francisco with Kids

Open up that Golden Gate . . . which can be crossed, on foot, or by bike, without a toll. Welcome to San Francisco!

THE BEST THINGS IN LIFE ARE FREE

In a city where Butt Plug Bingo is a legitimate fundraiser, parade themes include Weapons of Ass Destruction, and starting your weekend with an Irish coffee for breakfast at the Buena Vista Café is de rigueur, it's pretty much guaranteed that you'll have a great time in San Francisco. Where else in the world will you find a giant bridge painted orange? Where it's considered good clean fun to get airborne in your car on our famously steep streets? Or where locals don't even pause for earthquakes under 5.0 on the Richter scale?

But I know what you're thinking: Whoever came up with that bogus line that the best things in life are free has never been to San Francisco. How could anyone possibly have a great time in one of the most expensive cities in the world on just a few bucks per day? This is, after all, a city whose cost of living is so high that most locals can only dream of owning a home, where shopping at Whole Foods is considered a splurge.

But if there's one thing we underpaid travel writers know well, it's how to live large and spend little. As a San Francisco local for 17 years, I've perfected the art of having a lot of fun while spending hardly any cash. Some of my advice is obvious (skip the Ritz-Carlton brunch), some comes from experience (avoid a certain dirt-cheap Indian restaurant on Polk St. unless you enjoy frequent trips to the toilet), and all of it is geared toward making sure that you will have a fantastic experience in the city regardless of your tax bracket.

This is a guide that blurs the boundaries, straddles the lines: It's for the visitor who wants a rock-bottom, dirt-cheap (but fun!) trip to San Francisco; for the potential resident who is wondering how the heck the people who live here can manage to eat, sleep, *and* enjoy themselves; and for the resident, new or longtime, who is always looking for a good bargain, a happy hour, a class or lecture, or a city program he or she hasn't discovered yet to make life in this beautiful city a little more beautiful.

Yes, $16 martini lounges and eye-poppingly expensive restaurants are plentiful in the city, but that's not where we, the locals, hang out or dine. Going out to play on a tight budget here means doing what most of its denizens do every day: eating at the city's many affordable restaurants, enjoying the wonderful parks and neighborhoods, and taking advantage of its wide variety of free or inexpensive attractions, events, and performances. And if you do as the locals do, you're far more likely to experience the hidden secrets of San Francisco that only a frugal adventurer such as yourself will discover.

The best advice we can give you about San Francisco is to just *go.* Enjoy the cool blast of salty air as you stroll across the Golden Gate. Read *Howl* in a North Beach coffeehouse. Stuff yourself with cheap dim sum in Chinatown. Browse the vintage clothing shops along Haight Street. Watch a Giants game from the nosebleed seats. Walk along the beach, pierce your nose, skate through Golden Gate Park, ride the cable cars: It's all happening every day in San Francisco, and everyone, whether filthy rich or in the red, is invited. With this guidebook in hand, a transit pass, comfortable shoes, and a yearning for urban adventures, you'll have everything a cheap (or broke) sojourner needs in order to have a fantastic time in San Francisco.

San Francisco awaits . . . and it doesn't have to cost a fortune for you to have the time of your life.

1 THE BEST OF FREE & DIRT-CHEAP SAN FRANCISCO

Sure, you can pay through the nose for dinner at our finest restaurants, or stay at world-class hotels, and get an "only in San Francisco" experience. But some of the moments, and the sights, sounds, and smells, are free as the air, or won't set you back more than a few bucks. Here are our favorite things to see, do, taste, and experience, and the experience is worth a million bucks (pretax).

1 The Best Free Only-in-San Francisco Experiences

- **A Walk across the Golden Gate Bridge.** Don your windbreaker and walking shoes and prepare for a wind-blasted, exhilarating journey across San Francisco's most famous landmark. It's simply one of those things you have to do at least once in your life. See p. 78.
- **A Stroll through Chinatown.** Chinatown is a trip. I've been through it at least 100 times, and it has never failed to entertain me. Skip the ersatz camera and luggage stores and head straight for the food markets, where a cornucopia of critters that you'll never see at Safeway sit in boxes waiting for the wok. (Is that an armadillo?) See p. 79.
- **Spending a Soul-Stirring Sunday Morning at Glide Church.** The high-spirited singers and hand-clapping worshipers at Glide turn churchgoing into a spiritual party that leaves you feeling elated, hopeful, and at one with mankind. All walks of life attend the service, which focuses not on any particular religion but on what we all have in common. It's great fun, with plenty of singing, whooping, and roof raising. See p. 82.
- **Hangin' in the Haight.** Though the power of the flower has wilted, the Haight is still, more or less, the Haight: a sort of resting home for aging hippies, dazed ex-Deadheads, skate punks, and an eclectic assortment of rather pathetic young panhandlers. Think of it as visiting a people zoo as you walk down the rows of used-clothing stores, hip boutiques, and leather shops, trying hard not to stare at that girl (at least I *think* it's a girl) with the pierced eyebrows and shaved head.
- **Cruising the Castro.** The most populated and festive street in the city isn't just for gays and lesbians. There are some great shops and inexpensive cafes—particularly **Café Flore** (p. 64) for lunch—but it's the abundance of positive energy that makes the trip to the legendary Castro District a must. And *please* make time to catch a flick (any flick, doesn't matter) at the **Castro Theatre** (p. 157), a beautiful 1930s Spanish colonial movie palace that puts all those ugly multiplexes to shame.
- **Soaking Up the Sun in Golden Gate Park.** Exploring Golden

Gate Park is a crucial part of the San Francisco experience. Its arboreal paths stretch from the Haight all the way to Ocean Beach, offering dozens of fun things to do along the way. Top sites are the **Conservancy of Flowers, Japanese Tea Garden,** and **Stow Lake,** where you can rent romantic paddle boats and feed the ducks. The best time to go is on Sunday, when portions of the park are closed to traffic (bring skates or a bike for the full effect). Toward the end of the day, head west to the beach and watch the sunset. See p. 115.

- **Hiking the Coastal Trail.** Walk the forested coastal trail from the Cliff House to the Golden Gate Bridge and you'll see why San Franciscans put up with living on a foggy fault line. Start at the parking lot just above Cliff House and head north. On a clear day you'll have incredible views of the Marin Headlands, but even on foggy days it's worth the trek to scamper over old bunkers and relish the crisp, cool air. Dress warmly. See p. 133.
- **Grazing at the Ferry Plaza Farmers' Market.** We San Franciscans take our farmers markets very seriously. Arrive hungry at the Ferry Building (Embarcadero at Market St.) on Saturday, Sunday, Tuesday, and Thursday, and join the locals as they shop for America's finest organic produce and nosh on free samples from the friendly vendors and complimentary cooking classes hosted by the city's top chefs. See p. 71.
- **Pretending to be a guest at the Palace or Fairmont hotels.** You may not be staying the night, but you can certainly feel like a million bucks when you sit awhile to people-watch in the public spaces at the **Palace Hotel** (2 New Montgomery St.). The extravagant creation of banker "Bonanza King" Will Ralston in 1875, the Palace Hotel has one of the grandest rooms in the city: the **Garden Court.** Running a close second is the magnificent lobby at Nob Hill's **Fairmont Hotel & Tower** (950 Mason St.; p. 247)—it's so over-the-top ornate it will blow your mind.
- **Meandering along the Marina's Golden Gate Promenade.** There's something about walking along the promenade that just feels right. The combination of beach, bay, boats, Golden Gate views, and clean, cool breezes is good for the soul. See p. 122.
- **Climbing the Filbert Street Steps.** San Francisco is a city of

stairs, and the crème de la crème of steps is on Filbert Street between Sansome Street and the east side of Telegraph Hill. The terrain is so steep here that Filbert Street becomes Filbert Steps, a 377-step descent that wends its way through flower gardens and some of the city's oldest and most varied housing. It's a beautiful walk down, and great exercise going up. See p. 80.

2 The Best Dirt-Cheap Only-in-San Francisco Experiences

- **Watching the San Francisco Giants play at AT&T Park.** If it's baseball season, then you *must* spend an afternoon or evening watching the National League's Giants lose at one of the finest ballparks in America. For only $10 you can buy a bleacher-seat ticket on the day of a game. Even cheaper (like *free*!), you can always join the "knot-hole gang" at the Portwalk (located behind right field) to catch a free glimpse of the game through cut-out portholes into the ballpark. Even if the season's over, you can still take a guided tour of the stadium. See p. 102.
- **Catching an Early-Morning Cable Car.** Skip the boring California line and take the Powell-Hyde cable car down to Fisherman's Wharf—the ride is worth the wait. When you reach the top of Nob Hill, grab the rail in one hand and hold the camera with the other, because you're about to see a view of the bay that'll make you a believer. It's $5 a ride . . . but if no one collects your fare, count it as a freebie.
- **Visiting the Museum of Modern Art.** Ever since the SFMOMA opened in 1995, it has been the best place to go for a quick dose of culture. If you go on the first Tuesday of the month, admission is free. There's also no admission charge after 6pm on Thursdays. Start by touring the museum, then head for the gift shop (oftentimes more entertaining than the rotating exhibits). Have a light lunch at Caffè Museo, where the food is a vast improvement over most museums' mush, and then finish the trip with a stroll through the Yerba Buena Gardens across from the museum (the Martin Luther King, Jr., memorial is particularly inspiring). See p. 99.

Best Sort-Of Splurge That's Completely Worth It

Alcatraz Island: Even if you loathe tourist attractions, you'll dig Alcatraz. Just looking at The Rock from across the bay is enough to give you the heebie-jeebies—and the park rangers have put together an excellent audio tour. Actual admission to the park is free . . . the catch is that you have to pay to ride the boat there. But it's a very cool ride. You'll spend about $26 for the trip, unless you're a senior or in a family group (two adults, two children). See p. 105.

- **Starting the Day with North Beach Coffee.** One of the most pleasurable smells of San Francisco is the aroma of roasted coffee beans wafting down Columbus Avenue in the early morning. Start the day with a cup of Viennese on a sidewalk table at **Caffè Grecco** (423 Columbus Ave.; ✆ **415/397-6261**), followed by a walk down Columbus Avenue to the bay.
- **Sipping a Cocktail in the Clouds.** Some of the best ways to view the city are from top-floor lounges in the high-end hotels such as the **Sir Francis Drake** (450 Powell St.; ✆ **415/392-7755**), the **Grand Hyatt San Francisco** (345 Stockton St.; ✆ **415/398-1234**), and the **Mark Hopkins InterContinental** (1 Nob Hill; ✆ **415/392-3434**). Drinks aren't cheap, but it beats paying for a dinner. Besides, if you nurse your drink (or order a soda), the combo of atmosphere, surroundings, and view is a bargain.
- **Skating through Golden Gate Park on a Weekend.** C'mon! When's the last time you went skating? And if you've never tried skating before, there's no better place to learn than on the wide, flat main street through Golden Gate Park, which is closed to vehicles on weekends. You can rent skates for cheap at **Golden Gate Park Skate & Bike.** See p. 132.

3 The Best Dirt-Cheap Dining in San Francisco

- **Best Value.** Crepes. Yes, crepes. Cheap crepes that are bigger than your head and filled with everything from cheddar cheese and onions to spinach, ham, eggplant, pesto, tomatoes, roasted peppers, smoked salmon, mushrooms, sausage, and even scallops. **Crepes on Cole** (100 Carl St.; ✆ **415/664-1800;** p. 67), in the Haight, makes them for about $7, including a side of home fries. **Ti Couz** (3108 16th St.; ✆ **415/252-7373;** p. 63), in the Mission, makes even better crepes, but they are a bit more expensive.

- **Best Grease Pit.** Anyone who's a connoisseur of funky little ethnic eateries will love **Tú Lan** (8 Sixth St.; ✆ **415/626-0927;** p. 45), one of the greasiest little holes-in-the-wall in the city. But even Julia Child was a fan of their Vietnamese imperial rolls. For late-night noshing on tomato beef with noodles and house-special chow mein, **Sam Wo** (813 Washington St.; ✆ **415/982-0596;** p. 47) is my favorite Chinatown dive.
- **Best Pizza by the Slice.** It's a tie: The best by-the-slice experience in North Beach is **Golden Boy Pizza** (542 Green St.; ✆ **415/982-9738;** p. 48), where everyone watches with envy as you stroll down the sidewalk while savoring the doughy square of deliciousness. Equally good is **ZA Pizza** (1919 Hyde St.; ✆ **415/771-3100;** p. 52), in Russian Hill, a hugely popular by-the-slice neighborhood pizza joint.
- **Best Burritos.** It's impossible to deem one burrito the king in this town, but there's a reason people come from across town to line up at **Taquerias La Cumbre** (515 Valencia St.; ✆ **415/863-8205**), in the Mission. See p. 62.
- **Best Place for Picnic Supplies.** If you're anywhere near North Beach, head to San Francisco's legendary **Molinari Delicatessen** (373 Columbus Ave.; ✆ **415/421-2337;** p. 73), which offers an eye-popping selection of cold salads, cheeses, and sandwiches packaged and priced to go (the Italian subs are big enough for two hearty appetites). Another good sunny-day option is a picnic on Marina Green, but first stop by the **Marina Safeway** (15 Marina Blvd.; ✆ **415/563-4946**) to pick up fresh-baked breads, gourmet cheeses, and other foodstuffs (including fresh cracked crab when in season).
- **Best Coffee Shop or Cafe.** With all the wonderfully unique coffee shops throughout this cafe town, there can be no one winner. I do, however, love the authentic atmosphere at **Mario's Bohemian Cigar Store** (566 Columbus Ave.; ✆ **415/362-0536;** p. 50) and **Caffe Trieste** (601 Vallejo Ave.; ✆ **415/392-6739;** p. 173).

- **Best Happy Hour Spread.** At the top of Nob Hill inside the Fairmont Hotel is the beloved **Tonga Room** (950 Mason St.; ✆ **415/772-5278**). Every weekday from 5 to 7pm both locals and tourists rub elbows while getting stuffed at the all-you-can-eat buffet (chicken wings, chow mein, pot stickers, and much more) for $9.50. See p. 40.
- **Best Burger.** For the price, **Mo's Gourmet Burgers** (1322 Grant Ave.; ✆ **415/788-3779**) in North Beach is hard to beat, but everyone has a different opinion on this subject. See p. 50.
- **Best Dim Sum.** You could dine on dim sum for hours at **Lichee Garden** (1416 Powell St.; ✆ **415/397-2290**) and not rack up a bill over $20 per person. You'll be wowed by the variety of dumplings and mysterious dishes. It's a favorite even among Chinatown residents. See p. 46.

4 The Best Low-Cost Lodging in San Francisco

- **Best Overall Value.** This is a tough choice. The **Marina Inn** (3110 Octavia St.; ✆ **800/274-1420;** p. 29) is one of the best low-priced hotels in San Francisco, but its Marina location puts it far from the downtown scene. The **San Remo Hotel** (2237 Mason St.; ✆ **800/352-REMO** [352-7366]; p. 26) has an ideal North Beach location, friendly staff, and low prices, but the bathrooms are all shared. The best downtown deals are the **Hotel des Arts** (447 Bush St.; ✆ **800/956-4322;** p. 23) and the groovy **Mosser** (54 Fourth St.; ✆ **800/227-3804;** p. 25).
- **Best Cheap Hotel with Free Parking.** The peach-colored, Spanish-style stucco **Marina Motel** (2576 Lombard St.; ✆ **800/346-6118**) has far more old-fashioned character than the other Marina District motels. See p. 30.
- **Best View.** Hard to believe but true: You can get bay views in San Francisco for a mere $20-and-change nightly at the **Hostelling International San Francisco—Fisherman's Wharf** (Fort Mason, Bldg. 240; ✆ **415/771-7277**). See p. 28.
- **Best for Families. Cow Hollow Motor Inn & Suites'** (2190 Lombard St.; ✆ **415/921-5800**) one- and two-bedroom suites have full kitchens and dining areas, as well as antique furnishings and surprisingly tasteful decor. See p. 29.

San Francisco Top 10 Best-Kept Free & Cheap Secrets

1. Tickets to the de Young Museum ain't cheap (unless you go on the first Tues of each month, which is a free day), but you can always climb to the top of the museum's 144-foot tower for free. The panoramic views from the observation floor span much of the Bay Area.
2. The Boudin Demonstration Bakery at the Wharf has a nifty little free museum hidden upstairs that explains the symbiotic relationship between San Francisco and its unique sourdough loaf. The story and science behind the "mother dough" is fascinating, as is their demonstration—bakery visitors can watch the entire baking process from a 30-foot observation window along Jefferson Street.
3. Hard to find, but worth the effort, is a funky little bar in North Beach called Specs'. It looks like a maritime museum that imploded, with walls covered with historically eclectic seafaring oddities brought back by long-dead sailors who dropped in between voyages (dried whale penis, anyone?).
4. If you log onto **www.calacademy.org/webcams/penguins**, you can see what the California Academy of Sciences' penguins are up to via their PenguinCams, which offer three real-time views of the new penguin exhibit. It's mesmerizing.
5. If you want to watch a Giants game for free, you can join the "knothole gang" at the Portwalk (located behind right field) to catch a free glimpse of the game through cut-out portholes

- **Best for a Budget Romantic Rendezvous.** If the mini-penthouse at the **San Remo Hotel** (2237 Mason St.; ✆ **800/352-7366**) is available, book it: You won't find a more romantic place to stay in San Francisco for so little money. See p. 26.
- **Best Moderately Priced Hotel.** I've received nothing but kudos from satisfied guests who stayed at the **Golden Gate**

into the ballpark. In the spirit of sharing, Portwalk peekers are encouraged to take in only an inning or two before giving way to fellow fans.

6. Free steak sandwiches! Well, kinda. You have to buy at least one drink at Morton's Steakhouse (400 Post St. at Powell St.; ✆ 415/986-5830). Every Monday through Friday from 5-7pm they host a Carnivore Happy Hour, where you can stuff yourself on all-you-can-eat filet mignon sandwiches at the bar. Ask any local in-the-know—it's the best happy hour deal in the city.
7. Every second Thursday of the month you can watch free movies at Dolores Park, located at 20th and Dolores streets. Bring a blanket and even your dog if you'd like, as well as a little cash to buy the world's best tamales from the Tamale Lady.
8. The Good Vibrations sex-toy shop is worth visiting just to see their Antique Vibrator Museum. Who knew that vibrators have been around since 1869 and were prescribed by physicians to treat "hysteria?" Fascinating.
9. If you're looking for a buddy to ride bikes with, the 511 Bike Buddy Ridematch Service will pair you up with someone at your skill level at no cost. Log onto **www.ridematch.511.org**, click on "Bicycling," and then click on Bike Buddy Matching.
10. If city life is stressing you out, take some free tai chi lessons. Log onto **www.sfnpc.org/taichi** for a list of places and times that the free lessons are offered. There's no need to register; just dress comfortably and show up.

Hotel (775 Bush St.; ✆ **800/835-1118**). Just 2 blocks from Union Square, this 1913 Edwardian hotel is a real charmer and a fantastic value. See p. 19.

- **Best Budget B&B.** The 28-room **Hayes Valley Inn** (417 Gough St.; ✆ **800/930-7999**), an Edwardian-style B&B, is a find. Okay, so you'll have to share the very clean toilets and showers, but the price is right. See p. 30.

The Hotel des Arts (p. 23) features "Painted Rooms," each individually decorated by an emerging local artist.

2 CHEAP SLEEPS

You can score some amazing lodging bargains in San Francisco. With a little research and a lot of walking around, I managed to find numerous lodgings that are both inexpensive enough to be included in this guidebook (every place listed offers at least some room at under $100 per night) and respectable enough that even a cheap snob like me would be willing to stay there.

Of course, there's a catch. You can kiss mints-on-your-pillow luxuries goodbye, because most budget hotels keep their prices down by offering the bare essentials—phone, TV, bed, and bathroom—and in the Union Square district, even a private bathroom is considered an upgrade. One option is to avoid the heavily touristed areas such as Union Square and Fisherman's Wharf, and instead hang your hat at the city's outlying districts such as the Marina and take a bus into more central areas. Not only are the room rates far lower (and the chances of having your own bathroom doubled), but also the clientele is usually more, shall we say, "polished" as well.

We give the listed "rack rates" for the hotels in this chapter, but by all means look for better deals on the hotels' websites, as well as the major booking sites and packagers.

We also include several hostels in this chapter (see section below), depending on just how cheap you are willing to sleep; if you require your own room, then you'll pay more than for a room shared with other travelers-on-the-cheap. (Remember, too, that many hostels also offer private rooms.)

The cheapest option of all, of course, is to couch-surf; but if you don't have friends, relatives, friends-of-friends, or some other connection for a free roof over your head, start here and plan accordingly.

I'll Trade Ya . . .

It's sort of like leaving your keys in the basket by the door . . . but different. You swap apartments instead of partners. Somebody who's as frugal and/or broke as you offers his or her apartment for a few days in exchange for your apartment. It's usually done by online classifieds such as craigslist.org (**www.sfbay.craigslist.org/sfc/swp/**). Here's a good one: "6br - Gorgeous house in Paris (FRANCE) to swap for House in San Francisco. My parents own a very large gorgeous house in downtown Paris (14th arrondissement) near a park. (6 bedrooms, 3.5 bathrooms, terrace, huge living room, kitchen, dining room. . . . They would like to lend their house for 2 to 3 weeks in exchange for a place in San Francisco of similar size. The date would be approximatively [sic] August 12th to Sept 3rd 2009."

Paris, here I come!

HOSTEL? THEY WERE VERY NICE TO ME . . .

Hostels are not just for Europe! If you did the backpack/Eurailpass thing at some point, you know about hostels, which at their best can be homey places where you meet nice people, get great information, and find a free or dirt-cheap breakfast. At their worst, they are noisy flophouses. (And we're not even talking about those horror films *Hostel* and *The Saw*!) You don't even have to be a yout' to stay at a hostel (most are not called "youth hostels" anymore). Other misconceptions we can correct: You don't need to bring your own bedding, and most hostels no longer have a daytime "lockout" period, but are accessible 24/7. (But you should bring a lock, since most hostels provide lockers or other storage space you can secure.)

If you haven't stayed at a hostel, here's what you can expect: Most offer shared rooms (either same sex or mixed; Hostelling International hostels have only single-sex dorm rooms) with shared bathrooms, usually for less than (sometimes a *lot* less than) $50 a night; prices can vary by season. Some hostels offer private rooms for one, two, or three people, or en suite bathrooms, with the price going up accordingly, though the top end for private rooms is still usually well under $100.

HI hostels offer free breakfast; the **Green Tortoise** (p. 27) offers free breakfast *and* free dinner 3 nights a week. Most hostels have a communal kitchen/dining area, free Wi-Fi, a lounge, lockers or other locked storage, and free or low-cost organized activities, ranging from local tours, movies, and pub crawls, to day or overnight trips. The staff members are usually pretty good at helping you plan individual activities based on your interests. Many hostels also offer free or discounted airport/train station/bus station pickup, if you're arriving without a car.

There are several recommendable (and *non*recommendable) places in San Francisco, both HI hostels and private hostels or "backpackers." You can count on clean, safe, and well-managed properties with a Hostelling International hostel, all of which are part of an international nonprofit that "promote[s] international understanding of the world and its people through hostelling." You don't have to be a member of HI to stay, but you do get a slight discount if you are a member.

There are three HI hostels in San Francisco proper (in City Center, Downtown, and Fisherman's Wharf), and several more within public transit or driving distance if you're looking for a cheap overnight trip.

For information on how to join **Hostelling International USA** (which also gives you membership in all international HI hostels), visit **www.hiusa.org**. Membership is free if you're 17 or under, $28 annually for people 18 to 54. As a member, you can make prepaid reservations at HI hostels, and are eligible for a lot of discounts, from long-distance calling to bus travel to organized tours.

Private hostels can be just as inexpensive as, and sometimes more laid-back than, HI places. You may stay in a co-ed dorm room, find a bar on premises, and find a bulletin board offering rides or temp jobs. You may find a noisier, more partying crowd at a backpacker, which could be a plus or minus, depending on what you're looking for.

You'll find a comprehensive listing of hostels, both HI and backpacker (as well as budget hotels and guesthouses), at **www.hostels.com**, which claims to list "every hostel, everywhere." The website gives properties a "satisfaction rating," based on user reviews (which you can read). Granted, like most Internet reviews, they can be artificially inflated, but you can at least get an idea of what to expect and, if you like it, make reservations through that website, or go directly to the hostel's site.

In addition to the hostels we list in this chapter (HI and Green Tortoise, as well as Elements), some of the other top-rated hostels in the San Francisco area at press time include these:

- **Pacific Tradewinds Backpacker Hostel,** 680 Sacramento St. (✆ **888/SFHOSTEL** [734-6783]; www.pactradewinds.com), selected as the number one hostel in the U.S. by Hostelworld.com in 2007. Prices start at $24 per night ($23 if booked online), in co-ed dorms. BART: Montgomery St.; Bus: 15.
- **USA Hostels San Francisco,** 711 Post St. (✆ **877/483-2950;** www.usahostels.com), features an "all you can make" pancake breakfast daily, a game room, and an on-site laundry. Rates start from $25 ($24 if booked online) for single-sex and co-ed dorms, and they also offer private rooms with bathroom starting at $75 ($72 online). BART: Powell St.
- The **Dakota Hostel,** 606 Post St. (✆ **415/931-7475**), and the **Adelaide Hostel and Hotel,** 5 Isadora Duncan Lane, at Post and Taylor (✆ **877/359-1915;** www.adelaidehostel.com), are owned by the same management, and located near each other, though the Dakota gets warmer reviews on Hostels.com. In a landmark 1914 building, the

Dakota's rooms all have private bathrooms, with rates ranging from $28 and up for a four-bed room to $75 and up for a single room. The Adelaide offers both single-sex and co-ed dorm rooms from $23, with single, twin, and double en suite rooms starting from $45, going up to about $75. BART: Powell St.

1 Union Square

The Cornell Hotel de France Its quirks make this small French-style hotel more charming than many others in this price range. Pass the office, where a few faces will glance in your direction and smile, and embark on a ride in the old-fashioned elevator (we're talking *seriously* old-school here) to get to your basic room. Each floor is dedicated to a French painter and decorated with reproductions. Rooms are all plain and comfortable, with desks and chairs, and are individually and simply decorated. Smoking is not allowed. The full American breakfast included in the rate is served in the cool, cavern-like provincial basement restaurant, **Jeanne d'Arc.** Union Square is just a few blocks away.

715 Bush St. (btw Powell and Mason sts.), San Francisco, CA 94108. ✆ **800/232-9698** or 415/421-3154. Fax 415/399-1442. www.cornellhotel.com. 55 units. $85–$155 double. Rates include full American breakfast. AE, DC, DISC, MC, V. Parking across the street $17. Bus: 2, 3, 4, 30, or 45. Cable car: Powell-Hyde or Powell-Mason line. **Amenities:** Restaurant; computer w/Internet in lobby. *In room:* TV, dataport, Wi-Fi (for a fee), hair dryer.

The Golden Gate Hotel San Francisco's stock of small hotels in historic turn-of-the-20th-century buildings includes some real gems, and the Golden Gate Hotel is one of them. It's 2 blocks north of Union Square and 2 blocks down (literally) from the crest of Nob Hill, with cable car stops at the corner for easy access to Fisherman's Wharf and Chinatown. The city's theaters and best restaurants are also within walking distance. But the best thing about the 1913 Edwardian hotel—which definitely has a B&B feel—is that it's family run: John and Renate Kenaston and daughter Gabriele are hospitable innkeepers who take obvious pleasure in making their guests comfortable. Each individually decorated room has recently been repainted and carpeted and has handsome antique furnishings (plenty of wicker) from the early 1900s, quilted bedspreads, and fresh flowers. Request a room with a claw-foot tub if you enjoy a good, hot soak. Afternoon

CHEAP SLEEPS IN SAN FRANCISCO

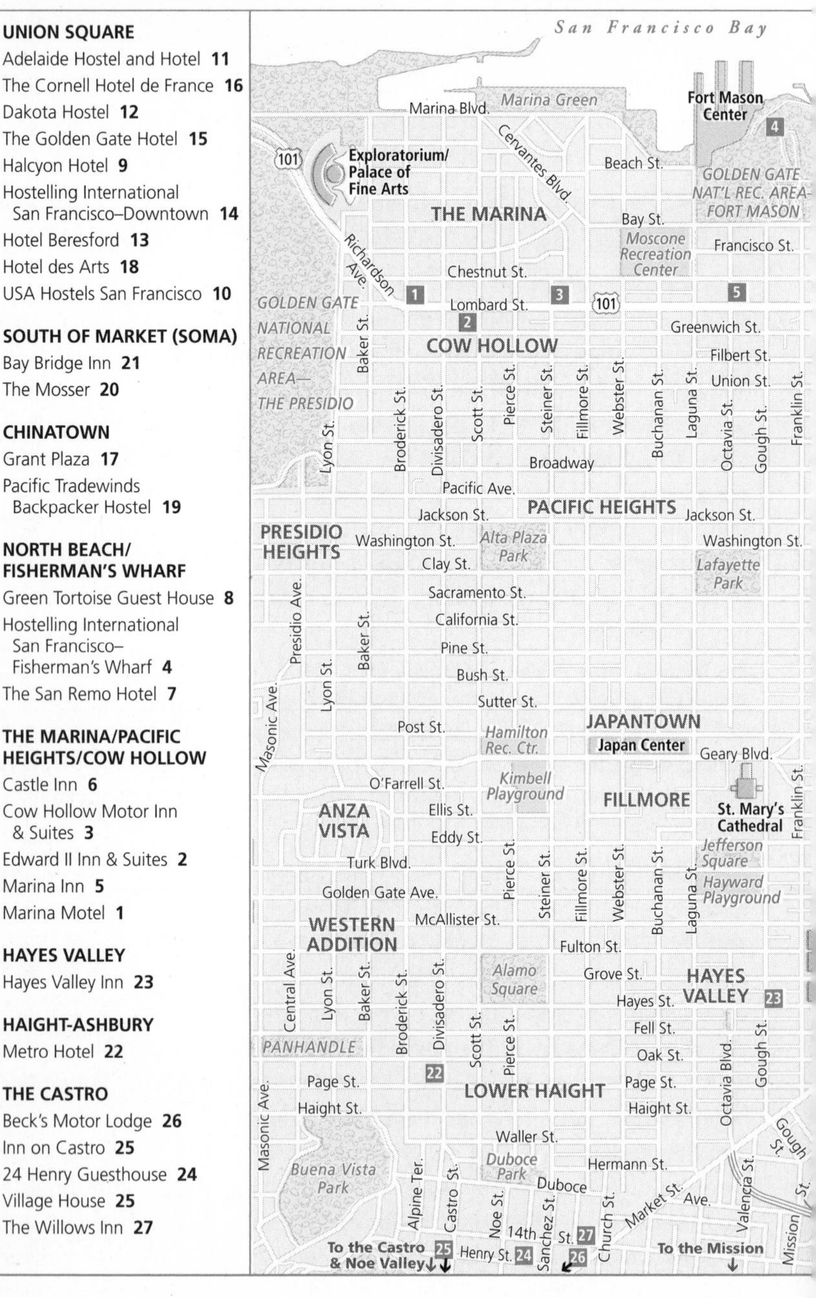

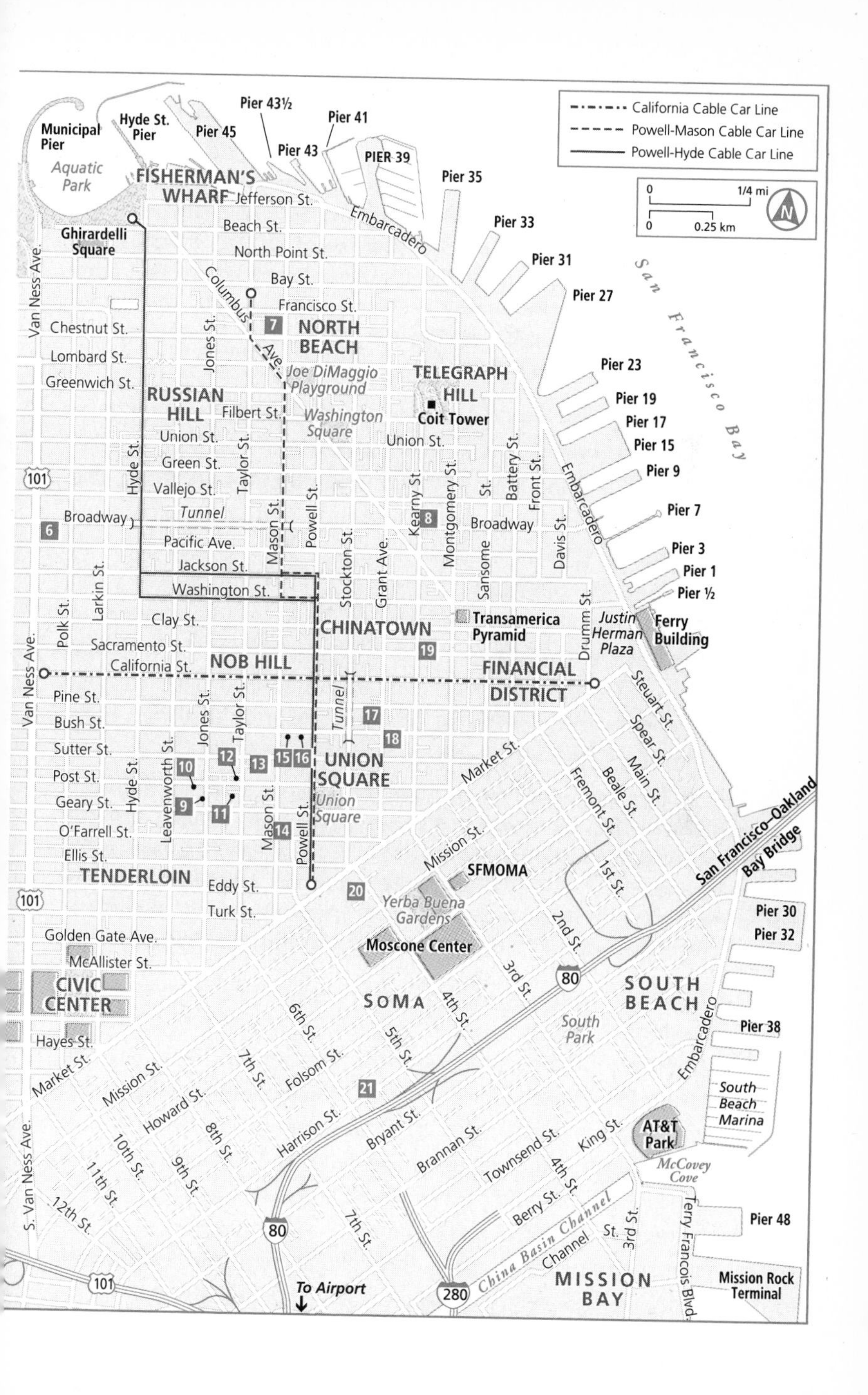
California Cable Car Line
Powell-Mason Cable Car Line
Powell-Hyde Cable Car Line
0
1/4 mi
0
0.25 km
N
San Francisco Bay
Municipal Pier
Hyde St. Pier
Pier 45
Pier 43½
Pier 41
Pier 43
PIER 39
Pier 35
Pier 33
Pier 31
Pier 27
Pier 23
Pier 19
Pier 17
Pier 15
Pier 9
Pier 7
Pier 3
Pier 1
Pier ½
Aquatic Park
FISHERMAN'S WHARF
Ghirardelli Square
NORTH BEACH
TELEGRAPH HILL
Coit Tower
RUSSIAN HILL
Joe DiMaggio Playground
Washington Square
CHINATOWN
Transamerica Pyramid
Justin Herman Plaza
Ferry Building
NOB HILL
FINANCIAL DISTRICT
UNION SQUARE
Union Square
TENDERLOIN
SFMOMA
Yerba Buena Gardens
Moscone Center
CIVIC CENTER
SoMa
SOUTH BEACH
South Park
San Francisco–Oakland Bay Bridge
Pier 30
Pier 32
Pier 38
South Beach Marina
AT&T Park
McCovey Cove
Pier 48
Mission Rock Terminal
MISSION BAY
China Basin Channel
To Airport
Jefferson St.
Beach St.
North Point St.
Bay St.
Francisco St.
Chestnut St.
Lombard St.
Greenwich St.
Filbert St.
Union St.
Green St.
Vallejo St.
Broadway
Tunnel
Pacific Ave.
Jackson St.
Washington St.
Clay St.
Sacramento St.
California St.
Pine St.
Bush St.
Sutter St.
Post St.
Geary St.
O'Farrell St.
Ellis St.
Eddy St.
Turk St.
Golden Gate Ave.
McAllister St.
Hayes St.
Van Ness Ave.
S. Van Ness Ave.
Polk St.
Larkin St.
Hyde St.
Leavenworth St.
Jones St.
Taylor St.
Mason St.
Powell St.
Stockton St.
Grant Ave.
Kearny St.
Montgomery St.
Sansome St.
Battery St.
Front St.
Davis St.
Drumm St.
Columbus Ave.
Embarcadero
Steuart St.
Spear St.
Main St.
Beale St.
Fremont St.
1st St.
2nd St.
3rd St.
4th St.
5th St.
6th St.
7th St.
8th St.
9th St.
10th St.
11th St.
12th St.
Market St.
Mission St.
Howard St.
Folsom St.
Harrison St.
Bryant St.
Brannan St.
Townsend St.
King St.
Berry St.
Channel St.
Terry Francois Blvd.
101
80
280
6
7
8
9
10
11
12
13
14
15
16
17
18
19
20
21

tea is served daily from 4 to 7pm, and guests are welcome to use the house fax and computer with wireless Internet free of charge.

775 Bush St. (btw Powell and Mason sts.), San Francisco, CA 94108. ✆ **800/835-1118** or 415/392-3702. Fax 415/392-6202. www.goldengatehotel.com. 25 units, 14 with bathroom. $85–$105 double without bathroom; $150 double with bathroom. Rates include continental breakfast and afternoon tea. AE, DC, MC, V. Self-parking $20. Bus: 2, 4, 30, 38, or 45. Cable car: Powell-Hyde or Powell-Mason line (1 block east). BART: Powell and Market. **Amenities:** Access to health club 1 block away; activities desk; laundry service/dry cleaning next door. *In room:* TV, dataport, free Wi-Fi, hair dryer, iron upon request.

Halcyon Hotel This small four-story brick building is a penny pincher's dream come true, the kind of place where you'll find everything you need, yet won't have to pay through the nose to get it. The small but clean studio guest rooms are equipped with microwave ovens, refrigerators, flatware and utensils, toasters, alarm clocks, coffeemakers and coffee, phones with free local calls, mail delivery, and voice mail—all the comforts of home in the heart of Union Square. A coin-operated washer and dryer are in the basement, along with free laundry soap and irons. The managers are usually on hand to offer friendly, personal service, making this option a great deal for cheap lodgings. Be sure to ask about special rates for weekly stays.

649 Jones St. (btw Geary and Post sts.), San Francisco, CA 94102. ✆ **800/627-2396** or 415/929-8033. Fax 415/441-8033. www.halcyonsf.com. 25 units. $79–$99 double year-round; $450–$600 weekly. AE, DC, DISC, MC, V. Parking garage nearby $14–$16 per day. Bus: 2, 3, 4, 9, 27, or 38. Pets accepted. **Amenities:** Access to nearby health club; concierge; tour desk; laundry facilities; free fax available in lobby. *In room:* TV, dataport, kitchen, fridge, coffeemaker, hair dryer, iron, voice mail.

Hotel Beresford The small, less expensive sister property of the Hotel Beresford Arms, the seven-floor Hotel Beresford is another good, moderately priced choice near Union Square. Perks are the same: satellite TV, phone, radio, private bathrooms with either a tub or a shower, and stocked fridges. The guest rooms are decorated in Victorian style and well kept, with plenty of personal touches you don't often find in a budget hotel. Rates even include continental breakfast. The on-site **White Horse Tavern,** a quaint replica of an old English pub, serves dinner Tuesday through Saturday and is a favorite for folks who like less trendy hullabaloo with their meal.

635 Sutter St. (near Mason St.), San Francisco, CA 94102. ✆ **800/533-6533** or 415/673-9900. Fax 415/474-0449. www.beresford.com. 114 units. $89–$165 double.

Cheap Hotel Chains

If all the recommendations in this chapter are booked and you don't mind going generic, you can try one of the following chains, which all have hotels either in the city or nearby: **Best Western** (✆ 800/528-1234), **Comfort Inn** (✆ 800/228-5150), **Days Inn** (✆ 800/325-2525), **Doubletree Hotels** (✆ 800/222-TREE [222-8733]), **Econo Lodges** (✆ 800/55-ECONO [553-2666]), **Holiday Inn** (✆ 800/HOLIDAY [465-4329]), **Howard Johnson** (✆ 800/654-2000), **La Quinta Motor Inns** (✆ 800/531-5900), **Motel 6** (✆ 800/466-8356), **Ramada** (✆ 800/2-RAMADA [272-6232]), **Rodeway Inns** (✆ 800/228-2000), **Super 8** (✆ 800/800-8000), and **Travelodge** (✆ 800/255-3050).

Extra person $10. Rates include continental breakfast. Children 11 and under stay free in parent's room. AE, DC, DISC, MC, V. Valet parking $20. Bus: 2, 3, 4, 30, 38, or 45. Cable car: Powell-Hyde line (1 block east). **Amenities:** Restaurant/pub; access to nearby health club ($10 a day); free high-speed Internet access in kiosk in lobby; laundry service. *In room:* TV, dataport, minibar, hair dryer upon request, iron.

★ **Hotel des Arts** While this bargain find has the same floor plan as San Francisco's numerous other Euro-style hotels—small lobby, narrow hallways, cramped rooms—the owners of the des Arts have made an obvious effort to distance themselves from the competition by including a visually stimulating dose of artistic license throughout the hotel. The lobby, for example, hosts a rotating art gallery featuring contemporary works by emerging local artists and is outfitted with groovy furnishings, while the guest rooms are soothingly situated with quality furnishings and tasteful accouterments. There's one suite that can sleep up to four persons at no additional charge. You'll love the lively location as well: right across the street from the entrance to Chinatown and 2 blocks from Union Square. There's even a French brasserie right downstairs. Considering the price (rooms with a very clean shared bathroom start at $59), quality, and location, it's quite possibly the best budget hotel in the city. ***Tip:*** Log onto the hotel's website to check out the "Painted Rooms" designed by artists, then call the hotel directly to book your favorite.

447 Bush St. (at Grant St.), San Francisco, CA 94108. ✆ **800/956-4322** or 415/956-3232. Fax 415/956-0399. www.sfhoteldesarts.com. 51 units, 26 with private bathroom. $79-$159 double with bathroom; $59-$79 double without bathroom. Rates include continental breakfast. AE, DC, MC, V. Nearby parking $18. Cable car: Powell-Hyde and Powell-Mason lines. **Amenities:** 24-hr. concierge, fax, and copy services; laundry and valet service. *In room:* TV, 2-line direct-dial telephone w/dataport and voice mail, minifridge and microwave in many rooms, hair dryer, iron/ironing board.

SUPER-CHEAP SLEEPS

Hostelling International San Francisco-Downtown For less than $30 per person, you can reexperience dorm life in an old San Francisco–style building in the heart of Union Square. Occupying five sparsely decorated floors, rooms here are simple and clean. Each has two or three bunk beds with linens, a sink, a closet, and lockers (bring your own locks or buy one at the front desk). Although most private rooms share hallway bathrooms, a few have private facilities. Prices are per person in the dorm rooms and per double bed in the private room. Among several common rooms is a large kitchen-style room with refrigerator space, toasters, and a microwave, but no stoves or ranges. There are laundry facilities in the building and a helpful information desk where you can book tours and sightseeing trips. The hostel is open 24 hours, and reservations are essential, especially during the summer.

312 Mason St. (btw Geary and O'Farrell sts.), San Francisco, CA 94102. ✆ **888/GOHIUSA** (464-4872) or 415/788-5604. Fax 415/788-3023. www.sfhostels.com. 105 units (86 private, 180 dorm beds). Hostelling members $27-$29 per person in dorm; nonmembers $30-$32 per person in dorm; hostelling members $79-$89 in private room with shared bathroom; nonmembers $72-$82 in private room with shared bathroom; hostelling members $89-$99 in private room with private bathroom; nonmembers $92-$102 in private room with private bathroom. Rates include continental breakfast. AE, DC, DISC, MC, V. Bus: 2, 3, 4, 30, 38, or 45. **Amenities:** Free Wi-Fi; Internet access at kiosk for a small fee; laundry facilities; TV lounge; limited kitchen. *In room:* Lockers, no phone.

2 South of Market (SoMa)

Bay Bridge Inn The South of Market region is woefully short on budget accommodations, which is why we give the Bay Bridge Inn only a nominal recommendation. The only reason you might want to stay in this part of town is if you're here for a convention (the Moscone Convention Center and Museum of Modern Art are a few blocks away), you're a major Giants fan (AT&T Park is down the street), or you're a serious party hound who prefers to stay within stumbling distance of SoMa's club scene. The rooms score zero points for character, but they're quite clean and in good condition (think of it as a privately owned Motel 6). Queen-size beds are standard, and rooms with king-size beds run an extra $25. Parking is free (there's $25 a night saved), as are wireless Internet access, local calls, pastries, and coffee, and buses to nearly every corner of the city depart from the nearby Transbay Terminal.

966 Harrison St. (btw Fifth and Sixth sts.), San Francisco, CA 94107. ✆ **415/397-0657.** www.baybridgeinn.com. Fax 415/495-5117. 22 units. $85–$150 double. AE, DISC, MC, V. Free parking. Bus: 10, 20, 30, 42, 45, 50, 60, 70, or 80. *In room:* A/C, TV, free Wi-Fi.

★ **The Mosser** "Hip on the Cheap" might best sum up the Mosser, a highly atypical budget hotel that incorporates Victorian architecture with modern interior design. It originally opened in 1913 as a luxury hotel only to be dwarfed by the far more modern high-rise hotels that surround it. But a multimillion-dollar renovation a few years back transformed this aging charmer into a sophisticated, stylish, and surprisingly affordable SoMa lodging. Guest rooms are replete with original Victorian flourishes—bay windows and hand-carved moldings—that juxtapose well with the contemporary custom-designed furnishings, granite showers, stainless steel fixtures, ceiling fans, Frette linens, double-paned windows, and modern electronics. The least expensive rooms are quite small and share a bathroom, but are an incredible deal for such a central location. The hotel's restaurant, **Annabelle's Bar & Bistro,** serves lunch and dinner, and the Mosser even houses Studio Paradiso, a state-of-the-art recording studio. The location is excellent—3 blocks from Union Square, 2 blocks from the MOMA and Moscone Convention Center, and half a block from the cable car turnaround. It also borders on a "sketchy" street, but then again, so do most hotels a few blocks west of Union Square.

54 Fourth St. (at Market St.), San Francisco, CA 94103. ✆ **800/227-3804** or 415/986-4400. Fax 415/495-7653. www.themosser.com. 166 units, 112 with bathroom. $169–$259 double with bathroom; $79–$99 double without bathroom. Rates include safe-deposit boxes at front desk. AE, DC, DISC, MC, V. Parking $30, plus $10 for oversize vehicles. Streetcar: F, and all underground Muni and BART. **Amenities:** Restaurant; bar; 24-hr. concierge; same-day laundry service/dry cleaning. *In room:* TV, dataport, Wi-Fi ($9.95/day), hair dryer, iron/ironing board, AM/FM stereo w/CD player, voice mail, ceiling fan.

3 Chinatown

Grant Plaza This no-frills spot sits in the heart of bustling Chinatown, 1 block from the Chinatown gate and 3 blocks from Union Square. The bare-bones rooms are compact and most of the tiny bathrooms have showers only; but it is one of the few places downtown where you'll find a room for under $100 (rooms with two double beds start at $99). That said, I recommend staying only on the top floor, where the rooms are newer and farther from the street noise. The hotel has no kitchen, but cafes and restaurants are just steps away from the hotel lobby. ***Note:*** If the Grant Plaza is fully booked, try the nearby **Hotel Astoria** (510 Bush St.; ✆ **800/666-6696** or 415/434-8883; www.hotelastoria-sf.com), which has similar rates.

465 Grant Ave. (at Pine St.), San Francisco, CA 94108. ✆ **800/472-6899** or 415/434-3883. Fax 415/434-3886. www.grantplaza.com. 72 units. $69–$119 double; $139 suite. AE, DC, DISC, MC, V. Self-parking $20. Bus: 15, 30, or 45. *In room:* TV, high-speed Internet access, hair dryer, iron (on request).

4 North Beach/Fisherman's Wharf

★ **The San Remo Hotel** This small, European-style *pensione* is one of the best budget hotels in San Francisco. In a quiet North Beach neighborhood, within walking distance of Fisherman's Wharf, the Italianate Victorian structure originally served as a boardinghouse for dockworkers displaced by the Great Fire of 1906. As a result, the rooms are small and bathrooms are shared, but all is forgiven when it comes time to pay the bill. Rooms are decorated in cozy country style, with brass and iron beds; oak, maple, or pine armoires; and wicker furnishings. The immaculate shared bathrooms feature tubs and brass pull-chain toilets with oak tanks and brass fixtures. If the penthouse—which has its own bathroom, TV, fridge, and patio—is available, book it: You won't find a more romantic place to stay in San Francisco for so little money.

2237 Mason St. (at Chestnut St.), San Francisco, CA 94133. ✆ **800/352-7366** or 415/776-8688. Fax 415/776-2811. www.sanremohotel.com. 62 units, 61 with shared bathroom. $65–$90 double; $175–$185 penthouse suite. AE, DC, MC, V. Self-parking $13–$14. Bus: 10, 15, 30, or 47. Streetcar: F. Cable car: Powell-Mason line. **Amenities:** Access to nearby health club; Internet kiosk in lobby; 2 massage chairs; self-service laundry; TV room. *In room:* Ceiling fan.

Accommodations with Free Parking

Despite our exhortations to leave the driving to locals and use the public transportation system to get around, we know that some of you will still want to drive the crazy streets of San Francisco, or at least arrive by car. But with parking fees averaging $30 a night at most hotels, the extra charges can add up for visitors with wheels. So if you're going to rent a car or bring your own, you might want to consider staying at one of the following affordable choices, which all offer free parking:

- Bay Bridge Inn, SoMa, p. 24
- Beck's Motor Lodge, the Castro, p. 32
- Castle Inn, Cow Hollow, p. 28
- Cow Hollow Motor Inn & Suites, Marina District/Cow Hollow, p. 29
- Hostelling International San Francisco–Fisherman's Wharf p. 28
- Marina Motel, Marina District/Cow Hollow, p. 30

SUPER-CHEAP SLEEPS

★ **Green Tortoise Guest House** This cheery and cheap North Beach facility attracts lots of young international travelers on tight budgets. It's part hostel, part hotel, with a variety of rooms and beds to choose from depending on your budget: Mixed Dorm, Female Dorm, Private Double, Private Triple, and Twin Private, all with mattresses, pillows, and linens. Perks include free breakfast and wireless Internet access, sauna, pool table and foosball, and a large fully equipped kitchen for cooking your own meals. The best part? It's smack-dab in the middle of the Broadway bar scene, just around the corner from one of Kerouac's favorite bars, Vesuvio's. The Green Tortoise Adventure Travel office is also located here; you can book trips throughout the region or cross-country, as well as catch regularly scheduled buses to Los Angeles and Las Vegas.

494 Broadway, San Francisco, CA 94133. ✆ **800/867-8647** or 415/834-1000. www.greentortoise.com. 100 beds, 17 rooms with shared bathroom. $29 dorm

beds per person; $58–$87 double and triple. Rates include continental breakfast. No credit cards. Bus: 15 or 30.

Hostelling International San Francisco–Fisherman's Wharf Unbelievable but true—you can get bay views in San Francisco for a mere $20 and change nightly. What sets this place apart from other hostels is its location in the middle of a national park at Fort Mason. Through the windows of this converted army barracks, trees frame a view of Alcatraz and the San Francisco Bay. Beds here are bunked dorm-style, and bathrooms are down the hall. Although most rooms hold 8 to 12 beds, a few rooms have only 3 or 4 beds. These smaller rooms have the best vistas and can be reserved for families. You'll find small lockers in lieu of closets, so bring a lock. All guests have access to a full kitchen, free continental breakfast, and a common area with a cozy fireplace. An on-site cafe serves lunch and dinner, and the friendly volunteers at the information desk can book tours. Heck, the breakfast alone practically makes it worth the price. Make reservations well in advance.

Fort Mason, Bldg. 240, San Francisco, CA 94123. ✆ 415/771-7277. Fax 415/771-1468. http://sfhostel.com. 150 beds. $23–$29 per person per night. Rates include breakfast. MC, V. Free limited parking. Bus: 28, 30, 47, or 49. Amenities: Free Wi-Fi; computer kiosks for small fee, self-service laundry and kitchen; meeting room; baggage storage; secure lockers.

5 The Marina/Pacific Heights/ Cow Hollow

Castle Inn The Castle Inn is a good choice away from Union Square and the worst traffic on Van Ness Avenue. Units at this clean, convenient, friendly motel have been upgraded with maple furniture and new carpeting. They include in-room VCRs, microwave ovens, small refrigerators, continental breakfast, and even complimentary Wi-Fi. Guests are within walking distance of Polk Street's bars and restaurants and Fisherman's Wharf. If you have a car to park and want to avoid the exorbitant garage fees in Union Square and around Fisherman's Wharf, the Castle Inn is a smart pick, but it's not so great if you want to be closer to shops and theater.

1565 Broadway (at Van Ness Ave.), San Francisco, CA 94109. ✆ 800/822-7853 or 415/441-1155. www.castleinnsf.com. $85–$145 double. AE, DC, DISC, MC, V. Free parking.

Cow Hollow Motor Inn & Suites If you're less interested in being downtown than in playing in and around the beautiful bayfront Marina, check out this modest brick hotel on busy Lombard Street. There's no fancy theme, but each room has cable TV, free local phone calls, free covered parking, and a coffeemaker. Families will appreciate the one- and two-bedroom suites, which have full kitchens and dining areas as well as antique furnishings and surprisingly tasteful decor.

2190 Lombard St. (btw Steiner and Fillmore sts.), San Francisco, CA 94123. ✆ **415/921-5800.** Fax 415/922-8515. www.cowhollowmotorinn.com. 129 units. $72–$125 double. Extra person $10. AE, DC, MC, V. Free parking. Bus: 28, 30, 43, or 76. **Amenities:** Laundry and dry cleaning within a block. *In room:* A/C, TV, dataport, free high-speed DSL and Wi-Fi, full kitchens in suites only, coffeemaker, hair dryer.

Edward II Inn & Suites This three-story "English country" inn has a room for almost anyone's budget, ranging from *pensione* units with shared bathrooms to luxuriously appointed suites and cottages with whirlpool bathtubs and fireplaces. Originally built to house guests who attended the 1915 Pan-Pacific Exposition, it's still a good place to stay in spotless and comfortably appointed rooms with cozy antique furnishings. They've recently added a small fitness center and the Café Maritime, a seafood restaurant open for dinner. Room prices even include a full continental breakfast. Nearby Chestnut and Union streets offer some of the best shopping and dining in the city. The adjoining pub serves drinks nightly. The only caveat is that the hotel's Lombard Street location is usually congested with traffic.

3155 Scott St. (at Lombard St.), San Francisco, CA 94123. ✆ **800/473-2846** or 415/922-3000. Fax 415/931-5784. www.edwardii.com. 29 units, 21 with bathroom. $69–$99 double with shared bathroom; $115–$139 double with private bathroom; $179–$199 junior suite. Extra person $25. Rates include continental breakfast and evening sherry. AE, DISC, MC, V. Self-parking $12 1 block away. Bus: 28, 30, 43, or 76. **Amenities:** Pub; fitness center ($10 a day); computer station (for a nominal fee). *In room:* TV, free high-speed Internet access and Wi-Fi, hair dryer and iron available on request.

Marina Inn Marina Inn is one of the best low-priced hotels in San Francisco. How it offers so much for so little is mystifying. Each guest room in the 1924 four-story Victorian looks like something from a country furnishings catalog, complete with rustic pine-wood furniture, a four-poster bed with silky-soft comforter, pretty wallpaper, and soothing tones of rose, hunter green, and pale yellow. You also get remote control televisions discreetly hidden in pine cabinetry—all for as little as $75 a night. Combine that with continental breakfast, friendly service, a business center in the lobby with an Internet kiosk, free Wi-Fi, and an armada of shops and restaurants within easy walking distance, and there you have it: one of my top choices for best overall value. ***Note:*** Traffic can be a bit noisy here, so the hotel added double panes on windows facing the street.

3110 Octavia St. (at Lombard St.), San Francisco, CA 94123. ✆ 800/274-1420 or 415/928-1000. Fax 415/928-5909. www.marinainn.com. 40 units. Nov–Feb $75–$115 double; Mar–May $85–$135 double; June–Oct $95–$145 double. Rates include continental breakfast. AE, DC, DISC, MC, V. Bus: 28, 30, 43, or 76. *In room:* TV, free Wi-Fi, hair dryer and iron on request.

★ **Marina Motel** Established in 1939, the Marina Motel is one of San Francisco's first motels, built for the opening of the Golden Gate Bridge. The same family has owned this peach-colored, Spanish-style stucco building for three generations, and they've taken exquisite care of it. All rooms look out onto an inner courtyard, which is awash with beautiful flowering plants and wall paintings by local artists. Though the rooms show minor signs of wear and tear, they're all quite clean, bright, quiet, and pleasantly decorated with framed lithographs of old San Francisco—a thoughtful touch that adds to the motel's old-fashioned character and that makes these budget accommodations stand out from all the rest along busy Lombard Street. Two-bedroom suites with fully equipped kitchens are also available. Location-wise, the Presidio and Marina Green are mere blocks away, and you can easily catch a bus downtown. The only downside is the street noise, which is likely to burden light sleepers. ***Bonus:*** All rooms include a breakfast coupon valid for two entrees for the price of one at **Judy's Restaurant,** a short walk from the motel.

2576 Lombard St. (btw Divisadero and Broderick sts.), San Francisco, CA 94123. ✆ 800/346-6118 or 415/921-9406. Fax 415/921-0364. www.marinamotel.com. 38 units. $89–$159 double; $199 suite. Lower rates in winter. Rates include 2-for-1 breakfast coupon at nearby cafe. AE, DISC, MC, V. Free covered parking. Bus: 28, 29, 30, 43, or 45. Dogs accepted with $10 nightly fee. *In room:* Dataport, fridge, coffeemaker, hair dryer, iron.

6 Hayes Valley

Hayes Valley Inn Hotel choices are severely limited in Hayes Valley, but for budget travelers—or people who would prefer to spend

Elements: A Hip Mission District Hotel-ish

Bad credit? No problem. There's finally a place for the perpetually young and broke to stay and play in the heart of the Mission District. The Elements Hotel is sort of a cross between a boutique hotel and a hostel, offering both private rooms and shared dorms, all with private bathrooms. Add to that Wi-Fi Internet access throughout the hotel, a free Internet lounge, rooftop parties, free movie nights, lockers, free continental breakfast, luggage storage and laundry facilities, free linens, TVs (in private rooms), a lively restaurant and lounge called **Medjool,** and a plethora of inexpensive ethnic cafes in the neighborhood, and baby, you've got it made. The hotel is at 2524 Mission St., between 21st and 22nd streets (✆ **866/327-8407** or 415/647-4100; www.elementssf.com). Rates per person are between $25 and $30; expect higher rates and minimum stays during holidays.

their dough on good meals or local designers—this 28-room Edwardian B&B is a find. Yes, you'll have to share the very clean toilets and showers, but you can brush your teeth at the sink/vanity in your sweetly decorated room. Expect to meet European tourists over cereal, bagels, orange juice, and coffee (included in the rates). Streetside rooms are larger, but noisier. The Van Ness Muni station or F-Market streetcars are a short walk east. The Asian Art Museum, opera, ballet, and symphony are a short walk north.

417 Gough St. (near Hayes St.), San Francisco, CA 94102. ✆ **800/930-7999** or 415/431-9131. www.hayesvalleyinn.com. 28 units. $84–$105 double. MC, V.

7 Haight-Ashbury

Metro Hotel It's not exactly in the heart of the Haight, but from this remodeled Victorian you can walk to the Castro, Golden Gate Park, or upper or lower Haight in under 30 minutes. Buses stop a block away and blast downtown and to the Haight every few minutes. The neighborhood isn't the best in town, but it beats Civic Center by a long shot and has plenty of cheap restaurants nearby. The high-ceilinged hotel is reminiscent of a European *pensione*—smallish rooms, nothing too fancy, but clean and friendly with everything you need to get by. There's a garden out back, too. ***Note:*** You're out of luck when it comes to parking around here, so if you have a car I'd skip this one.

319 Divisadero St. (btw Oak and Page sts.), San Francisco, CA 94117. © **415/861-5364.** Fax 415/863-1970. www.metrohotelsf.com. 23 units. $76 double with twin bed; $87 double with two twin beds; $87–$130 double with queen beds. AE, DISC, MC, V. Bus: 6, 7, 16, 24, 66, or 71. **Amenities:** Nepalese restaurant. *In room:* TV.

8 The Castro

Beck's Motor Lodge In a town where DINK (double income, no kids) tourists happily spend fistfuls of money, you'd think someone would create a gay luxury hotel—or even a moderate hotel, for that matter. But absurdly, the most commercial and modern accommodations in the touristy Castro is this run-of-the-mill motel. Standard but contemporary, the ultratidy rooms include low-Levitz furnishings, a sun deck overlooking upper Market Street's action, and free parking. Unless you're into homey B&Bs, this is really your only choice in the area—fortunately, it's very well maintained. But be warned that this is a party spot; party people stay here, and the staff can be brusque.

2222 Market St. (at 15th St.), San Francisco, CA 94114. © **800/227-4360** in the U.S., except CA, 800/955-2325 within CA, or 415/621-8212. Fax 415/241-0435. www.becksmotorlodgesf.com. 58 units. $93–$151 double. AE, DC, DISC, MC, V. Free parking. Bus: 8 or 37. Streetcar: F. **Amenities:** Coin-operated washing machines. *In room:* TV, dataport, free Wi-Fi, fridge, coffeemaker.

Inn on Castro One of the better choices in the Castro, half a block from all the action, is this Edwardian-style inn decorated with contemporary furnishings, original modern art, and fresh flowers throughout. It definitely feels more like a home than an inn, so if you like less commercial abodes, this place is for you. Most rooms share a small back patio, and the suite has a private entrance and an outdoor sitting area. The inn also offers access to six individual nearby apartments ($125–$190) with complete kitchens. Note that rates include a full breakfast, and that the least expensive rooms share a bathroom.

321 Castro St. (at Market St.), San Francisco, CA 94114. © **415/861-0321.** Fax 415/861-0321. www.innoncastro.com. 8 units, 2 with bathroom across the hall;

6 apts. $105–$165 double. Rates include full breakfast and evening brandy. AE, DC, MC, V. Streetcar: F, K, L, or M. **Amenities:** Hall fridges stocked w/free sodas and water. *In room:* Flatscreen TV, DVD/CD, dataport, free Wi-Fi, hair dryer.

24 Henry Guesthouse & Village House Its central Castro location is not the only thing that makes 24 Henry a good choice for gay travelers. The 24 Henry building, an 1870s Victorian on a serene side street, is quite charming, as is the Village House sister property 4 blocks away. All of the individually decorated guest rooms have high ceilings and period furniture; most have shared bathrooms. A continental breakfast is served each morning in the parlor. All rooms are nonsmoking.

24 Henry St. (near Sanchez St.), San Francisco, CA 94114. ✆ **800/900-5686** or 415/864-5686. Fax 415/864-0406. www.24henry.com. 10 units, 3 with bathroom. $75–$100 double with shared bathroom; $119–$139 double with private bathroom. Extra person $20. Rates include continental breakfast. AE, MC, V. Bus: 8, 22, 24, or 37. Streetcar: F, J, K, L, M, or N. **Amenities:** Wi-Fi throughout.

The Willows Inn Right in the heart of the Castro, the all-nonsmoking Willows Inn employs a staff eager to greet and attend to visitors. The country and antique willow furnishings don't strictly suit a 1903 Edwardian home, but everything's quite comfortable—especially considering the extras, which include an expanded continental breakfast (fresh fruit, yogurt, baked goods, gourmet coffee, eggs, assorted teas, and orange juice), the morning paper, nightly cocktails, a sitting room (with a DVD player), and a pantry with limited kitchen facilities. The homey rooms vary in size from large (queen-size bed) to smaller (double bed) and are priced accordingly. Each room has a vanity sink, and all the rooms share eight water closets and shower rooms.

710 14th St. (near Church and Market sts.), San Francisco, CA 94114. ✆ **800/431-0277** or 415/431-4770. Fax 415/431-5295. www.willowssf.com. 12 units, none with bathroom. $99–$160 double; from $145 suite. Rates include continental breakfast. AE, DC, DISC, MC, V. Bus: 22 or 37. Streetcar: Church St. station (across the street) or F. *In room:* TV/VCR, free Wi-Fi, fridge.

San Francisco's many ethnic restaurants offer some of the best bargains in town.

3 CHEAP EATS

Afghan, Burmese, Cambodian, Cajun, Moroccan, Persian, Ethiopian—whatever cuisine you're in the mood for, this city serves it. With more than 4,000 reasons to avoid cooking at home, more San Franciscans eat out than any other city's citizens in the U.S. And all you need to join the dinner party is a little money and an adventurous palate, because half the fun of visiting San Francisco is the opportunity to sample the flavors of the world in one fell swoop. Best of all, many of the city's greatest eating experiences are its small, affordable neighborhood haunts, the kind you'll never find unless someone (that would be me) lets you in on San Francisco's cheap dining secrets.

Frugal Feasting at the Food Courts

Remember when Templeton the Rat from the movie *Charlotte's Web* discovered the joy of feasting on a multitude of junk food at the fairground? That's sort of what the feeling is like at San Francisco's top food courts, where you can sample wonderfully prepared dishes from around the globe for less than $10 a pop, and you never have to tip a waiter. In the SoMa District, the 800-seat food court in the **Westfield San Francisco Centre** at 5th and Mission streets is phenomenal. You can choose from Andale Mexican cuisine, Askew Grill, Bistro Burger, and, what may become the food court's most coveted destination, Out the Door, part of famed chef Charles Phan's collection of restaurants such as the Slanted Door.

In the Union Square area, the **Crocker Galleria** (50 Post St. at Montgomery St.) has a terrific food court on the third level, open Monday through Friday until 6pm and Saturdays until 5pm. It's always packed at lunch with office workers seeking a quick, inexpensive bite. At the Fountain Café you'll find breakfast bagels, eggs, and baked goods in the morning, and sandwiches and burgers at lunch. Get a chili fix at Chili Up; the different versions come with tortillas or corn bread. You'll also find counters for Leila Mediterranean Cuisine, 360 Degree Gourmet Burritos, New Asia Restaurant, and Niji Japanese Grill, among other international options. To avoid the rush, arrive before 11:30am or after 1pm and grab a table in the light-filled atrium.

The sexiest food court in the city is **Rincon Center,** at 101 Spear St., between Mission and Howard streets. The 1930s Moderne/Art Deco building is on the National Register of Historic Places and contains an 85-foot waterfall inside the dramatic atrium and murals in the former post office lobby. For a truly cosmopolitan experience, you can nosh at Arabi for top-notch Middle Eastern salads, Sorabol for Korean grilled meats and soup, Thai to Go for pad Thai, Wazwan for Indian dishes and naan bread, and Taqueria Pepe's for burritos. Burgers, pizzas, sandwiches, and soups are also to be had. Seat-yourself tables are dispersed throughout the pretty indoor courtyard. The restaurants in Rincon Center are open weekdays from 11am to 3pm.

We've tried to list places that offer a good meal for $10 or less per person (not including drinks), as well as a couple of good-value splurges. And that's what the prices were at press time; as everyone knows, pretty much everything went *way* up in the summer and fall of 2008, so you might find items a few bucks higher than when we wrote this. Or not. By early 2009, a lot of places were dealing with the economic downturn by keeping prices steady or even lowering them.

And, before you head out on the streets of San Francisco to your culinary destiny, there are a few things you should keep in mind:

- It's against the law to smoke in any restaurant in San Francisco, even if it has a separate bar or lounge. You're welcome to smoke outside, however.
- Plan on dining early. Most restaurants close their kitchens around 10pm.
- If there's a long wait for a table, ask if you can order at the bar, which often has faster service and a more affordable menu.
- Note that a lot of the places we list are smaller "mom and pop" style and may not take credit cards. So make sure you have some cash on you *before* you order.
- If you're driving to a restaurant, add extra time into your itinerary to find parking, which can be an especially infuriating exercise in areas like the Mission, downtown, the Marina, and most everywhere else for that matter.

1 Union Square & the Tenderloin

Blondie's Pizza *PIZZA* The staff here cuts and sells huge wedges of thick-crusted pizzas slathered with tomato sauce, cheese, and various toppings at a constant pace. At $2.75 a slice, you can feed an army and still have change left over for a cable car ticket. You can order pepperoni, but if you ask for carrots and broccoli, you've even got yourself a reasonably healthy meal for under $3. You won't find tables here, but the benches at Union Square are just 2 blocks away.

CHEAP EATS IN SAN FRANCISCO

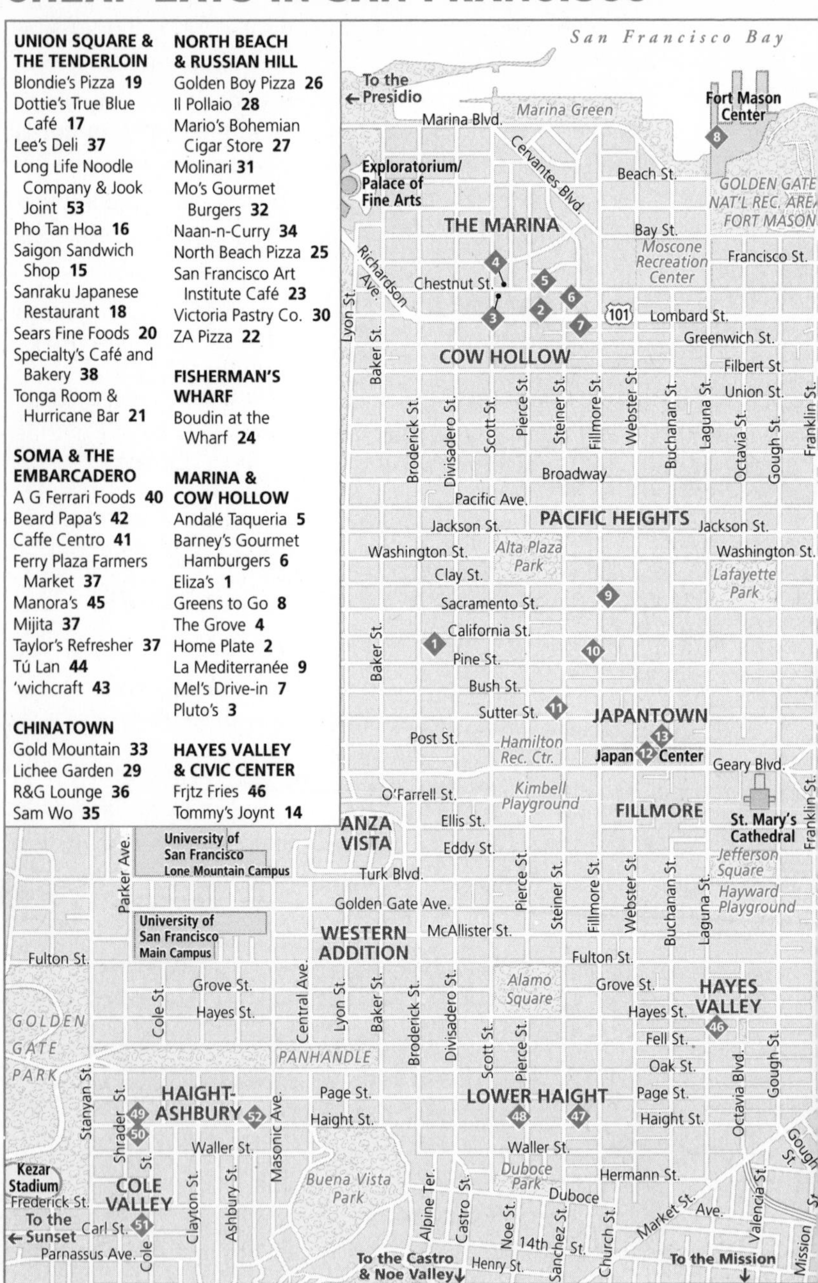

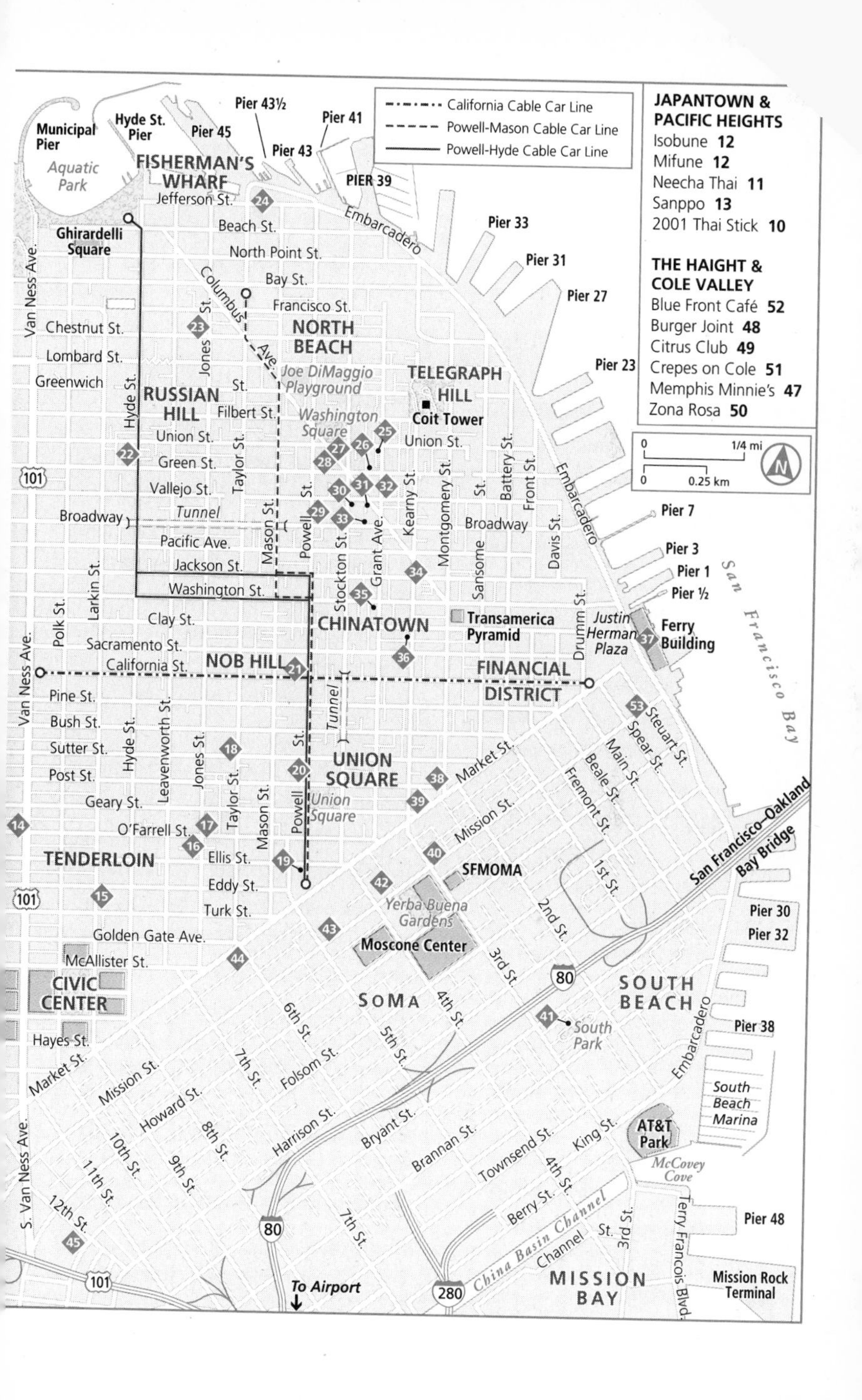

California Cable Car Line
Powell-Mason Cable Car Line
Powell-Hyde Cable Car Line
JAPANTOWN & PACIFIC HEIGHTS
Isobune 12
Mifune 12
Neecha Thai 11
Sanppo 13
2001 Thai Stick 10
THE HAIGHT & COLE VALLEY
Blue Front Café 52
Burger Joint 48
Citrus Club 49
Crepes on Cole 51
Memphis Minnie's 47
Zona Rosa 50
0
1/4 mi
0
0.25 km
N
Municipal Pier
Hyde St. Pier
Pier 45
Pier 43½
Pier 41
Pier 43
PIER 39
Pier 33
Pier 31
Pier 27
Pier 23
Pier 7
Pier 3
Pier 1
Pier ½
Aquatic Park
FISHERMAN'S WHARF
Jefferson St.
Ghirardelli Square
Beach St.
North Point St.
Embarcadero
Bay St.
Columbus Ave.
Francisco St.
Van Ness Ave.
Chestnut St.
Lombard St.
Greenwich St.
Jones St.
NORTH BEACH
Joe DiMaggio Playground
TELEGRAPH HILL
Coit Tower
RUSSIAN HILL
Hyde St.
Filbert St.
Washington Square
Union St.
Green St.
Taylor St.
Vallejo St.
Kearny St.
Montgomery St.
Sansome St.
Battery St.
Front St.
Broadway
Tunnel
Pacific Ave.
Jackson St.
Washington St.
Mason St.
Powell St.
Stockton St.
Grant Ave.
Davis St.
Drumm St.
Larkin St.
Polk St.
Clay St.
CHINATOWN
Transamerica Pyramid
Justin Herman Plaza
Ferry Building
Sacramento St.
California St.
NOB HILL
FINANCIAL DISTRICT
San Francisco Bay
Pine St.
Bush St.
Sutter St.
Post St.
Geary St.
O'Farrell St.
Ellis St.
Eddy St.
Turk St.
Leavenworth St.
UNION SQUARE
Union Square
Market St.
Steuart St.
Spear St.
Main St.
Beale St.
Fremont St.
Mission St.
1st St.
2nd St.
3rd St.
4th St.
5th St.
6th St.
7th St.
8th St.
9th St.
10th St.
11th St.
12th St.
San Francisco–Oakland Bay Bridge
TENDERLOIN
SFMOMA
Yerba Buena Gardens
Moscone Center
Golden Gate Ave.
McAllister St.
CIVIC CENTER
Hayes St.
SOMA
SOUTH BEACH
South Park
Pier 30
Pier 32
Pier 38
Folsom St.
Howard St.
Harrison St.
Bryant St.
Brannan St.
Townsend St.
King St.
Berry St.
Channel St.
China Basin Channel
South Beach Marina
AT&T Park
McCovey Cove
Terry Francois Blvd.
Pier 48
S. Van Ness Ave.
MISSION BAY
Mission Rock Terminal
To Airport
101
80
280

(btw Ellis and Market sts.). ✆ **415/982-6168.** Pizza $2.75–$3 per t cards for regular orders. (AE, MC, V accepted on orders over $30.) n–10pm; Sun 10am–9:30pm. Muni: Powell-Hyde or Powell-Mason cable ca... Ellis St.

Low-Price Meal in High-Price Setting!

For a measly $9.50 and a one-drink minimum each, you can feed the kids (or yourself) at the *very* high-end Fairmont Hotel's **Tonga Room & Hurricane Bar** during Happy Hour from 5 to 7pm on weekdays. The all-you-can-eat buffet offers myriad Polynesian appetizers, including mini shiitake egg rolls with Tonga's secret sauce, chicken wontons with chili sauce, Kalua pork garlic noodles, king prawn crackers with Portuguese sausage dip, macadamia nut pineapple rice, Big Island orzo, and assorted tropical fruit with piña colada dip.

The tropical storm cued to thunder on the half-hour will provide entertainment. There's nothing else like it. The Fairmont is at 950 Mason St. at California Street in Nob Hill. Cable car: California St. You can reserve your spot at the hurricane by calling ✆ **415/772-5278** or online at www.opentable.com.

★ **Dottie's True Blue Café** *AMERICAN/BREAKFAST* This family-owned breakfast restaurant is one of my favorite downtown diners. This is the kind of place you'd expect to see off old Rte. 66, where customers are on a first-name basis with the staff and everyone is welcomed with a hearty "hello" and steaming mug of coffee. Dottie's serves far-above-average American morning fare (big portions of French toast, pancakes, bacon and eggs, omelets, and the like), delivered to tables laminated with old movie-star photos on rugged, diner-quality plates. Whatever you order arrives with delicious homemade bread, muffins, or scones, as well as house-made jelly. There are also daily specials and vegetarian dishes.

In the Pacific Bay Inn, 522 Jones St. (at O'Farrell St.). ✆ **415/885-2767.** Breakfast $5–$11. DISC, MC, V. Wed–Mon 7:30am–3pm (lunch 11:30am–3pm). Bus: 2, 3, 4, 27, or 38. Cable car: Powell-Mason line.

★ **Pho Tan Hoa** *VIETNAMESE* Although it's only a few blocks off of Union Square, the walk to this simple Vietnamese restaurant in the downtrodden Tenderloin District can be quite an adventure, often characterized by crack-smoking loiterers (literally) and plenty of people down on their luck. Thing is, the folks along the way are usually friendly enough and your arrival at the restaurant brings the promise of huge, killer bowls of Vietnamese soup with all the classic fixings (basil, bean sprouts, and so on) at absurdly low prices. Any of the dozens of selections is a meal in itself, be it my favorite—the seafood soup with rice noodles—or those with beef, chicken, shrimp, or flank steak. There are also plenty of rice dishes—with beef, vegetables, deep-fried egg rolls, or barbecued pork, and intensely strong iced coffee. For a cheap, hearty, but light meal, this is my favorite downtown option, and could be yours too, provided you can overlook the fact that they use MSG and that the atmosphere is nothing more than clean cafeteria style.

431 Jones St. (btw O'Farrell and Ellis sts.). ✆ **415/673-3163.** Soups and main courses $5–$10. No credit cards. Daily 8am–7pm. Bus: 27, 31, or 38.

Saigon Sandwich Shop *VIETNAMESE/DELI* This Civic Center takeout deli is one of my favorite downtown options for a cheap, satisfying meal. For around $3 you get these wonderful Vietnamese sandwiches—baguettes full of pork or chicken with spicy sauces, cilantro, and peppers, or the popular Vietnamese-style meatball sandwiches. There's not much in the way of seating, so order it to go and wolf it down on the sidewalk.

560 Larkin St. (at Turk St.). ✆ **415/474-5698.** Main courses $3–$6. Mon–Sat 7am–5pm; Sun 7am–4:30pm. No credit cards. Bus: 19, 31, or 38.

★ **Sanraku Japanese Restaurant** *JAPANESE/SUSHI* A perfect combination of great cooked dishes and sushi at bargain prices makes this straightforward, bright, and busy restaurant the best choice in the area for Japanese food. The friendly, hardworking staff does its best to keep up with diners' demands, but the restaurant gets quite busy during lunch, when a special box lunch of the likes of California roll, soup, salad, deep-fried salmon roll, and beef with noodles with steamed rice comes at a very digestible $9.50. The main menu, which is always available, features great sesame chicken with teriyaki sauce and rice; tempura; a vast selection of *nigiri* (raw fish sushi) and rolls; and great combination plates of sushi, sashimi, and teriyaki. Dinner sees brisk business, too, but there always seems to be an available table.

704 Sutter St. (at Taylor St.). ✆ 415/771-0803. www.sanraku.com. Main courses $7–$13 lunch, $10–$26 dinner; 7-course fixed-price dinner $55. AE, DC, DISC, MC, V. Mon–Sat lunch 11am–4pm and dinner 4–10pm; Sun dinner 4–10pm. Bus: 2, 3, 4, 27, or 38. Cable car: Powell-Mason line.

★ **Sears Fine Foods** *AMERICAN* Sears is not just another downtown diner—it's an old-fashioned institution, famous for its crispy, dark-brown waffles, light sourdough French toast served with housemade strawberry preserves, and silver-dollar–size Swedish pancakes (18 per serving!). As the story goes, Ben Sears, a retired clown, founded the diner in 1938. His Swedish wife, Hilbur, was responsible for the legendary pancakes, which, although the restaurant is under new ownership, are still whipped up according to her family's secret recipe. Sears also offers classic lunch and dinner fare—try the Reuben for lunch and codfish and chips for dinner, followed by a big slice of pie for dessert. Breakfast is served until 3pm every day, and plan on a brief wait to be seated on weekends.

439 Powell St. (btw Post and Sutter sts.). ✆ 415/986-0700. www.searsfinefood.com. Reservations accepted for parties of 6 or more. Breakfast $3–$8; salads and soups $3–$8; main courses $6–$10. AE, DC, MC, V. Daily 6:30am–10pm (breakfast until 3pm). Cable car: Powell-Mason and Powell-Hyde lines. Bus: 2, 3, 4, or 38.

2 SoMa & the Embarcadero

★ **Beard Papa's** *BAKERY* When this Japanese chain of cream puffs hit the U.S., it became an overnight sensation. Outside of Japan, Beard Papa's can be enjoyed in Hawaii, New York, L.A., and now San Francisco. What's the secret to these luscious cream puffs? Beard Papa's claims it could be their special 2-hour process: mixing custard cream, real whipped cream, and Madagascar vanilla beans to produce the filling, a procedure that's repeated several times a day. Or maybe it's the ultrafresh crust. Or the interesting way the cream puffs are just a little less sweet than you'd expect them to be. Well, you'll just have to come find out for yourselves. You can get the traditional cream puffs served plain or dipped in chocolate on any day, but unusual fillings like strawberry, green tea, or pumpkin are strictly seasonal.

99 Yerba Buena Lane (at Mission St., btw 3rd and 4th sts.). ✆ 415/978-9972. Westfield San Francisco Centre, 865 Market St. (at 5th St.). ✆ 415/978-9972. www.beardpapasf.com. Cream puffs $1.75 each or $20 per dozen. AE, MC, V.

Mon-Sat 10am-8pm; Sun 10am-6:30pm. Muni: No. 30-Stockton or no. 45-Union-Stockton bus to Mission St.

Caffe Centro *CAFE* If it's a sunny day and you're in the mood for a little SoMa adventure, you'll find no place as relaxing as this hidden cafe retreat. Caffe Centro's limited kitchen and dining room inhibits it from becoming a destination restaurant, but its simple, cozy space, too-quaint sidewalk seating, and view of a grassy minipark and Old San Francisco–style homes make it the perfect place to catch a few rays, read the paper, and relax. The only reminder that you're in a big city is the dwindling cadre of city workers who come in for a dose of high-octane java and a salad or sandwiches for lunch. In the morning stop in for a breakfast of pastries, fruit, granola, and poached eggs, all priced well under $10.

102 South Park (btw Second and Third sts. and Bryant and Brannan sts.). ✆ 415/882-1500. Main courses under $9. AE, MC, V. Mon-Fri 7am-5pm; Sat 8:30am-2:30pm. Bus: 9, 15, 30, 45, 76, or 81X.

Long Life Noodle Company & Jook Joint *ASIAN* If you want good, cheap noodles, this is the place. Although nothing here will wow you, you will get a better-than-average meal for little money. The theme is noodles from all over Asia prepared in a variety of ways. Egg, rice, and wheat noodles are served with soup, stir-fried, cold, or over salad in dishes with names like Buddha's Bliss (ramen noodles in miso broth with smoked trout, tofu, and enoki mushrooms) or Dragon's Breath (garlicky lo mein noodles wok-tossed with button mushrooms and parsley). You'll also find dishes made with rice or *jook* (rice porridge) and other pan-Asian favorites such as pot stickers, spring rolls, and fried wontons. The decor at this location of the small, regional chain is hypermodern with too much neon. But with all entrees under $9, who's complaining? (You can also slurp Long Life noodles at their Sony Metreon food court branch.)

139 Steuart St. (at Mission St.). ✆ 415/281-3818. Reservations not accepted. Main courses $6.25-$8.75. MC, V. Mon-Fri 11:30am-9pm. Muni: F-Market streetcar to Steuart St., and then walk 1½ blocks south.

★ **Manora's** *THAI* Manora's cranks out some of the best Thai food in town and is well worth a jaunt to SoMa. But this is no relaxed affair: It's perpetually packed (unless you come early), and you'll be seated sardine-like at one of the cramped but well-appointed tables. During the dinner rush, the noise level can make conversation among larger parties almost impossible, but the food is so darned good, you'll probably prefer to turn toward your plate and stuff your face anyway. Start with a Thai iced tea or coffee and tangy soup or chicken satay, which comes with decadent peanut sauce. Follow these with any of the wonderful dinner dishes—which should be shared—and a side of rice. There are endless options, including a vast array of vegetarian plates. Every remarkably flavorful dish arrives seemingly seconds after you order it, which is great if you're hungry, a bummer if you were planning a long, leisurely dinner. ***Tip:*** Come before 7pm or after 9pm if you don't want a loud, rushed meal.

1600 Folsom St. (at 12th St.). ✆ 415/861-6224. www.manorathai.com. Reservations recommended for 4 or more. Main courses $7–$12. MC, V. Mon–Fri 11:30am–2:30pm; Mon–Sat 5:30–10:30pm; Sun 5–10pm. Bus: 9, 12, or 47.

★ **Mijita** *MEXICAN* Tracy des Jardins, the talent behind this gem, is best known for her hyperelegant establishment Jardiniere, which serves dinner to the black-tie set en route to the opera, symphony, or ballet. But this unpretentious joint serving simply prepared Mexican "street food" is a great way to enjoy des Jardins's culinary talents. Not only will you get hearty morsels like a freshly grilled fish taco with cilantro-avocado cream or a carnitas taco with crisped braised pork at amazing prices (under $5), but you'll also enjoy a terrific view to boot. Located on the backside of the Ferry Building, Mijita looks out to the San Francisco Bay. Watch commuters catching ferries back home while you enjoy "queso fundido," melted Mexican cheeses and chorizo sausage served with soft tortillas. If it's warm enough to sit outside, take your time sipping a cold beer and munching spiced pumpkin seeds. Des Jardins is dedicated to supporting local farmers, fisherman, and ranchers who produce food sustainably, but the most amazing part is the tiny bill. *"Otra cerveza, por favor!"*

One Ferry Bldg., No. 44 (at the Embarcadero). ✆ 415/399-0814. www.mijitasf.com. Highchairs. Reservations not accepted. Brunch main courses $6.50–$7. Lunch/dinner main courses $4–$5. Kids' menu $2. AE, MC, V. Mon–Wed 11am–7pm; Thurs–Fri 11am–8pm; Sat 9am–8pm; Sun 10am–4pm. Muni: F-Market streetcar.

★ **Taylor's Refresher** *AMERICAN/HAMBURGERS* This must be what diner food tasted like 50 years ago, when cows still roamed pastures and a tomato still tasted like a tomato. Eating here made me understand how diners got to be so popular in the first place. The hamburgers, made with local, naturally raised beef, are mouthwatering, as are the sweet potato fries. Even the cherry tomatoes on the garden salad were sweet and delicate, not the tasteless, hard-skinned variety one expects at a typical diner. Then again, this diner isn't exactly typical. The first, and still existing, Taylor's Refresher was established in 1949 in the heart of the Napa Valley, with plenty of nearby family farms to draw on for fresh, local ingredients. This site, in the Ferry Building, takes advantage of the neighboring Farmer's Market for its raw materials. Despite the gourmet touch, the food still comes on trays, the music is loud, and the price is right. On a sunny day, choose an outdoor table and order one of the awesome milkshakes or a root beer float—all made with San Francisco's luscious Double Rainbow ice cream.

One Ferry Bldg. (at Embarcadero). ✆ **866/328-3663.** www.taylorsrefresher.com. Highchairs. Reservations not accepted. Main courses $4–$14. AE, DC, DISC, MC, V. Daily 10:30am–8:30pm. Muni: F-Market streetcar.

★ **Tú Lan** *VIETNAMESE* Only adventurous foodies interested in a cheap midday snack need to read this review. You'll have to brave the winos, weirdos, and street stench to get to this total dive in an unsavory neighborhood bordering Union Square and SoMa, but I do it happily to get my hands on the best imperial rolls on the planet. Alas, the atmosphere inside isn't much better—it's about as greasy as greasy spoons get, and if you head to the upstairs bathroom you might even catch an unsavory glimpse of kitchen staff hovering over mounds of ground meat meant for tonight's dinner piled high on a banquet table. But once I get a bite of the crisp, thick imperial rolls, which are served over rice noodles and accompanied by lettuce, mint, peanuts, and a yummy dipping sauce, I couldn't care less. There's also a good selection of stir-fried rice plates—including awesome barbecued pork, which can be washed down with intense iced coffee. In any case, you'll feel brave just eating here.

8 Sixth St. (at Market St.). ✆ **415/626-0927.** Main courses $4–$7.50. No credit cards. Mon–Sat 11am–9:30pm. Bus: 6, 7, 27, 31, 66, or 71. Streetcar: F, J, K, L, M, or N. Cable car: Powell-Mason and Powell-Hyde lines.

★ **'wichcraft** *SANDWICHES* New Yorkers know Tom Colicchio for his lauded restaurants Gramercy Tavern and Craft. You may know the award-winning chef for his role as head judge on the TV show *Top Chef.* Now it's time to get to know him for his . . . um, sandwiches. Yes, Colicchio's West Coast debut is based on slices of bread with stuff inside. The "'wich" in "'wichcraft" is short for sandwich, get it?

When you bite into his juicy BBQ flank steak sandwich with roasted shitake mushrooms and grilled red onions on a pressed ciabatta roll, you'll definitely get it. Vegetarians may like the grilled gruyere and caramelized onions on rye, or even a tasty vegan option with chickpeas and roasted peppers.

868 Mission St. (btw 4th and 5th sts.). ✆ 415/593-3895. www.wichcraftnyc.com. Highchairs, boosters. No reservations. Sandwiches $5-$10. AE, DC, DISC, MC, V. Mon-Fri 8am-9pm; Sat 10am-9pm; Sun 10am-6pm. Muni: No. 30-Stockton or no. 45-Union-Stockton bus to Mission St.

3 Chinatown

★ **Gold Mountain** *CHINESE/DIM SUM* This gymnasium-size restaurant is a must-visit for anyone who's never experienced what it's like to dine with hundreds of Chinese-speaking patrons conversing loudly at enormous round tables among glittering chandeliers and gilded dragons while dozens of white-shirted waitstaff push around stainless steel carts filled with small plates of exotic-looking edible adventures. (Was that sentence long enough for you?) Chicken feet, pork buns, shrimp dumplings, honey-walnut prawns (yum), the ubiquitous chicken-in-foil, and a myriad of other quasi-recognizable concoctions that range from appealing to revolting (never ate beef tripe, never will) whiz about at eye level. I remember coming here as a kid on late Saturday mornings and being infatuated with the entire cacophonous event. And even if you eat until you're ill, you'll never put down more than $20 worth of food, making Gold Mountain a real bargain as well, especially for large groups. Don't even bother with the regular menu: It's the dim sum service from 8am to 3pm on weekends and 10:30am to 3pm on weekdays that you want.

664 Broadway (btw Grant Ave. and Stockton St.). ✆ 415/296-7733. Main courses $3-$9. AE, MC, V. Mon-Fri 10:30am-3pm and 5-9:30pm; Sat-Sun 8am-3pm and 5-9:30pm. Bus: 12, 15, 30, or 83.

Lichee Garden *CHINESE/DIM SUM* This longtime, consistently good Cantonese restaurant is even a favorite among Chinatown residents. Lichee Garden's lengthy menu is filled with familiar items like egg foo yong, sweet-and-sour pork, wonton soup, and every other dish you remember from your childhood, assuming you weren't raised in China. The kitchen caters to those who can't make the leap from American broccoli to Chinese broccoli by offering both, but the menu includes more adventurous fare as well. The list of seafood showcases many scallop inventions, and live lobster and crab in season—both highly recommended. The excellent dim sum makes a great lunch option. Large and bright, the dining room has seen many families over the 25-plus years it's been open. Service is businesslike and you won't have to wait long for your meal. Technically, it's not in Chinatown, but it's just 1 block west of it.

1416 Powell St. (btw Broadway and Vallejo sts.). ✆ 415/397-2290. http://lichee garden.citysearch.com. Highchairs. Reservations recommended. Main courses $5.50–$14. MC, V. Daily 7am–9:15pm. Muni: No. 30-Stockton or no. 45-Union-Stockton bus to Broadway.

★ **R&G Lounge** *CHINESE* It's tempting to take your chances and duck into any of the exotic restaurants in Chinatown, but if you want a sure thing, go directly to the three-story R&G Lounge. During lunch, all three floors are packed with hungry neighborhood workers who go straight for the $5.50 rice-plate specials. Even then, you can order from the dinner menu, which features legendary deep-fried salt-and-pepper crab (a little greasy for my taste); and wonderful chicken with black-bean sauce. A personal favorite is melt-in-your-mouth R&G Special Beef, which explodes with the tangy flavor of the accompanying sauce. I was less excited by the tired chicken salad, house specialty noodles, and bland spring rolls. But that was just fine since I saved room for generous and savory seafood in a clay pot and classic roast duck.

631 Kearny St. (at Clay St.). ✆ 415/982-7877. www.rnglounge.com. Reservations recommended. Main courses $9.50–$30. AE, DC, DISC, MC, V. Daily 11am–9:30pm. Parking validated across the street at Portsmouth Sq. garage 24 hr. or Holiday Inn after 5pm. Bus: 1, 9AX, 9BX, or 15. Cable Car: California St.

Sam Wo *CHINESE* Very handy for late-nighters, Sam's is a total dive that's usually packed at 1am with party people trying to sober up (I've been pulling all-nighters here since I was a teen). The century-old restaurant's two pocket-size dining rooms are located on top of each other, on the second and third floors—take the stairs past the grimy first-floor kitchen. You'll probably have to share a table, but this place is for mingling almost as much as for eating (the bossy waitresses are pure comedy). The house specialty is *jook,* known as *congee* in its native Hong Kong—a thick rice gruel flavored with fish, shrimp, chicken, beef, or pork; the best is Sampan, made with rice and

Dim Sum 101

If you're looking for the most bang for your dining buck, you'll be hard-pressed to find a better deal than a dim sum dining experience in Chinatown. In many Chinese restaurants, dim sum is served from late morning until around 2pm, but not later. In fact, if you arrive past 1pm, you run the risk of the kitchen losing interest in providing much of anything to eat. It's best to arrive around 11am. Dim sum generally enters on carts wheeled about the room by waitresses (otherwise, you order from a menu). Ask for a table near the kitchen in order to get first crack at whatever's on its way around the room. The ladies with their carts will stop by your table and show you what they have. If it looks appealing to you, nod or say, "Yes"; if not, just say, "No thanks." It's okay to order slowly—finishing one plate, sipping tea, and then ordering something else. By the way, if you run out of tea, open the teapot lid.

In Chinatown, **Gold Mountain** (p. 46) is typical of the cavernous dim sum parlors that serve hundreds of families on the weekends. **Lichee Garden** (p. 46) is another very good spot for dim sum in the sometimes-confusing array of Chinatown choices. It's the favorite of one of San Francisco's most prominent chefs, as well as

seafood. Try sweet-and-sour pork rice, wonton soup with duck, or a roast-pork/rice-noodle roll. More traditional fried noodles and rice plates are available, too, but I always end up ordering the same thing: tomato beef with noodles and house-special chow mein.

813 Washington St. (by Grant Ave.). ✆ 415/982-0596. Reservations not accepted. Main courses $3.50–$6. No credit cards. Mon–Sat 11am–3am; Sun 11am–9:30pm in summer and on holidays. Bus: 9x, 15, 30, or 45.

4 North Beach & Russian Hill

★ **Golden Boy Pizza** *ITALIAN/PIZZA* Pass by Golden Boy when the bars are hopping in North Beach and you'll find a crowd of inebriated sots savoring steamy slices of wondrously gooey pizza. But you don't have to be on a red wine buzz to enjoy the big, doughy plenty of Chinatown workers on their morning break. Here's a rundown of dim sum that first-timers will probably enjoy:

- *Har Gau:* Shrimp dumplings encased in a translucent wrapper and steamed
- *Sui Mai:* Rectangles of pork and shrimp in a sheer noodle wrapper
- *Gau Choi Gau:* Chives, alone or with shrimp or scallop
- *Jun Jui Kau:* Rice pearl balls with seasoned ground pork and rice
- *Law Mai Gai:* Sticky rice with bits of meat and mushrooms wrapped in a lotus leaf
- *Char Siu Bau:* Steamed pork buns—bits of barbecued meat in a doughy roll
- *Guk Char Siu Ban:* Baked pork buns—bits of barbecued meat in a glazed roll
- *Chun Guen:* Spring rolls—smaller, less-crowded version of egg roll
- *Gau Ji:* Pot stickers—a thick, crescent-shaped dough filled with ground pork

squares of Italian-style pizzas, each enticingly placed in the front windows (the aroma alone is irresistable). Locals have flocked here for years to fill up on one of the cheapest and cheesiest meals in town. Expect to take your feast to go on busy nights, as there are only a few bar seats inside.

542 Green St. (btw Stockton St. and Grant Ave.). ✆ **415/982-9738.** Pizza slice $2.50–$3.50. No credit cards. Sun–Thurs 11:30am–11pm; Fri–Sat 11:30am–2am. Bus: 15, 30, 39, 41, or 45.

★ **Il Pollaio** *ITALIAN/ARGENTINE* Simple, affordable, and consistently good is the winning combination at Il Pollaio. When I used to live in the neighborhood, I ate here at least once a week, and I still can't make chicken this good. Seat yourself in the tiny, unfussy room, order, and wait expectantly for the fresh-from-the-grill lemon-infused chicken, which is so moist it practically falls off the bone. Each meal comes with a choice of salad or fries. If you're not in the mood for chicken, you can opt for rabbit, lamb, pork chop, or Italian sausage. On a sunny day, get your goods to go and picnic across the street at Washington Square.

555 Columbus Ave. (btw Green and Union sts.). ✆ 415/362-7727. Reservations not accepted. Main courses $8–$15. DISC, MC, V. Mon–Sat 11:30am–9pm. Bus: 15, 30, 39, 41, or 45. Cable car: Powell-Mason line.

★ **Mario's Bohemian Cigar Store** *ITALIAN* Across the street from Washington Square is one of North Beach's most venerable neighborhood hangouts. The century-old corner cafe—small, well worn, and perpetually busy—is one of the oldest and best original cappuccino cafes in United States. I stop by at least once a month for a hot meatball or eggplant focaccia sandwich and a slice of Mario's house-made ricotta cheesecake, then recharge with a cappuccino as I watch the world stroll by the picture windows. You can also get the sandwiches to go and make a picnic of it at Washington Square across the street. And no, they don't sell cigars.

566 Columbus Ave. (at Union St.). ✆ 415/362-0536. www.mariosbohemiancigarstore.com. Sandwiches $7.75–$8.50. MC, V. Mon–Sat 10am–midnight; Sun 10am–11pm. Bus: 15, 30, 41, or 45.

★ **Mo's Gourmet Burgers** *AMERICAN* This simple diner offers a straightforward but winning combination: big, thick, grilled patties of fresh-ground, best-quality, center-cut chuck; fresh french fries; and choice of cabbage slaw, sautéed garlic mushrooms, or chili. *Voilà!* You've got the city's burger of choice. The other food—spicy chicken sandwiches; steak with veggies, garlic bread, and potatoes; and token veggie dishes—is also up to snuff, but that messy, memorable burger is what keeps the carnivores captivated (the sinisterly sweet shakes are fantastic, too). Bargain-diners will appreciate prices, with burgers ranging from $5.95 for a classic to $7.95 for an "Alpine" burger with Gruyère cheese and sautéed mushrooms. Entrees start at $9 for meatloaf with mashed potatoes, garlic bread, and a vegetable, and top out at $17 for New York steak. The classic breakfast menu is also a bargain. A second location, at SoMa's Yerba Buena Gardens, 772 Folsom St., between Third and Fourth streets (✆ **415/957-3779**), is open Monday from 10am to 5pm, Tuesday through Friday from 10am to 8pm, Saturday from 9am to 8pm, and Sunday from 9am to 5pm. It features breakfast and burgers.

1322 Grant Ave. (btw Vallejo and Green sts.). ✆ **415/788-3779.** Main courses $5.95–$17. MC, V. Mon–Thurs 11:30am–10:30pm; Fri 11:30am–11:30pm; Sat 9am–11:30pm; Sun 9am–10:30pm. Bus: 9X, 15, 30, 39, 41, or 45.

Naan-N-Curry *INDIAN/PAKISTANI* When San Franciscans want good, inexpensive Indian/Pakistani food, they come to Naan-N-Curry. Flavorful tandoori-oven-baked meats, spicy curries, a great selection of vegetarian options, and plenty of naan breads are on offer here. A favorite here is the tikka masala, which is cooked in a mild yogurt sauce, and vegetable biryani, or vegetables with rice. With a casual atmosphere and hearty portions for just pennies, it's worth branching out from pizza, noodles, and the other usual suspects.

533 Jackson St. (at Columbus Ave.). ✆ **415/693-0499.** Main courses $4–$10. MC, V. Mon–Fri 11am–11:30pm; Sat–Sun noon–11:30pm. Muni: No. 15 bus to Jackson St.

★ **North Beach Pizza** *ITALIAN/PIZZA* Whenever I order a North Beach pizza, I'm always disappointed by the measly amount of toppings that they always skimp on. Then I eat the entire damn thing in one sitting. There's something about that uniquely gooey whole-milk mozzarella and hand-spun dough with thick, chewy edges that's so addictive it's been the most awarded and widely beloved pizza in the city for 2 decades. You *can* get a better pizza in the city—Pauline's has them beat—but not in North Beach, not via free delivery throughout the city, and not at 2:30am on Sunday when you're drunk and/or starving. Either create your own pizza from their list of 20 fresh ingredients (the sausage with black olives is the *bomb*), or choose from the house's 10 specialties such as the San Francisco Special—clams, garlic, cheese, and one brutal case of halitosis. There are numerous satellite NBPs throughout the city offering fast, free delivery until the wee hours. ***Tip:*** The lunch special, daily from 11am to 4pm, gets you an individual 8-incher for under $5.

1499 Grant St. (at Union St.). ✆ **415/433-2444.** www.northbeachpizza.com. Main courses $9–$21. AE, DC, DISC, MC, V. Sun–Thurs 9am–1am; Fri–Sat 9am–3am. Cable car: Powell-Mason line. Bus: 15, 30, 41, or 45.

San Francisco Art Institute Café *AMERICAN* Never in a million years would you stumble upon the Art Institute Café by accident. One of the best-kept secrets in San Francisco, this cafe offers fresh, affordable cafe standards for in-the-know residents and visitors as well as Art Institute students: a wide array of hearty breakfast dishes, fresh salads, s on homemade bread, daily ethnically inspired specials, ing with caffeine in it—all priced at or under $7. The view, tends from Alcatraz Island to Coit Tower and beyond, is so phenomenal that the exterior served as the outside of Sigourney Weaver's chic apartment in the movie *Copycat*. The cafe has an open kitchen, sleek aluminum tables, and weekly rotating student art shows. A large courtyard with cement tables (and the same Hollywood view) is the perfect spot for an alfresco lunch high above the tourist fray.

800 Chestnut St. (btw Jones and Leavenworth sts.). ✆ **415/749-4567.** Main courses $4–$6. No credit cards. Fall–spring Mon–Thurs 8am–5pm, Fri 8am–4pm; summer Mon–Fri 9am–2pm. Closed Sat–Sun. Hours dependent on school schedule; please call to confirm. Bus: 30 or 49. Cable car: Powell-Hyde or Powell-Mason line.

★ **ZA Pizza** *PIZZA* On a tree-lined section of Hyde Street along the cable car route, this is a favorite neighborhood gathering spot serving some of the biggest and best slices in the city. Locals hang out at the counter of this tiny establishment and watch a game on TV or take a seat at one of the few indoor and outdoor tables. The thin-crust pizzas are named after luminary characters such as the Pesto Picasso, with roasted chicken, sun-dried tomatoes, and fresh pesto; and the Popeye the Greek, with spinach and feta cheese. Two salads are also on the menu, but the house salad wins out over the plain-tasting Caesar. Good beers on tap as well.

1919 Hyde St. (btw Green and Union sts.). ✆ **415/771-3100.** Highchairs. Slices $3.50–$4.50. AE, DISC, MC, V. Sun–Wed noon–10pm; Thurs–Sat noon–11pm. Muni: Powell-Hyde cable car to Green St.

5 Fisherman's Wharf

Boudin at the Wharf *DELI/AMERICAN* This industrial-chic Fisherman's Wharf shrine to the city's famous tangy French-style bread is impossible to miss. Even if you're not hungry, drop in to see bakers at work making 3,000 loaves daily or take the tour and learn about the city sourdough bread's history (Boudin is the city's oldest continually operating business). Good, strong coffee is served at **Peet's Coffee** (another Bay Area great), and at **Bakers Hall** you'll find picnic possibilities such as handcrafted cheeses, fruit spreads, and chocolates, as well as a wall map highlighting the town's best places to spread a blanket and feast. There's also a casual **self-serve cafe** serving inexpensive sandwiches, clam chowder bowls, salads, and pastries, and the more formal **Bistro Boudin** restaurant, which offers Alcatraz views with its Dungeness crab Louis, pizza, crab cakes, and burgers on sourdough buns.

160 Jefferson St., near Pier 43½. ✆ 415/928-1849. www.boudinbakery.com. Reservations recommended at bistro. Main courses cafe $6–$10, bistro $11–$33. AE, DC, DISC, MC, V. Cafe daily 8am–10pm; bistro Mon–Fri noon–10pm, Sat 11:30am–10pm, Sun 11:30am–9pm. Bus: 10, 15, or 47. Streetcar: F.

6 Marina & Cow Hollow

★ **Andalé Taqueria** *MEXICAN* Andalé (Spanish for "hurry up") offers *muy bueno* high-end fast food for the health-conscious and the just plain hungry. As the long menu explains, this small California chain prides itself on its fresh ingredients and low-cal options. Lard, preservatives, and canned items are eschewed; Andalé favors salad dressings made with double virgin olive oil, whole vegetarian beans (not refried), skinless chicken, salsas and *aguas frescas* made from fresh fruits and veggies, and mesquite-grilled meats. Add the location (on a sunny shopping stretch), sophisticated decor, full bar, and check-me-out patio seating (complete with corner fireplace), and it's no wonder that good-looking, fitness-fanatic Marina District residents consider this place home. Cafeteria-style service keeps prices low.

2150 Chestnut St. (btw Steiner and Pierce sts.). ✆ 415/749-0506. Reservations not accepted. Most dishes $4.25–$11. MC, V. Daily 10am–10pm. Bus: 22, 28, 30, 30X, 43, 76, or 82X.

★ **Barney's Gourmet Hamburgers** *HAMBURGERS* If you're on a perpetual quest for the best burger in America, a mandatory stop is Barney's Gourmet Hamburgers. Once you get past all the framed awards for the Bay Area's best burger, you're bombarded by a mind-boggling menu of beef, chicken, turkey, and vegetarian burgers to choose from, as well as sandwiches and salads. The ultimate combo is a humungous basket of fries (enough for a party of three), one-third-pound burger, and thick shake. Popular versions are the California Burger with jack cheese, bacon, Ortega chiles, and sour cream, or the Popeye Burger made with chicken, sautéed spinach, and feta cheese. Be sure to dine alfresco in the hidden courtyard in back.

3344 Steiner St. (btw Chestnut and Lombard sts.). ✆ 415/563-0307. www.barneys hamburgers.com. Main courses $5–$8. No credit cards. Mon–Thurs 11am–9:30pm; Fri–Sat 11am–10pm; Sun 11am–9pm. Bus: 22, 28, 30, 30X, 43, 76, or 82X.

★ **Eliza's** *CHINESE* Despite the curiously colorful design of modern architecture, whimsy, and glass art, this perennially packed neighborhood haunt serves some of the freshest California-influenced Chinese food in town. Unlike comparable options, here the atmosphere (albeit unintentionally funky) and presentation parallel the food. The fantastically fresh soups, salads, seafood, pork, chicken, duck, and such specials as spicy eggplant are outstanding and are served on beautiful English and Japanese plates. (Get the sea bass with black-bean sauce and go straight to heaven!) I often come at midday and order the wonderful kung pao chicken lunch special (available weekdays only): a mixture of tender chicken, peanuts, chile peppers, subtly hot sauce, and perfectly crunchy vegetables. It's one of 32 main-course choices that come with rice and soup for around $6. The place is also jumping at night, so prepare to stand in line. A second location, in Potrero Hill at 1457 18th St. (✆ **415/648-9999**), is open Monday through Friday 11am to 3pm and daily 5 to 9pm.

2877 California St. (at Broderick St.). ✆ 415/621-4819. Reservations accepted for parties of 4 or more. Main courses $5.30–$6.15 lunch, $7.15–$15 dinner. MC, V. Mon–Thurs 11am–3pm and 5–9:30pm; Fri 11am–3pm and 5–10pm; Sat 4:30–10pm; Sun 4:30–9pm. Bus: 1 or 24.

★ **The Grove** *CAFE* The Grove is the kind of place you go just to hang out and enjoy the fact that you're in San Francisco. That the heaping salads, lasagna, pasta, sandwiches, and daily specials are predictably good is an added bonus. I like coming here on weekday mornings for the easygoing vibe, strong coffee, and friendly, fast service. Inside you can sit at one of the dark wood tables on the scuffed hardwood floor and people-watch through the large open windows, but on sunny days the most coveted seats are along the sidewalk. It's the perfect place to read the newspaper, sip an enormous mug of coffee, and be glad you're not at work right now. A second Pacific Heights location is at 2016 Fillmore St. between California and Pine sts. (✆ **415/474-1419**).

2250 Chestnut St. (btw Scott and Pierce sts.). ✆ 415/474-4843. Most main courses $6–$7. MC, V. Mon–Fri 7am–11pm; Sat–Sun 8am–11pm. Bus: 22, 28, 30, 30X, 43, 76, or 82X.

★ **Home Plate** *BREAKFAST* Dollar for dollar, Home Plate just may be the best breakfast place in San Francisco. Many Marina residents kick off their hectic weekends by carbo-loading here on big piles of buttermilk pancakes and waffles smothered with fresh fruit, or hefty omelets stuffed with everything from apple wood–smoked ham to spinach. You'll always start off with a coveted plate of freshly baked scones, best eaten with a bit of butter and a dab of jam. Be sure to look over the daily specials scrawled on the little green chalkboard before you order. And as every fan of this tiny cafe knows, it's best to call ahead and ask to have your name put on the waiting list before you slide into Home Plate.

2274 Lombard St. (at Pierce St.). ✆ 415/922-HOME (922-4663). Main courses $3.95–$7. DC, DISC, MC, V. Daily 7am–4pm. Bus: 28, 30, 43, or 76.

★ **La Méditerranée** *MEDITERRANEAN* With an upscale-cafe ambience and quality food, La Méditerranée has long warranted its reputation as one of the most appealing inexpensive restaurants in upper Fillmore. Here you'll find freshly prepared traditional Mediterranean food that's worlds apart from the Euro-eclectic fare many restaurants now call "Mediterranean." Baba ghanouj, tabbouleh, dolmas, and hummus start out the menu. My favorite dish here is the chicken Cilicia, a phyllo-dough dish that's hand-rolled and baked with cinnamon-y spices, almonds, chickpeas, and raisins. Also recommended are the zesty chicken pomegranate drumsticks on a bed of rice. Both come with green salad, potato salad, or soup for around $9.50. Ground lamb dishes, quiches, and Middle Eastern combo plates round out the affordable menu, and wine comes by the glass and in half or full liters. A second location is at 288 Noe St., at Market Street (✆ **415/431-7210**).

2210 Fillmore St. (at Sacramento St.). ✆ 415/921-2956. www.cafelamed.com. Main courses $7–$10 lunch, $8–$12 dinner. AE, MC, V. Sun–Thurs 11am–10pm; Fri–Sat 11am–11pm. Bus: 1, 3, or 22.

★ **Mel's Drive-In** *AMERICAN* Sure, it's contrived, touristy, and nowhere near healthy, but when you get that urge for a chocolate shake and banana cream pie at the stroke of midnight, no other place in the city comes through like Mel's Drive-In. Modeled after a classic 1950s diner, right down to the jukebox at each table, Mel's harkens back to the halcyon days when cholesterol and fried foods didn't jab your guilty conscience with every greasy, wonderful bite. Too bad the prices don't reflect the '50s; a burger with fries and a coke costs about $12. Another Mel's at 3355 Geary St., at Stanyan Street (✆ **415/387-2244**), is open from 6am to 1am Sunday through Thursday and

6am to 3am Friday and Saturday. Additional locations are 1050 Van Ness (✆ **415/292-6357**), open Sunday through Thursday 6am to 3am and Friday through Sunday 6am to 4am; and 801 Mission St. (✆ **415/227-4477**), open Sunday through Wednesday 6am to 1am, Thursday 6am to 2am, and Friday and Saturday 24 hours.

2165 Lombard St. (at Fillmore St.). ✆ **415/921-3039.** www.melsdrive-in.com. Main courses $6.50–$12 breakfast, $7–$10 lunch, $8–$15 dinner. MC, V. Sun–Wed 6am–1am; Thurs 6am–2am; Fri–Sat 24 hr. Bus: 22, 30, or 43.

★ **Pluto's** *CALIFORNIA* Catering to the Marina District's DINK (double income, no kids) crowd, Pluto's combines assembly-line efficiency with high quality. The result is cheap, fresh fare: huge salads with a dozen choices of toppings; oven-roasted poultry and grilled meats (the tri-tip is great); sandwiches; and a wide array of sides like crispy garlic potato rings, seasonal veggies, and barbecued chicken wings. Pluto's serves teas, sodas, bottled brews, and Napa wines, as well as homemade desserts. The ordering system is bewildering to newcomers: Grab a checklist, and then hand it to the servers, who check off your order and relay it to the cashier. Seating is limited during the rush, but the turnover is fairly fast. A second Inner Sunset location is at 627 Irving St., at Eighth Avenue (✆ **415/753-8867**).

3258 Scott St. (at Chestnut St.). ✆ **415/7-PLUTOS** (775-8867). www.plutosfreshfood.com. Reservations not accepted. Main courses $3.50–$5.75. MC, V. Mon–Fri 11am–10pm; Sat–Sun 10:30am–10pm. Bus: 28, 30, or 76.

7 Hayes Valley & Civic Center

★ **Frjtz Fries** *BELGIAN* Although they serve great sandwiches and salads, Frjtz is best known for its addictively crisp french fries, piled high in a paper cone (how Euro!) and served with a barrage of exotic dipping sauces such as chipotle rémoulade and balsamic mayo. I'm also a fan of their crepes—try the grilled rosemary chicken and Swiss cheese—their big, leafy salad, or the chunky focaccia sandwich packed with roasted peppers, red onions, pesto mayo, grilled eggplant, and melted Gorgonzola. Wash it down with creamy Chimay Belgian ale. There's also a second Frjtz Fries at 590 Valencia St. (at 17th St.; ✆ **415/863-8272**), in the Mission.

581 Hayes St. (at Laguna St.). ✆ **415/864-7654.** www.frjtzfries.com. Reservations not accepted. Fries $3–$4.50; crepes $5–$8; sandwiches $7–$8.25. AE, DC, DISC, MC, V. Mon–Thurs 11am–10pm; Fri–Sat 11am–midnight; Sun 11am–9pm. Bus: 21.

★ **Tommy's Joynt** *AMERICAN* With its colorful mural exterior, it's hard to miss Tommy's Joynt, a 58-year-old haven for cholesterol-be-damned holdouts from America's halcyon days and a late-night favorite for those in search of a cheap and hearty meal. The restaurant's exterior is tame in comparison to the interior, which looks like a Buffalo Bill museum that imploded: a wild collage of stuffed birds, a mounted buffalo head, an ancient piano, rusty firearms, fading prints, a beer-guzzling lion, and Santa Claus masks. The hofbrau-style buffet offers a cornucopia of rib-clinging a la carte dishes such as their signature buffalo stew (via a buffalo ranch in Wyoming), which resides under heat lamps among the stainless steel trays of turkeys, hams, sloppy Joes, oxtails, corned beef, meatballs, mashed potatoes, and other classics. There's also a slew of seating on two levels, almost 100 varieties of beer, and a most interesting clientele of almost exclusively 50-something pre-cardiac-arrest males (some of whom have been coming to the "Joynt" for more than 40 years). It's all good stuff in a 'merican kind of way, the kind of place you take Grandpappy when he's in town just to show him that San Francisco's not entirely sissy.

1101 Geary Blvd. (at Van Ness Ave.). ✆ **415/775-4216.** www.tommysjoynt.com. Reservations not accepted. Main courses $4–$7. No credit cards. Daily 10am–2am. Bus: 2, 3, 4, or 38.

8 Japantown & Pacific Heights

★ **Isobune** *SUSHI* Unless you arrive early, there's almost always a short wait to be seated around Isobune's enormous oval sushi bar. But once you're situated, the culinary adventure begins. Right before your eyes, plate after plate of sushi passes by on circling tugboats floating in a minuscule canal that encircles the sushi bar. If you see something you like, just grab it off the boat and enjoy; the service staff will tally up the damages at the end. (They can tell how much you've eaten by the number of empty plates.) It's not the best sushi in town, but it's relatively cheap, you get to see it before you eat it, and the atmosphere is fun.

In the Japan Center, 1737 Post St. ✆ **415/563-1030.** Sushi $1.20–$2.95 each. MC, V. Daily 11:30am–10pm. Bus: 2, 3, 4, 22, or 38.

Mifune *JAPANESE* Mifune has been serving traditional Japanese food for 15 years and has a steady clientele of folks who are happy with the fare, and ecstatic about the prices. Slide into one of the Japanese-style booths and order the house specialty, a homemade udon and soba noodles dinner. The *donburi* dishes and tempura dinner are popular as well.

In the Japan Center, 1737 Post St. ✆ 415/922-0337. Main courses $4-$17. AE, DC, DISC, MC, V. Daily 11am-9pm. Bus: 2, 3, 4, 22, or 38.

★ **Neecha Thai** *THAI* I've been coming here for many years for very simple reasons: The food's consistently good, the ambience is homey, the prices are low, and I lived down the street. A few years back, the old, dark decor was replaced by a brighter but not-quite-harmonious modern style (unfortunately, they kept the ugly fake-brick paneling). The fare is standard but well-prepared Thai, with more than 70 choices, including satay; salads; lemon grass soup; coconut-milk curries; and exotic meat, chicken, seafood, and vegetable dishes—and yes, the ever-popular pad Thai, too. My favorite dishes here are the shrimp in red curry and the salmon wrapped in banana leaf.

2100 Sutter St. (at Steiner St.). ✆ 415/922-9419. Most dishes $5-$8. AE, MC, V. Mon-Fri 11am-3pm and 5-10pm; Sat-Sun 5-10pm. Bus: 2, 4, or 38.

Sanppo *JAPANESE* This simple, unpretentious restaurant located across from the Japan Center serves standard Japanese fare at a great price. You may be asked to share one of the few tables that surround a square counter in the small dining room, but at these prices, it's worth it. Lunch items range from fresh, thick-cut sashimi to teriyaki, tempura, beef donburi, and *gyoza* (dumplings filled with savory meat and herbs). Lunches and dinners all include miso soup, rice, and pickled vegetables. Combination dishes, including tempura, sashimi, and *gyoza,* or tempura and teriyaki, are also available.

1702 Post St. (at Laguna St.). ✆ 415/346-3486. Main courses $6-$15; combination dishes $10-$17. MC, V. Daily 11am-midnight. Bus: 2, 3, 4, or 38.

★ **2001 Thai Stick** *THAI* The name of this place is so bad that I passed by it for years before a friend who lives in the neighborhood assured me that the food is actually quite good, and perfect for a casual, inexpensive meal. He was right. My green curry with chicken was lightly spiced and had the rich creaminess of coconut milk without being too rich. Also good was the pork in peanut sauce, but even better was the price.

2001 Fillmore St. (at Pine St.). ✆ 415/885-6100. Highchairs, boosters. Reservations not accepted. Main courses $5.95-$11. Sun-Thurs 11am-10pm; Fri-Sat 11am-11pm. AE, DC, DISC, MC, V. Muni: No. 1-California bus to California St., and then walk 1 block south.

9 The Mission District

Angkor Borei *CAMBODIAN* One of the first destinations on your San Francisco ethnic-food adventure tour should be Angkor Borei, a small, unpretentious neighborhood restaurant that serves fine Cambodian cuisine. It's the perfect place to sample Cambodia's intricate cuisine at the modest price tag locals have come to expect in the Mission District. The combination of spices in most any dish on the menu is intriguing—typically, sweet basil and tangy lemongrass are the first to hit the tongue, then a short blast of hot chili pepper bursts through, and, finally, soothing coconut milk brings the whole blend together. Try the delicate vegetable-filled spring rolls to warm up, then go for a spicy noodle dish or duck in a clay pot.

3471 Mission St. (at Courtland Ave.). ✆ **415/550-8417.** Main courses $6–$12. AE, DISC, MC, V. Daily 11am–10pm. Bus: 14 or 49.

★ **Dolores Park Cafe** *AMERICAN/BREAKFAST* The setting alone, across the street from Dolores Park with a spacious front deck, would probably be enough to guarantee this cafe's popularity. But it also happens to serve a terrific cafe latte, and plenty of other inexpensive and satisfying items, like albacore tuna melts on whole-grain bread and Niman Ranch honey-glazed ham sandwiches. Breakfast items, soups, and salads are all worth stopping by for as well. Enjoy your meal in the sunshine, alongside other diners rocking strollers or perusing the newspaper. Their live music show Friday nights from 7:30 to 9:30pm is a big hit, so make sure to eat your dinner before the crowds stream in.

501 Dolores St. (at 18th St.). ✆ **415/621-2936.** www.doloresparkcafe.org. Highchairs. Reservations not accepted. Sandwiches and salads $5–$7.50. No credit cards. Daily 7am–8pm. Fri music nights until 9:30pm. Muni: J-Church streetcar to 18th, and then walk 1 block east.

El Nuevo Frutilandia *CUBAN/PUERTO RICAN* El Nuevo Frutilandia is one of the few places in the city to get home-cooked Puerto Rican and Cuban food (the fresh-fruit shakes are wonderful, as are the Puerto Rican dumplings made of crushed plantain and yuca, filled with shredded pork). It's an unpretentious little place, serving reasonably priced plates of chicken in green sauce, roast pork with rice and yucca, and shrimp in garlic sauce. It's also well off the beaten path, so the odds of running into tourists here are slim.

3077 24th St. (at Folsom St.). ✆ **415/648-2958.** Main courses $6–$12. MC, V. Mon–Sun noon–3pm and 5–8:45pm. Metro: 24th St. station.

El Trebol Restaurante *SALVADORAN/NICARAGUAN* This delightful little family-run Salvadoran/Nicaraguan eatery in the Mission District is one of the best deals in the city, and a local favorite that the locals would prefer to remain secret. It's a Formica-table kind of place that serves Salvadoran/Nicaraguan treats like *pupusas* (handmade corn patties stuffed with cheese or meat or both) for less than a dollar and full meals (including rice and beans) for less than $7. Be sure to try the fried plantains as well, washed down with a $1 glass of wine.

3324 24th St. (at Mission St.). ✆ **415/285-6298.** Main courses $4–$8. No credit cards. Mon–Fri noon–9pm; Sat noon–8pm. 24th St. Mission BART station.

★ **La Corneta Taqueria** *MEXICAN* Taquerias abound in the Mission, so it may be useful to clarify what they actually sell, especially if you are not from the Southwest. They do not sell the crunchy, uniformly shaped "tacos" that break into a million pieces when you bite them, such as you find at the fast-food chains Del Taco or Taco Bell. Mission taquerias sell flavorful tacos on soft corn or flour tortillas, in addition to tostadas, enchiladas, and even plated dinners. But the biggest reason most San Franciscans come to a taqueria is for the burritos. And at La Corneta, in addition to a more colorful, spacious, and clean-feeling dining room than you find at many neighborhood taquerias, you'll get a darn good burrito. Stand in line to choose beans (black, pinto, refried), a filling (beef, beef tongue, chicken, pork, shrimp, vegetarian), and your salsa preference (mild or hot). Make sure to ask for guacamole and sour cream as well. After that, you won't need to eat until tomorrow.

2731 Mission St. (btw 23rd and 24th sts.). ✆ **415/643-7001.** www.lacorneta.com. Highchairs. Main courses $1.25–$13. MC, V. Daily 10am–10pm. BART to 24th and Mission.

★ **Pancho Villa Taqueria** *MEXICAN* This is an old standby and one of the best taquerias in the city. The ever-present line testifies to the quality and consistency of the burritos, tacos, quesadillas, and enormous combination plates of prawns, *carne asada,* and chicken. The dining room isn't much to look at—utilitarian comes to mind—but who cares? With a choice of meats, beans, tortillas, salsas, and extras like sour cream or avocado, your eyes will be on your plate. Portions are substantial, and a late lunch will easily serve for dinner.

CHEAP EATS & NIGHTLIFE AROUND THE CASTRO & THE MISSION

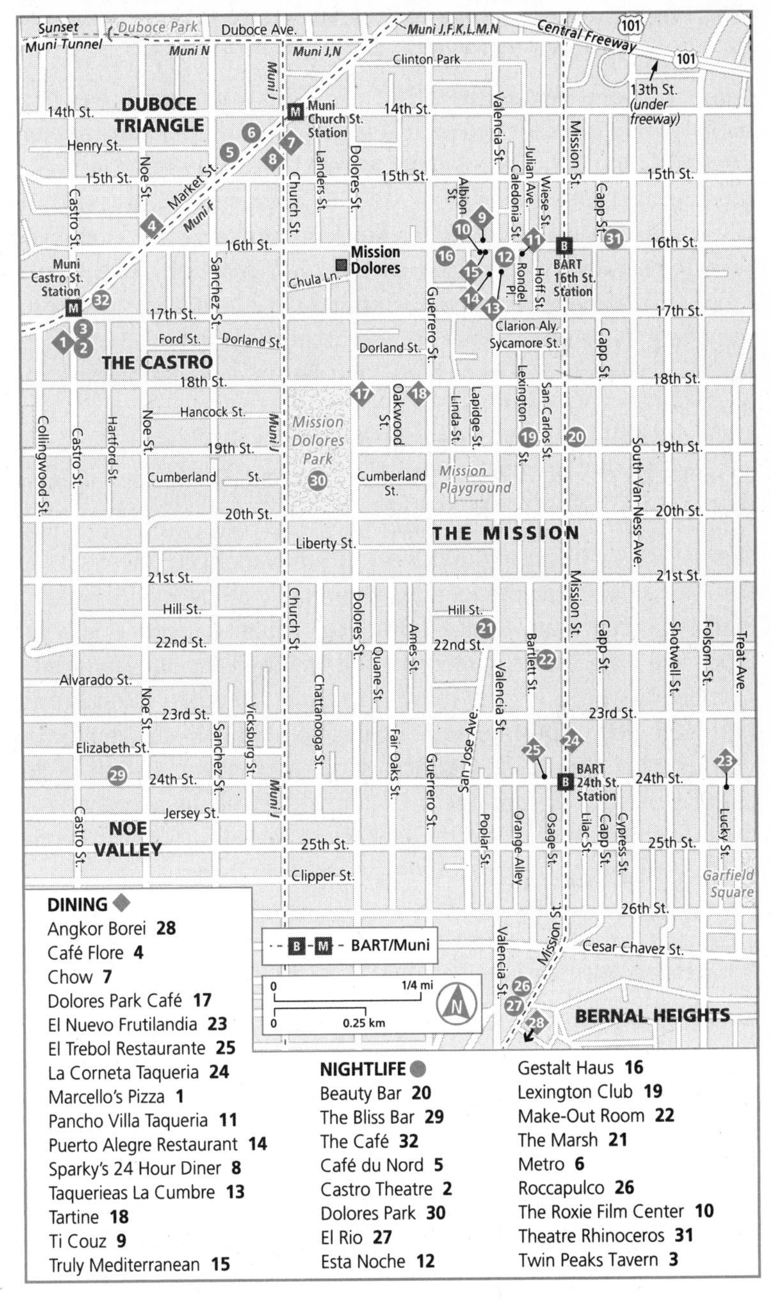

3071 16th St. (btw Mission and Valencia sts.). ✆ 415/864-8840. www.panchovillasf.com. Highchairs. Main courses $1.35–$10. AE, MC, V. Daily 10am–midnight. Muni: BART to 16th and Mission sts., and then walk 1 block west.

Puerto Alegre Restaurant *MEXICAN* This would hardly be a popular spot were it not for two critical factors: Pitchers of margaritas are a mere $11, and the dive-restaurant prices come with a more festive and intimate atmosphere than other Mexican restaurants in the 'hood. This is not a place for wolfing down a quick burrito; this is the kind of joint where you gather with friends, suck back a few slushy 'ritas, and get loose amid the plastic-covered seats and tables. And you order a burrito or combination plate not because it's the best in town but because it's *good enough* and dirt cheap, and because you're bound to get hammered if you don't soak up that tequila with something.

546 Valencia St. (btw 16th and 17th sts.). ✆ 415/255-8201. Main courses $3.85–$6.35. DC, MC, V. Mon 11am–10pm; Tues 5–11pm; Wed–Sun 11am–11pm. BART: Mission. Bus: 14, 22, 33, 49, or 53.

Taquerias La Cumbre *MEXICAN* If San Francisco commissioned a flag honoring its favorite food, we'd probably all be waving a banner of the Golden Gate Bridge bolstering a giant burrito—that's how much we love the mammoth tortilla-wrapped meals. Taquerias La Cumbre has been around forever and still retains its "Best Burrito" title, each deftly constructed using fresh pork, steak, chicken, or vegetables, plus cheese, beans, rice, salsa, and maybe a dash of guacamole or sour cream. The fact that it's served in a cafeteria-like brick-lined room with overly shellacked tables featuring a woman with overflowing cleavage makes it taste even better.

515 Valencia St. (btw 16th and 17th sts.). ✆ 415/863-8205. Reservations not accepted. Tacos and burritos $3.50–$6.50; dinner plates $5–$7. No credit cards. Mon–Sat 11am–9pm; Sun noon–9pm. Bus: 14, 22, 33, 49, or 53. BART: Mission.

★ **Tartine** *BAKERY* Crowds from far and near are drawn by the smell of freshly baked bread at Tartine, considered by many (myself included) to be the best bakery in San Francisco. You could be forgiven for forgoing dinner and simply dining on a loaf of oven-fresh walnut bread, which comes out of the oven after 4pm and sells out quickly. If the walnut bread is gone, all is not lost: Tartine also has some wonderful toasted sandwiches and plenty of other mouthwatering baked goods to choose from.

eclectic and cost-conscious diners. After all, what's not to like about starting with a Cobb salad before moving on to Thai-style noodles with steak, chicken, peanuts, and spicy lime-chile garlic broth, or cioppino? Better yet, everything except the fish of the day costs under $15, especially the budget-wise daily sandwich specials, which range from meatball with mozzarella (Sun) to grilled tuna with Asian-style slaw, pickled ginger, and a wasabi mayonnaise (Mon); both come with salad, soup, or fries. Although the food and prices alone would be a good argument for coming here, beer on tap, a great inexpensive wine selection, and the fun, tavern-like environment clinch the deal. A second location, **Park Chow,** is at 1240 Ninth Ave. (✆ **415/665-9912**). You can't make reservations unless you have a party of eight or more, but if you're headed their way, you can call ahead to place your name on the wait list (recommended).

215 Church St. (near Market St.). ✆ **415/552-2469.** Reservations not accepted. Main courses $7–$15. DISC, MC, V. Mon–Thurs 11am–11pm; Fri 11am–midnight; Sat 10am–midnight; Sun 10am–11pm; brunch served Sat–Sun 10am–2:30pm. Bus: 8, 22, or 37. Streetcar: F, J, K, L, or M.

Marcello's Pizza *PIZZA* Marcello's isn't a fancy place, just a traditional pizza joint with a couple of tables, tasty pizza by the slice, and a few other basic dishes like burgers, salads, and calzones. Weekend nights there's a line out the door of drunk and/or stoned Castro Street partiers with the late-night munchies.

420 Castro St. (at Market St.). ✆ **415/863-3900.** www.marcellospizzasf.com. Pizza slices $2.25–$3; pies $11–$26. No credit cards. Sun–Thurs 11am–1am; Fri–Sat 11am–1am; Sun noon–midnight. Metro: K, L, or M to Castro St. Station.

Sparky's 24 Hour Diner *AMERICAN* Good ol' Sparky's is one of the few 24-hour greasy spoons in the city, a Church Street diner that serves a decent burger and a hearty breakfast to Castro and Upper Market locals. The lights are a tad too bright and the waitstaff a bit too dim, but at least the breakfasts here avoid the white-bread toast and frozen-hash-brown-type food substance that seem to be standard issue at all-night coffee shops. The wee-hours crowd at Sparky's can be a bit eccentric—and sometimes a tad inebriated—but just mind your own business and pass the ketchup. Hey, it was good enough for Queen Latifah when she was in town.

242 Church St. (at Market St.). ✆ **415/626-8666.** Main courses $7–$15. AE, MC, V. Daily 24 hr. Metro: K, L, or M to Castro St. Station.

11 The Haight & Cole Valley

Blue Front Cafe *AMERICAN/BREAKFAST/MEDITERRANEAN* The Blue Front's menu is as eclectic as the upbringing of its friendly owners, three Greek Orthodox Christian brothers who were raised in the Old City of Jerusalem. The specialties are Middle Eastern/Mediterranean—spit-roasted lamb gyros in pita bread and falafel wraps are among the choices—but you'll find all-American turkey, club, and Reuben sandwiches on the menu as well. The Blue Front is also a good breakfast spot, serving up three-egg omelets, toasted bagels, and breakfast wraps in Mediterranean *lavash* bread. The room is nothing fancy—wooden tables are close together with plenty of people reading their papers and nursing their coffees—but the huge Genie hanging out front blends in well with the colorful neighborhood.

1430 Haight St. (btw Masonic Ave. and Ashbury St.). © **415/252-5917.** www.bluefrontcafe.com. Highchairs. Reservations not accepted. Main courses $5.25–$9.75. MC, V. Sun–Thurs 7:30am–10pm; Fri–Sat 7:30am–11pm. Muni: 6-Parnassus, 7-Haight, or 71-Haight-Noreiga bus to Masonic Ave.

★ **Burger Joint** *HAMBURGERS* In a setting reminiscent of a '50s-era TV sitcom, with vinyl-covered chairs and vintage Formica patterns on the tables, you can enjoy a really good burger. They're made with naturally raised, hormone-free Niman Ranch beef and served on a bun that has enough personality to handle a juicy hand-formed patty. The only alternatives to a hamburger or cheeseburger are a hot dog, free-range chicken breast sandwich, or veggie burger, all served with crispy fries. Sinfully good milkshakes and root beer floats are made with San Francisco's Double Rainbow ice cream. Another location is in the Mission neighborhood.

700 Haight St. (at Pierce St.). © **415/864-3833.** Mission: 807 Valencia St. (btw 19th and 20th sts.). © **415/824-3494.** www.burgerjointsf.com. Boosters, highchairs. Main courses $5.45–$7.95. MC, V. Daily 9am–11:30pm. Muni: 6-Parnassus, 7-Haight, or 71-Haight-Noreiga bus to Pierce St.

★ **Citrus Club** *NOODLES* When you're a starving travel writer, you quickly discover that the cheapest, healthiest, and most satisfying things to eat in San Francisco are burritos and noodles. Citrus Club does noodles. Large, heaping bowls of thick Asian noodles, served hot in bone-warming broth or cool, minty, and refreshing. In typical Upper Haight fashion, the Club has sort of a cheap-Polynesian-chic feel—love those Vietnamese straw hat lamps—a young, hip staff and clientele, and the omnipresent world beat rhythms. Most items on the menu are unlike anything you've seen before, so take my advice and walk around the two dining rooms to see what looks good before ordering. A refreshing starter is the citrus salad made with mixed greens, mint, fried noodles, and a tangy citrus vinaigrette. Popular cold noodle selections are the spicy lime and coconut, and the orange-mint. For hot noodles, try the marmalade shrimp or sweet chile-glazed tofu and greens. If you're in a party mood, order a sake margarita; otherwise, a big pot of ginger tea goes well with any of the noodle dishes.

1790 Haight St. (at Shrader St.). ✆ 415/387-6366. Main courses $6–$10. MC, V. Mon–Thurs and Sun 11:30am–10pm; Fri–Sat 11:30am–11pm. Muni Metro: N. Bus: 6, 7, 66, 71, or 73.

Crepes on Cole *CREPES* If you're in the Cole Valley or Haight-Ashbury area and you're looking for a hearty, healthy, and very affordable meal, consider a crepe (yes, a crepe). These paper-thin, egg-based pancakes can be filled with a wide variety of ingredients—meats, veggies, sweets, and more—and enjoyed as either a main course or a dessert. You can either build your own crepe from the wide variety of fillings, or order from house specialties such as the Florentine crepe made with cheddar cheese, onions, spinach, and cottage cheese, or the Mediterranean crepe with cheddar, onion, eggplant, pesto, tomato, and roasted peppers. All options, including the less-celebrated omelets, come with a heaping pile of house potatoes. You can also order one of the simple sandwiches, bagels, or an enormous Caesar salad, all for under $8.

100 Carl St. (at Cole St.). ✆ 415/664-1800. Main courses $6–$8. No credit cards. Sun–Thurs 7am–11pm; Fri–Sat 7am–midnight; Sun 7am–11pm. Metro: N-Judah. Bus: 6, 7, 66, or 71.

★ **Memphis Minnie's** *BARBECUE* If you've got a hankering for a tender piece of slow-cooked meat, head straight to Memphis Minnie's. The owner smokes his brisket for 12 hours and adds his own spice rub for kick and flavor. Other options are finger-licking-good ribs and succulent pulled pork. The protocol is simple: Stand in line and choose your meat and two sides, such as sweet potato or corn muffin, and have a seat at one of the tables lined up against the bright yellow and red wall. Look around at the playful decor, which includes plastic pigs, black-and-white cow-print ceiling fans, pinned-up trucker hats, and pithy sayings like "Never Trust a Skinny Cook." Once your meal is ready, choose from one of the three sauces at your table: red Texan, North Carolina vinegar, and South Carolina yellow mustard. Fortunately, each table has a full roll of paper towels on it as well.

576 Haight St. (at Steiner St.). ✆ 415/864-7675. www.memphisminnies.com. Highchairs, boosters. Main courses $8–$15. AE, MC, V. Tues–Fri 11am–10pm; Sat 9am–10pm; Sun 9am–9pm. Muni: 6-Parnassus, 7-Haight, or 71-Haight-Noreiga bus to Steiner St.

★ **Zona Rosa** *MEXICAN* This is a great place to stop and get a cheap (and healthful) bite. The most popular items are the burritos, which are made to order and include your choice of beans (refried, whole pinto, or black), meats (the carnitas is great), or vegetarian ingredients. You can sit on a stool at the window and watch the Haight Street freaks strolling by, relax at one of five colorful interior tables, or take it to go and head to Golden Gate Park (just 2 blocks away). Zona Rosa is one of the best burrito shops around.

1797 Haight St. (at Shrader St.). ✆ 415/668-7717. Burritos $5.50–$7.50. No credit cards. Daily 11am–9:30pm. Muni Metro: N. Bus: 6, 7, 66, 71, or 73.

11 Sunset & Richmond Districts

Brothers Restaurant *KOREAN* At do-it-yourself Korean barbecue joints, the food is as much fun to cook as it is to eat. You barbecue marinated beef and pork on hibachis built into the tables, wrap the meat in a lettuce leaf, and add whatever condiments you like—kind of a Korean burrito. Brothers Restaurant, one of many popular Korean eateries along Geary Boulevard (Richmond District), caters to a primarily Korean clientele. It's the most popular Geary Boulevard place with local Koreans, and the staff sometimes proves its own authenticity when you're trying to make reservations in English. You can grill meats at your table's wood-fired hibachi or sample from the rest of the small menu.

4128 Geary Blvd. (at Fifth Ave). ✆ 415/387-7991. Main courses $6–$20. Daily 11am–2am. MC, V. Bus: 38.

★ **Burma Superstar** *BURMESE* Despite its gratuitous name, this basic dining room garners two-star status by offering exceptional Burmese food at rock-bottom prices. Unfortunately, the allure of the tealeaf salad, Burmese-style curry with potato, and sweet-tangy

CHEAP EATS IN THE RICHMOND & THE SUNSET

sesame beef is one of the city's worst-kept secrets. Add to that a no-reservations policy and you can count on waiting in line for up to an hour. (FYI, parties of two are seated more quickly than larger groups, and it's less crowded at lunch.) On the bright side, you can pencil your cellphone number onto the waiting list and browse the Clement Street shops until you receive a call.

309 Clement St. (at Fourth Ave.). ✆ 415/387-2147. www.burmasuperstar.com. Reservations not accepted. Main courses $8–$16. MC, V. Mon–Thurs 11am–3:30pm and 5:30–9:30pm; Fri–Sat 11am–3:30pm and 5:30–10pm; Sun 11am–3:30pm and 5:30–9:30pm. Bus: 2, 4, 38, or 44.

The Canvas Cafe/Gallery *BREAKFAST/ECLECTIC* This loftlike space across the street from Golden Gate Park triples as an art gallery, lounge, and cafe. Get there during daylight hours, and it's an optimal place to grab a bite before heading off to the Strybing Arboretum, the Japanese Tea Garden, or other park attractions within close walking distance. Munch on oatmeal or toasted bagels for breakfast, and for lunch choose from an assortment of salads, several cold or grilled sandwiches, focaccia pizzas, and even a few pasta entrees like macaroni and cheese and meat or veggie lasagna. While you await your meal, look around at the paintings and sculptures for sale. Another bonus: This is one of the few San Francisco cafes with its own parking lot.

1200 9th Ave. (at Lincoln Way). ✆ **415/504-0060.** www.thecanvasgallery.com. Highchairs, boosters. Reservations not accepted. Main courses $7-$11. AE, MC, V. Mon-Thurs 10am-10pm; Fri 10am-7:30pm; Sat 9am-7:30pm; Sun 9am-10pm. Live music Thurs-Sun evenings. Muni: N-Judah streetcar to 9th Ave., and then walk 2 blocks north toward the park, or no. 71 Haight-Noriega stops across the street at 9th and Lincoln.

Coriya Hot Pot City *TAIWANESE* This all-you-can-eat Taiwanese restaurant on Clement Street is sort of a cross between Japanese shabu-shabu and Korean barbecue. Load up your trays buffet-style with the makings of a hearty meal—piles of raw meats and vegetables—then play chef at your own table, where hot pots and grills are built in. Steam or sauté beef, pork, chicken, seafood, noodles, and vegetables to your heart's content. The place is loud, crowded (you'll have to wait in line on weekends), and festive, and does not serve parties of one, so bring a group of friends and split the bill. There are even free drink refills!

852 Clement St. (at 10th Ave.). ✆ **415/387-7888.** Main courses $13-$15. Sun-Thurs noon-11:30pm; Fri-Sat noon-1am. MC, V. Bus: 38.

★ **de Young Cafe** *CALIFORNIA* This is my new favorite lunch spot when visiting Golden Gate Park. Beyond inventively prepared soups, salads, and sandwiches—such as a Thai Beef sandwich with ginger roast beef, lemongrass, and sweet soy sauce—you can also enjoy tasty grilled options like fish tacos with cilantro-lime slaw and hot items such as pasta puttanesca or Dungeness crab cakes. The food is made with seasonal, local ingredients, most of which is produced, raised, or farmed within 150 miles of the cafe, such as their Niman Ranch hot dogs. Although the offerings are appetizing, the cafe's best asset is its location within the de Young Museum, where it's open to all visitors. On sunny days, you can sit outside by the sculpture garden. A sesame chicken salad is always nice, but a sesame chicken salad next to a Henry Moore sculpture is extra special.

FREE Amazing Grazing

There's no better way to enjoy a free breakfast on a sunny San Francisco morning than by strolling the Ferry Plaza Farmers Market and snacking your way through breakfast on some of America's finest organic produce. While poking among the 100 stalls crammed with northern California fruit, vegetable, bread, shellfish, and dairy items, you're bound to bump elbows with the dozens of Bay Area chefs (such as Alice Waters) who do their shopping here. The enthusiastic vendors are always willing to educate visitors about the benefits of organic produce, and often provide free samples. But wait, there's more: On Saturdays the market operates a **Shop with the Chef** program in which a guest restaurant chef browses the market for ingredients, then conducts a free cooking class at 10:30am (with free samples, of course). Several local restaurants, such as North Beach's Rose Pistola, also have food stalls promoting their organic cuisine, so skip breakfast before you come. You can also pick up locally made vinegars and oils, which make wonderful gifts. The Farmers' Market takes place year-round, rain or shine, every Saturday and Sunday from 8am to 2pm, Tuesdays from 10am to 2pm, and Thursdays from 3 to 7pm at the Ferry Building, on the Embarcadero at the foot of Market Street (about a 15-min. walk from Fisherman's Wharf). Call ✆ **415/353-5650** for more information or log onto www.ferryplazafarmersmarket.com.

1200 9th Ave. (at Lincoln Way). ✆ **415/750-2614.** www.famsf.org/deyoung/visiting. Highchairs. Salads and sandwiches $5.50–$14. AE, DC, DISC, MC, V. Tues–Sun 9:30am–4pm; Fri 9:30am–8:45pm. Muni: N-Judah streetcar to 9th Ave., and then walk north on 9th into the park, or 44-O'Shaughnessy bus to Concourse Dr.

★ **Giorgio's Pizzeria** *PIZZA* This festive, boisterous pizzeria has been serving consistently good thin-crust pizza for more than 35 years. Giorgio's lunchtime deals are fantastic: $5.95 for a big slice, salad, and refillable soda, and $6.95 for a pasta dish with the same sides (available up until 4pm).

Enjoying an Urban Picnic

You're not cheap, you're just a hopeless romantic who loves to picnic. So let's make it easy for you to play Don Juan for under $10. To start, hunt for sandwiches at **Specialty's Café and Bakery** (✆ 877/502-2837; 1 Post St. at Market St.) or **Lee's Deli** (✆ 415/421-0648; 648 Market St. between Kearny and Montgomery sts., among other Financial District locations). Specialty's bakes its own bread and offers deli-style sandwiches with some inventive options such as Thai chicken and turkey curry. Lee's is fast, inexpensive, and basic: tuna or thickly sliced real turkey. Once you've packed your bag, you're ready to head to 100 1st St. There you'll find the award-winning second-floor garden in the Delta Tower, a lush respite from busy Mission Street. The black-granite and green-glass fountain sculpture provides a soothing counterpoint to the street traffic. If you're in SoMa, stop by **A G Ferrari Foods** on 688 Mission St. (✆ 415/344-0644) to pick up Italian sandwiches on fresh focaccia bread. Then head to Yerba Buena Gardens (p. 50) for an alfresco urban retreat.

Then there's picnicking by the bay. Go to the **Ferry Building Marketplace** on the Embarcadero and purchase sandwiches from **Mastrelli's Delicatessen** (✆ 415/397-3354). Then go out behind the building, grab a bench, and enjoy your picnic as you watch the ferries head out across the bay. At Fort Mason, pick up vegetarian sandwiches like egg salad at **Greens to Go** (Bldg. A, Fort Mason

151 Clement St. (at 3rd Ave.). ✆ **415/668-1266.** www.giorgiospizza.com. Highchairs, boosters. Reservations not accepted. Minipizza $7–$12, large pizza $13–$22. MC, V. Sun–Thurs 11:30am–10pm; Fri–Sat 11:30am–11pm. Muni: 2-Clement, 3-Jackson, or 4-Sutter bus to 3rd Ave.; or 1-California bus to 3rd Ave., and then walk 1 block south to Clement St.

★ **Marnee Thai** *THAI* Fortunately for out-of-town visitors, it's now no longer necessary to trek to the outer Sunset to try the best Thai food in San Francisco. Marnee Thai's new location is just steps away from Golden Gate Park, so you can easily come in for an early dinner after spending the afternoon visiting the Strybing Arboretum or Japanese

Center, ✆ 415/771-6330) and then sit yourselves under a palm tree on the expansive lawn. If you're at **Crissy Field** (p. 120), grab a soup or sandwich at the **Warming Hut.** You'll find plenty of picnic spots outside.

North Beach provides more sources for dining outdoors on the cheap. **Molinari,** 373 Columbus Ave. at Vallejo Street (✆ 415/421-2337), is an Italian delicatessen with a fantastic assortment of imported foodstuffs and friendly staff who will create everything-on-'em sandwiches to go. Also consider takeout from **Mario's Bohemian Cigar Store** (p. 50). You can't pass on dessert if you're anywhere near **Victoria Pastry Co.,** 1362 Stockton St. at Vallejo (✆ 415/781-2015). The chewy almond cookies are divine, as are the cakes, all sold by the slice or whole. Walk over to Washington Square Park at the corner of Columbus Avenue and Union Street and let the feasting begin.

If you're headed out to Lincoln Park in the Richmond District, a convenient stop is **Angelina's Bakery** at 6000 California St., at 22nd Avenue (✆ 415/221-7801). Pick up sandwiches, salads, or quiches and hop back on the no. 1-California bus to 32nd Street. Then walk north 2 blocks to Eagle's Point at the end of the Land's End trail. Enjoy your picnic with a priceless view of the Marin Headlands and western side of the Golden Gate Bridge.

Tea Garden. The spicy Angel wings (deep-fried chicken wings topped with chili, garlic, and sweet basil) are hugely popular and not too spicy for most kids. All the soups, curries, and noodle dishes are also fabulous. Be adventurous, skip the pad Thai, and try one of the many other wonderful dishes. If you're lucky, the owner's wife will pop by when you're there. In addition to being very opinionated about what you should order, she'll gladly tell you your fortune, free of charge.

1243 9th Ave. (btw Irving St. and Lincoln Way). ✆ **415/731-9999.** www.marneethaisf.com. Highchairs, boosters. Reservations recommended on weekends. Main courses $8–$14. AE, MC, V. Daily 11:30am–10pm. Muni: N-Judah streetcar to 9th Ave., and then walk 2 blocks north toward the park.

★ **Park Chow** *AMERICAN* Just like Chow, its sister restaurant in the Castro (p. 64), Park Chow balances good ingredients, a lively atmosphere, and amazing value to deliver a great dining experience.

1238 9th Ave. (btw Irving St. and Lincoln Way). ✆ **415/665-9912.** Highchairs, boosters. Reservations not accepted. Main courses $6–$15. MC, V. Mon–Thurs 11am–10pm; Fri 11am–11pm; Sat 10am–11pm; Sun 10am–10pm. Muni: N-Judah streetcar to 9th Ave., and then walk 2 blocks north toward the park.

★ **Pizzetta 211** *PIZZA* When you arrive at this miniscule storefront on an otherwise residential street far from downtown, you'll feel like you've come upon a hidden gem. You have. The cozy pizzeria, with but a handful of indoor and outdoor tables, serves up thin-crust, wood-oven-fired pizzette from a weekly changing menu. Whenever possible, organic produce, dairy, and grains are used to make delectable, crispy pizzas with inspired toppings like oven-dried San Marzano tomatoes, prosciutto, and local goat cheese, or roasted cauliflower, garlic, and bread crumbs. Salads and Italian desserts are also available. The wait for a table can get brutal after 7pm; a better option is to come for lunch after a morning hike at Land's End and sit outside.

211 23rd Ave. (at California St.). ✆ **415/379-9880.** Reservations not accepted. Individual pizzas $9–$14. No credit cards. Mon 5–9pm; Wed–Fri lunch noon–2:30pm, dinner 5–9pm; Sat–Sun noon–9pm. Muni: 1-California bus to 23rd Ave.

★ **Yum Yum Fish** *SUSHI* Sure, Yum Yum Fish smells like a fish market, but that's only because it *is* a fish market. But those-in-the-know also come here for the freshest inexpensive sushi in the city, served at a little counter in the back and eaten at a folding table with two garage-sale/giveaway chairs. How inexpensive? The seven-piece inari combo (California, tofu, and mixed veggie) runs about $12 at most sushi restaurants—here, it's $4. If you want to be the life of the next potluck party, order the $40 party platter, which comes loaded with various rolls and nigiri. The staff here is superfriendly, and once you get used to the smell you're bound to stay awhile, stuffing yourself on top-notch sushi.

2181 Irving St. (btw 22nd and 23rd aves.). ✆ **415/566-6433.** www.yumyumfishsushi.com. Main courses $6–$20. DISC, MC, V. Daily 10:30am–7:30pm. Bus: 71.

It doesn't cost a thing to look at the view of the city from the top of the de Young Museum (which also has a "free day" every month).

4 EXPLORING SAN FRANCISCO

San Francisco may be one of the most expensive places to live in the world, but when it comes to seeing the city's sights and playing with all of its toys, you can have a ball for only a few dollars a day, and do like the natives do, and take advantage of the numerous free attractions and activities. Within this chapter are dozens and dozens of cool places and activities to see and experience—from mind-broadening talks, readings and lectures to $10 bleacher seats at the Giants' ballpark—all of which have been given my Cheap Guy 3¢ Stamp of Approval. Stick with these recommendations and you're guaranteed to have quite the adventure in San Francisco at very little expense.

1 San Francisco's Top 10 Free Attractions

1. The Golden Gate Bridge A mandatory awe-inspiring adventure is a bracing stroll across the Golden Gate Bridge—possibly the most beautiful, and certainly the most photographed, bridge in the world. There is simply no other way to truly appreciate its immense scale and beauty. The best part is that the weather is absolutely predictable: chilly and windy, so bring a jacket. With its gracefully suspended single span, spidery bracing cables, and zooming twin towers, the 1.7-mile bridge looks more like a work of abstract art than one of the 20th century's greatest practical engineering feats. You can actually feel it sway and vibrate as gusty ocean winds whip through its cables, but don't be alarmed. The bridge is not about to collapse. It held up under the ballast of more than a hundred thousand revelers who congregated there to celebrate its 50th anniversary in 1987, and it didn't even flinch during the 1989 earthquake. While you must pay a toll if you drive across, it costs you only shoe leather (or pleather, if you're vegan) to walk. Cyclists also cross free. FINE PRINT Skates and skateboards are not permitted; dogs on leashes are permitted; pedestrian access is from 5am to 9pm in summer, and 5am to 6pm in winter.

Hwy. 101 N. www.goldengatebridge.org. Bus: 28 or 29.

2. Lombard Street Known (erroneously) as the "crookedest street in the world," this whimsically winding block of Lombard Street draws thousands of visitors each year (much to the chagrin of neighborhood residents, most of whom would prefer to block off the street to tourists). The angle of the street is so steep that the road has to snake back and forth to make a descent possible. The brick-lined street zigzags around the residences' bright flower gardens, which explode with color during warmer months. This short stretch of Lombard Street is one-way, downhill, and fun to drive. Take the curves slowly and in low gear, and expect a wait during the weekend. You can also take staircases (without curves) up or down on either side of the street. In truth, most locals don't understand what the fuss is all about. I'm guessing the draw is the combination of seeing such a famous landmark, the challenge of negotiating so many steep curves, and a classic photo op (my advice: don't take photos while you're driving downhill!). ***FYI:*** Vermont Street, between 20th and

22nd streets in Potrero Hill, is even more crooked, but not nearly as picturesque.

Btw Hyde and Leavenworth sts. Cable car: Powell-Hyde.

3. Coit Tower In a city known for its great views and vantage points, Coit Tower is one of the best. Located atop Telegraph Hill, just east of North Beach, the round stone tower offers panoramic views of the city and the bay. Inside the base of the tower are impressive murals titled *Life in California* and *1934,* which were completed under the WPA during the New Deal. They are the work of more than 25 artists, many of whom had studied under Mexican muralist Diego Rivera. On weekends the narrow street leading to the tower is often clogged with tourist traffic. If you can, find a parking spot in North Beach and hoof it. It's actually a beautiful walk—especially if you take the Filbert Street Steps (see the box "The 377-Step Program"). FINE PRINT While admission to the building is free, if you want to see the view from the top of the tower, there's a charge for the elevator ride to the top.

Telegraph Hill. ✆ 415/362-0808. Free admission; elevator ride to the top is $4.50 adults, $3.50 seniors, $2 children 6–12. Daily 10am–6pm. Bus: 39 (Coit).

4. Chinatown Chinatown is one of the most popular tourist attractions in San Francisco, but it has never become merely a tourist trap—above all else it is a place where people live; in fact, it's the largest Chinese community outside of Asia. As soon as you cross under the ornate, dragon-crested gateway on Grant Avenue at Bush Street, you're no longer in the Western world. Street signs are marked in Chinese characters, lampposts are encircled by dragons, and store windows display strange medicinal herbs and animal parts you'd never find at a suburban drugstore. The best time to see this teeming neighborhood is early in the morning, when merchants deliver their wares in pushcarts and mothers rush down the street toting live chickens, gasping catfish, and very dead armadillos in pink plastic bags—always the pink plastic bags—for tonight's dinner (yes, I've seen boxes of dead armadillos for sale here). For more about exploring Chinatown see the "Chinatown" section later in this chapter.

5. Sea Lions at PIER 39 The attraction that draws the largest crowds at PIER 39 is also the attraction that fails to pay rent, smells up the neighborhood, and refuses to mind its manners: sea lions. The first

FREE The 377-Step Program

One of the best ways to enjoy San Francisco's topography is to tour the dozens of stairways that have been built into the city's steep sidewalks and pathways. The most popular is the Filbert Street Steps between Sansome Street and Telegraph Hill, a 377-step descent on the eastern face of Telegraph Hill (you can combine it with a trip to Coit Tower). The verdant path offers a blissful break from urban clamor as it winds past century-old cottages and lush gardens. The breathtaking view of the bay from the top of the hill has attracted artists, writers, and singers for years (Joan Baez and Armistead Maupin are among past residents). Start at Telegraph Hill Boulevard near Coit Tower and work your way down. When you cross Montgomery Street to the lower steps, take a look at the Art Deco apartment complex at 1930 Montgomery—you might recognize it from the movie *Dark Passage* (Humphrey Bogart and Lauren Bacall). You may want to take a sidetrack along Napier Lane, a narrow wooden walkway that leads to the public Grace Marchant Gardens, a particularly enchanting sight on Halloween when more than 200 jack-o'-lanterns light up the night for local trick-or-treaters. For more tips on the best city stairs log on to **www.sisterbetty.org/stairways.**

sea lions dropped by PIER 39's K Dock in 1989, and the ensuing battle between the sea lions and K Dock boat owners was handily won by the pinnipeds. The boats were relocated to another part of the marina, and when K Dock was eventually destroyed by the weight of all those lazy mammals, new floating docks were brought in to keep the boys fat and happy, much to the delight of the thousands of tourists who make the pilgrimage to watch them wallow. Weather permitting, the **Marine Mammal Center** (✆ **415/289-SEAL** [289-7325]) offers an educational talk at PIER 39 on weekends from 11am to 5pm that teaches visitors about the range, habitat, and adaptability of the California sea lion. FINE PRINT In winter, the population can top 900 sea lions. During the summer, they migrate south to the Channel Islands for breeding season, but in recent years a small group has been staying year-round (showoffs!).

On the waterfront at the Embarcadero and Beach St. ✆ 415/705-5500. www.pier39.com; www.marinemammalcenter.org.

6. Cable Car Museum If you've ever wondered how cable cars work, this nifty museum explains (and demonstrates) it all. It's the actual powerhouse, repair shop, and storage place of the entire cable car system and is in full operation. The exposed machinery, which pulls the cables under San Francisco's streets, looks like a Rube Goldberg invention. Stand in the mezzanine gallery and you'll be mesmerized by the massive groaning and vibrating winches as they thread the cable that hauls the cars through a huge figure-eight and back into the system using slack-absorbing tension wheels. For a better view, move to the lower-level viewing room, where you can see the massive pulleys and gears operating underground. Also on display here is one of the first grip cars (cable cars) developed by Andrew S. Hallidie, operated for the first time on Clay Street on August 2, 1873. Other displays include an antique grip car and trailer that operated on Pacific Avenue until 1929, and dozens of exact-scale models of cars used on the various city lines. There's also a shop where you can buy a variety of cable car gifts.

Polly Want a Latte!

If you're walking around San Francisco—especially Telegraph Hill or Russian Hill—and you suddenly hear lots of loud squawking and screeching overhead, look up. You're most likely witnessing a flyby of the city's famous green flock of wild parrots. These are the scions of a colony that started out as a few wayward house pets—mostly cherry-headed Conures, which are indigenous to South America—who found each other and bred. Years later they've become hundreds strong, speedily traveling in chatty packs through the city (with a few parakeets along for the ride) and stopping to rest on high tree branches. To learn just how special these birds are to the city, check out the book *The Wild Parrots of Telegraph Hill*, by Mark Bittner, or see the heart-warming movie of the same name. For more info about the wild parrots log onto **www.markbittner.net.**

shington St.). ✆ **415/474-1887.** www.cablecarmuseum.org. -Sept daily 10am–6pm; Oct–Mar daily 10am–5pm. Closed tmas, and New Year's Day. Cable car: Both Powell St. lines.

canique "Fun for all ages" isn't a trite expression when ng San Francisco's Musée Mécanique, a unique penny arcade museum containing one of the largest privately owned collections of antique coin-operated mechanical musical instruments in the world—160 machines dating back from the 1880s through the present (and they still work!). You can pay Grand-Ma Fortune Teller a quarter to see what she has to say about your future, or watch little kids cower in fear as Laughing "Fat Lady" Sal gives her infamous cackle of a greeting. Other yesteryear seaside resort games include antique movie machines, 19th-century music boxes, old-school strength testers, and mechanical cranes.

Pier 45 (at the end of Taylor St. at Fisherman's Wharf). ✆ **415/346-2000.** www.museemechanique.org. Free admission. Mon–Fri 10am–7pm; Sat–Sun 10am–8pm.

8. Sunday Sermon at Glide Memorial Church The best way to spend a Sunday morning in San Francisco is to visit this Tenderloin-area church to witness the exhilarating and lively sermons accompanied by an amazing gospel choir. Reverend Cecil Williams's enthusiastic and uplifting preaching and singing with the homeless and poor of the neighborhood has attracted nationwide fame over the past 40-plus years. In 1994, during the pastor's 30th-anniversary celebration, singers Angela Bofill and Bobby McFerrin joined comedian Robin Williams, author Maya Angelou, and talk-show queen Oprah Winfrey to honor him publicly. Even former President Bill Clinton has joined the crowd. Cecil Williams now shares pastor duties with Douglas Fitch and alternates presiding over the roof-raising Sunday services in front of a diverse audience that crosses all socioeconomic boundaries. Go for an uplifting experience and some hand-clapping, shoulder-swaying gospel choir music—it's an experience you'll never forget. FINE PRINT Arrive about 20 minutes early to make sure you get a seat; otherwise, it's SRO.

330 Ellis St. (west of Union Sq.). ✆ **415/674-6000.** www.glide.org. Services Sun at 9 and 11am. Bus: 27. Streetcar: Powell. BART: Powell.

9. The Painted Ladies at Alamo Square San Francisco's collection of Victorian houses are known as Painted Ladies, and the most

Money-Saving Tourist Passes

If you're the type who loves to cram as many attractions as possible into one trip, then you might want to consider purchasing a **San Francisco CityPass** or **GO San Francisco Card.** The CityPass includes 7 days of unlimited public transportation (including cable cars, Metro streetcars, and the entire bus system), and free access to some of the city's major attractions: the California Palace of the Legion of Honor and de Young museums, Aquarium of the Bay, the Asian Art Museum, the San Francisco Museum of Modern Art, the Exploratorium, and a Blue & Gold Fleet bay cruise. Discounts and coupons to other tourist-related attractions and activities are included as well. You can buy a CityPass at any of the above attractions or online at **www.citypass.net.** Current rates are $54 for adults and $44 for kids 5 to 17. For recorded information, call ✆ **888/330-5008.**

I think the better deal, however, is the **GO San Francisco Card** (✆ **800/887-9103;** www.gosanfranciscocard.com). It offers free or discounted admission to more than 45 of the most popular attractions, activities, and tours throughout the Bay Area and Wine Country; has far more flexibility (available in 1-, 2-, 3-, 5-, and 7-day increments over a 14-day period); and comes with a nifty little full-color guidebook that fits in your back pocket. In addition, some stores and restaurants offer discounts of up to 20% to GO San Francisco Card holders. The GO Cards are smart-technology enabled, which means they operate by calendar day and are activated the first time they are swiped, so you'll want to start your touring early in the morning to get the most value. The 2-day card costs $75 for adults ($35 for kids 3–12), and doesn't need to be used on consecutive days. You can purchase the GO Cards via their website or at the San Francisco Visitor Information Center (p. 260) or Red & Fleet Ticket Booth.

famous of them all are the "Six Sisters" perched along the 700 block of Steiner Street. If you stand in the middle of Alamo facing northeast, you'll see one of the most famous views of San Francisco, seen on postcards and posters all around the city: six nearly identical Victorian homes with the sharp-edged Financial District skyscrapers as a backdrop.

700 block of Steiner St. (btw Fulton and Hayes sts.).

10. Farmers' Market at the Ferry Building If you're heading to the Ferry Building Marketplace or just happen to be in the area at the right time (especially a sunny Sat), make a point of visiting the Farmers' Market, which is held in the outdoor areas in front of and behind the marketplace. This is where San Francisco foodies and many of the best local chefs—including the famed Alice Waters of Chez Panisse—gather, hang out, and peruse stalls hawking the finest Northern California fruits, vegetables, breads, dairy, flowers, readymade snacks, and complete meals by local restaurants (and lots of free samples). You'll be amazed at the variety and quality, and the crowded scene itself is something to behold. You can also pick up locally made vinegars, preserves, olives, and oils here—they make wonderful gifts. Drop by on Saturday from 9am to noon for a serious social fest, including interviews with local farmers and culinary demos by city chefs.

The Embarcadero, at Market St. ✆ **415/291-3276.** www.cuesa.org. Year-round Tues 10am-2pm, Sat 8am-2pm; May-Oct Tues 10am-2pm, Thurs 4-8pm, Sat 8am-2pm, Sun 10am-2pm. Bus: 2, 7, 12, 14, 21, 66, or 71. Streetcar: F. BART: Embarcadero.

2 Other Attractions & Museums

ALWAYS FREE

Boudin Demonstration Bakery at the Wharf After more than 30 years of being an inconspicuous bread shop in the heart of Fisherman's Wharf, the Boudin Bakery has been supersized. The new, ultramodern, 26,000-square-foot flagship baking emporium is nearly half a block long, housing not only their signature demonstration bakery but also a nifty museum, gourmet marketplace, cafe, espresso bar, and restaurant. The Boudin (pronounced Bo-*deen*) family has been baking sourdough French bread in San Francisco since the Gold Rush, using the same simple recipe and "mother dough" for more than 150 years. About 3,000 loaves a day are baked within the glass-walled bakery; visitors can watch the entire process from a 30-foot observation window along Jefferson Street or from a catwalk suspended directly over the bakery (it's quite entertaining, actually). You'll smell it before you see it, as the heavenly aroma emanating from the bread ovens is purposely blasted down onto the sidewalk.

The best time to arrive is in the morning when the demo bakery is in full swing. Watch (and smell) the action along Jefferson Street; then, when your appetite is stoked, head to the cafe for an inexpensive breakfast of sourdough French toast or their Bread Bowl Scrambler filled with eggs, bacon, cheddar, onions, and bell peppers. After breakfast, spend some time browsing the museum and marketplace. Tours of the bakery are available as well. ***Tip:*** If the line at the cafe is too long, walk across the parking lot to the octagon-shaped building, which serves the same items—Boudin chowder bowls, salads, pizzas—in a serve-yourself setting.

160 Jefferson St. (btw Taylor and Mason sts.). ✆ **415/928-1849.** www.boudinbakery.com. Bakery/cafe/marketplace daily 10am–7pm.

The Cannery The Cannery was built by Del Monte in 1907 as the world's largest fruit-canning plant. It was converted into a mall in the 1960s and now contains 30-plus shops and several restaurants, including **Jack's Cannery Bar** (✆ **415/931-6400**), which has a jaw-dropping selection of beers on tap. Vendors' stalls and sidewalk cafes occupy the courtyard amid a grove of century-old olive trees, and, weather permitting, street performers are usually out in force, entertaining tourists (but very few locals) for free. Shops are open daily at 10am and Sunday at 11am, while the restaurants generally open at 11:30am. Visit the website to download discount coupons to various restaurants and stores.

2801 Leavenworth St. (btw Beach and Jefferson sts.). ✆ **415/771-3112.** www.thecannery.com. Bus: 30 or 47. Cable car: F line to Hyde St.

Ferry Building Marketplace There's no better way to enjoy a San Francisco morning than strolling this gourmet marketplace in the Ferry Building and inexpensively snacking your way through breakfast or lunch. San Franciscans—myself included—can't get enough of this place; we're still amazed at what a fantastic job they did renovating the interior. The Marketplace is open daily and includes much of

EXPLORING SAN FRANCISCO

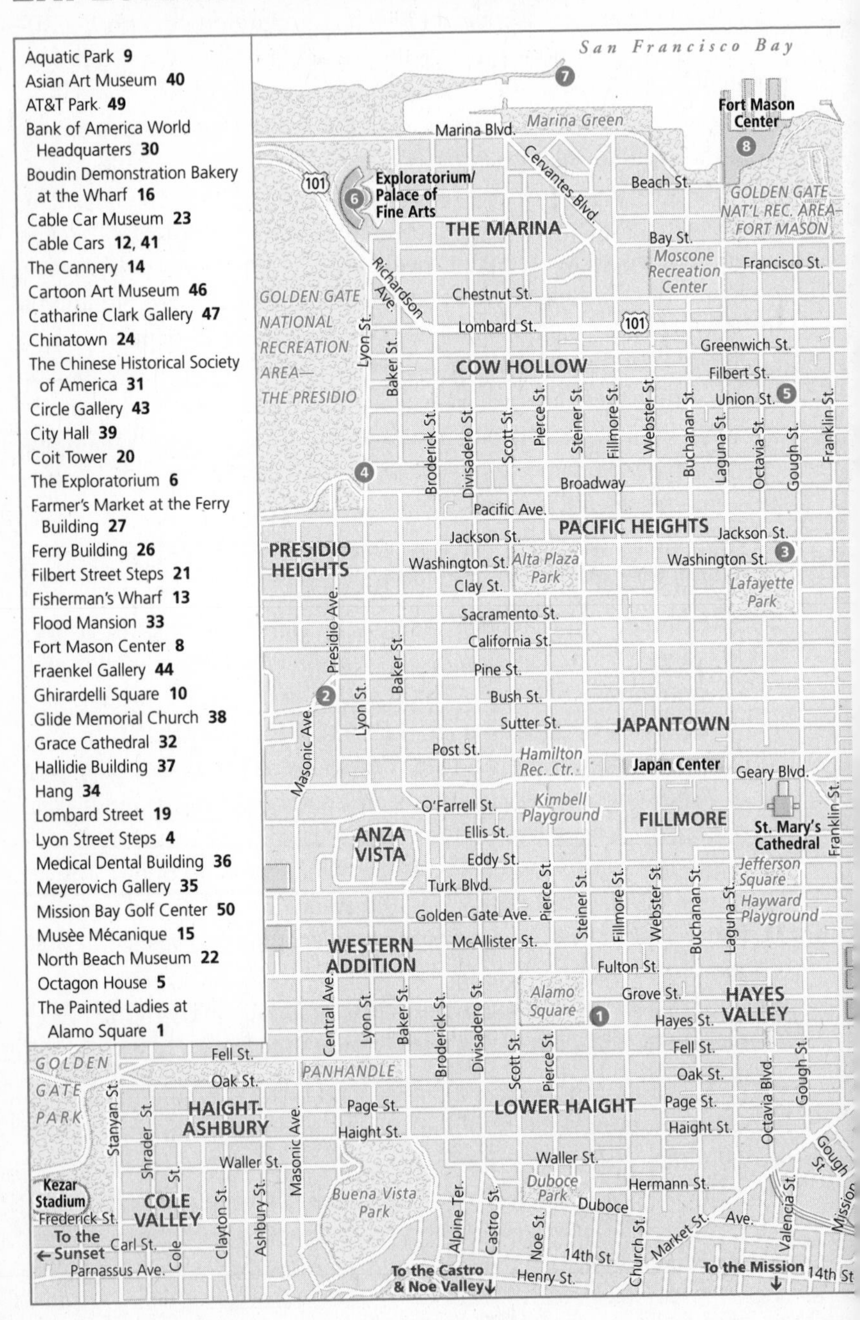

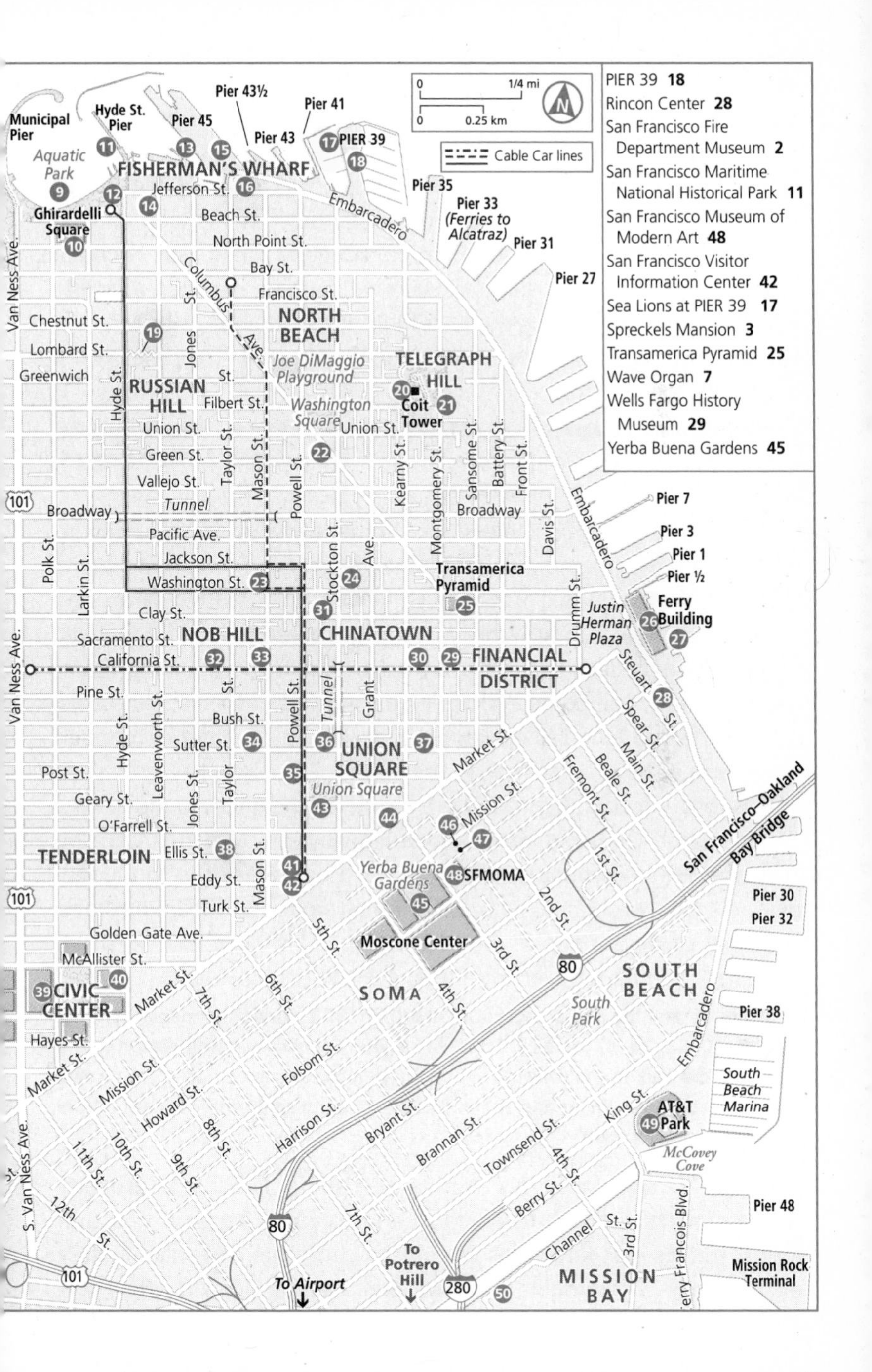

PIER 39 18
Rincon Center 28
San Francisco Fire Department Museum 2
San Francisco Maritime National Historical Park 11
San Francisco Museum of Modern Art 48
San Francisco Visitor Information Center 42
Sea Lions at PIER 39 17
Spreckels Mansion 3
Transamerica Pyramid 25
Wave Organ 7
Wells Fargo History Museum 29
Yerba Buena Gardens 45
Cable Car lines
1/4 mi
0.25 km
FISHERMAN'S WHARF
NORTH BEACH
TELEGRAPH HILL
RUSSIAN HILL
NOB HILL
CHINATOWN
FINANCIAL DISTRICT
UNION SQUARE
TENDERLOIN
CIVIC CENTER
SOMA
SOUTH BEACH
MISSION BAY
Municipal Pier
Hyde St. Pier
Pier 45
Pier 43½
Pier 43
Pier 41
Pier 35
Pier 33 (Ferries to Alcatraz)
Pier 31
Pier 27
Pier 7
Pier 3
Pier 1
Pier ½
Pier 30
Pier 32
Pier 38
Pier 48
Aquatic Park
Ghirardelli Square
Coit Tower
Transamerica Pyramid
Ferry Building
Justin Herman Plaza
Joe DiMaggio Playground
Washington Square
Union Square
Yerba Buena Gardens
SFMOMA
Moscone Center
South Park
South Beach Marina
AT&T Park
McCovey Cove
Mission Rock Terminal
San Francisco–Oakland Bay Bridge
To Airport
To Potrero Hill
Embarcadero
Jefferson St.
Beach St.
North Point St.
Bay St.
Francisco St.
Chestnut St.
Lombard St.
Greenwich
Filbert St.
Union St.
Green St.
Vallejo St.
Broadway
Tunnel
Pacific Ave.
Jackson St.
Washington St.
Clay St.
Sacramento St.
California St.
Pine St.
Bush St.
Sutter St.
Post St.
Geary St.
O'Farrell St.
Ellis St.
Eddy St.
Turk St.
Golden Gate Ave.
McAllister St.
Hayes St.
Market St.
Mission St.
Howard St.
Folsom St.
Harrison St.
Bryant St.
Brannan St.
Townsend St.
King St.
Berry St.
Channel St.
Van Ness Ave.
S. Van Ness Ave.
Polk St.
Larkin St.
Hyde St.
Leavenworth St.
Jones St.
Taylor St.
Mason St.
Powell St.
Stockton St.
Grant Ave.
Kearny St.
Montgomery St.
Sansome St.
Battery St.
Front St.
Davis St.
Drumm St.
Steuart St.
Spear St.
Main St.
Beale St.
Fremont St.
1st St.
2nd St.
3rd St.
4th St.
5th St.
6th St.
7th St.
8th St.
9th St.
10th St.
11th St.
12th St.
Columbus Ave.
Terry Francois Blvd.
101
80
280

Northern California's best gourmet bounty: **Cowgirl Creamery's Artisan Cheese Shop, Recchiuti Confections** (amazing), **Scharffen Berger Chocolate, Acme Breads,** Wine Country's gourmet diner **Taylor's Refresher,** and myriad other restaurants, delis, gourmet coffee shops, specialty foods, and wine bars. Check out the **Imperial Tea Court,** where you'll be taught the traditional Chinese way to steep and sip your tea; nosh on a nibble of premium sturgeon roe at **Tsar Nicoulai Caviar,** a small Parisian-style "caviar cafe"; grab a fish taco at **Mijita** and savor the bayfront views from the outdoor tables; or browse the **Farmers' Market** when it's up and running (p. 84). Trust me, you'll love this place.

The Embarcadero, at Market St. ✆ 415/693-0996. www.ferrybuildingmarketplace.com. Most stores daily 10am–6pm; restaurant hours vary. Bus: 2, 7, 12, 14, 21, 66, or 71. Streetcar: F. BART: Embarcadero.

Fisherman's Wharf Unless you come early in the morning to watch the few remaining fishing boats depart, you won't find many traces of the traditional waterfront life that once existed here—the only trolling going on at Fisherman's Wharf these days is for tourists' dollars. Nonetheless, everyone always seems to be enjoying themselves as they stroll down PIER 39 on a sunny day, especially the kids.

Some people love Fisherman's Wharf; others can't get far enough away from it. Most agree that, for better or for worse, it has to be seen at least once in your lifetime. There are still some traces of old-school San Francisco character here that I will always enjoy, particularly the convivial seafood street vendors who dish out piles of fresh Dungeness, clam chowder, and sourdough bread from their steaming stainless steel carts—it's one of the best dining deals in the city. In short, there's something for everyone here, even us snobby locals.

At Taylor St. and the Embarcadero. ✆ 415/674-7503. www.fishermanswharf.org. Bus: 15, 30, 32, 39, 42, or 82X. Streetcar: F line. Cable car: Powell-Mason to the last stop and walk to the wharf. If you're arriving by car, park on adjacent streets or on the wharf btw Taylor and Jones sts. for $16 per day, $8 with validation from participating restaurants.

Ghirardelli Square This National Historic Landmark property dates from 1864, when it served as a factory making Civil War uniforms, but it's best known as the former chocolate and spice factory of Domingo Ghirardelli (pronounced "*Gear*-ar-delly"), who purchased it in 1893. The factory has since been converted into an unimpressive three-level mall containing 30-plus stores and five dining establishments. Street performers entertain regularly in the West Plaza and fountain area. Incidentally, the Ghirardelli Chocolate Company still makes chocolate, but its factory is in a lower-rent district in the East Bay. Still, if you have a sweet tooth, you won't be disappointed at the mall's fantastic (though overpriced) old-fashioned soda fountain, which is open until midnight. Their "world famous" hot-fudge sundae is good, too. (Then again, have you ever had a bad hot-fudge sundae?)

900 N. Point St. (btw Polk and Larkin sts.). ✆ **415/775-5500.** www.ghirardellisq.com. Stores generally daily 10am–9pm in summer; Sun–Fri 10am–6pm, Sat 10am–9pm rest of year.

Grace Cathedral Although this Nob Hill cathedral, designed by architect Lewis P. Hobart, appears to be made of stone, it is in fact constructed of reinforced concrete beaten to achieve a stonelike effect. Construction began on the site of the Crocker mansion in 1928 but was not completed until 1964. Among the more interesting features of the building are its stained-glass windows, particularly those by the French Loire studios and Charles Counick, depicting such modern figures as Thurgood Marshall, Robert Frost, and Albert Einstein; the replicas of Ghiberti's bronze *Doors of Paradise* at the east end; the series of religious murals completed in the 1940s by Polish artist John de Rosen; and the 44-bell carillon. Along with its magical ambience, Grace lifts spirits with services, musical performances (including organ recitals on many Sundays), and its weekly Forum (Sun 9:30–10:30am except during summer and major holidays), where guests lead discussions about spirituality in modern times and have community dialogues on social issues.

1100 California St. (btw Taylor and Jones sts.). ✆ **415/749-6300.** www.gracecathedral.org.

North Beach Museum To get a virtually private glimpse of the history of one of San Francisco's most intriguing neighborhoods, go to the North Beach Museum, tucked away on the mezzanine of the Bay View Street Bank. This little museum traces North Beach's past with photos and artifacts dating back to the turn of the 20th century. Hardly anybody knows the museum is there, so you may have it all to yourself; but you must go during banking hours.

1429 Stockton St. (at Columbus Ave.). ✆ 415/391-6210. Free admission. Mon–Fri 10am–5pm. Bus: 15, 30, or 45.

Octagon House This unusual, eight-sided, cupola-topped house dates from 1861 and is maintained by the National Society of Colonial Dames of America. Its design was based on a past theory that people living in a space of this shape would live longer, healthier lives. Inside is a small museum where you'll find Early American furniture, portraits, silver, pewter, looking glasses, and English and Chinese ceramics. There are also some historic documents, including signatures of 54 of the 56 signers of the Declaration of Independence. Even if you're not able to visit the inside, this atypical structure is worth a look from the outside. FINE PRINT Admission is free, but there is a "suggested donation."

2645 Gough St. (at Union St.). ✆ 415/441-7512. Free admission; donation suggested. Feb–Dec 2 Sun, and 2nd and 4th Thurs of each month noon–3pm. Tours by appointment are the only way to see the house. Closed holidays. Bus: 41 or 45.

PIER 39 PIER 39 is a multilevel waterfront entertainment complex located a few blocks east of Fisherman's Wharf. Constructed on an abandoned cargo pier, it is, ostensibly, a re-creation of a turn-of-the-20th-century street scene, but don't expect a slice of old-time maritime life here: Today, PIER 39 is a busy outdoor mall visited by millions of tourists each year. It has more than 110 stores, 13 bayview restaurants, a two-tiered Venetian carousel, a Hard Rock Cafe, the Riptide Arcade, and the intriguing (though overpriced) Aquarium of the Bay. And everything here is slanted toward helping you part with your travel dollars. This is *the* place that locals love to hate, but kids adore it here. That said, it does have a few perks: absolutely beautiful natural surroundings and bay views, fresh sea air, and hundreds of sunbathing sea lions (about 900 in peak season) lounging along its neighboring docks. (See p. 80 for info about the free weekend talks by the Marine Mammal Center.)

On the waterfront at the Embarcadero and Beach St. ✆ 415/705-5500. www.pier39.com. Free admission. Shops daily 10am–8:30pm, with extended weekend hours during summer. Bus: 15, 30, or 42.

San Francisco Fire Department Museum This one-room museum next to a firehouse features display cases filled with artifacts tracing the history of San Francisco's fire departments, from volunteer firefighters to the beginnings of the professional squads of today. The floor display of antique equipment, including two steam engines, shows how far we've come.

655 Presidio Ave. (btw Bush and Pine sts.). ✆ 415/558-3546 (recorded info) or 415/563-4630 (during open hours). www.sffiremuseum.org. Free admission. Thurs–Sun 1–4pm. Muni: 43-Masonic, 4-Sutter, or 2-Clement bus.

San Francisco Maritime Museum The literally shipshape Maritime Museum looks like a set for an old Hollywood movie. Shaped like an Art Deco ship, the museum is filled with sailing, whaling, and fishing lore. Nautical types will go nuts when they see all the intricate ship models and scrimshaw. The collection of shipwreck photographs and historic marine scenes includes an 1851 snapshot of hundreds of abandoned ships, deserted by crews dashing off to participate in the Gold Rush. Beautifully carved, brightly painted wooden figureheads from old windjammers line the walls. ***Note:*** The museum was closed for extensive renovation as of press time but is supposed to reopen in early 2009. Visit the website for progress reports on the renovation.

900 Beach St. (at Polk St.). ✆ 415/447-5000. www.maritime.org. Free admission. Daily 10am–5pm. Bus: 15, 30, 42, or 69. Cable car: Powell-Hyde.

San Francisco Maritime National Historical Park This park includes several marine-themed sites within a few blocks of each other. Although the park's signature Maritime Museum—on Beach Street at Polk Street, shaped like an Art Deco ship, and filled with seafaring memorabilia—is undergoing its planned 2006 to 2009 renovations, it's worth walking by just to admire the building (see above). Head 2 blocks east to the corner of Hyde and Jefferson and you'll find SFMNHP's state-of-the-art Visitor's Center, which offers a fun, interactive look at the city's maritime heritage. Housed in the historic Haslett Warehouse building, the Center tells the stories of voyage, discovery, and cultural diversity. Across the street, at the park's Hyde Street Pier, are several historic ships, which are moored and open to the public. Make sure you visit the pier's small-boat shop, where visitors can follow the restoration progress of historic boats from the museum's collection. It's behind the maritime bookstore on your right as you approach the ships. FINE PRINT Admission to the park itself is free, but there's a small fee for boarding the ships.

Visitor's Center: Hyde and Jefferson sts. (near Fisherman's Wharf). ✆ 415/447-5000. www.nps.gov/safr. Free admission to Visitor's Center. Tickets to board

ships $5, free for children 15 and under. Visitor's Center: Memorial Day to Oct 15 daily 9:30am-7pm; Oct 16-May 30 9:30am-5pm. Ships on Hyde St. Pier: Memorial Day to Sept 30 daily 9:30am-5:30pm; Oct 16-May 27 daily 9am-5pm. Bus: 19, 30, or 47. Cable car: Powell-Hyde St. line to the last stop.

Wells Fargo History Museum Wells Fargo, one of California's largest banks, got its start in the Wild West. Its history museum, at the bank's head office, houses hundreds of genuine relics from the company's whip-and-six-shooter days, including pistols, photographs, early banking articles, posters, a stagecoach, and mining equipment.

420 Montgomery St. (at California St.). ✆ 415/396-2619. www.wellsfargohistory.com. Free admission. Mon-Fri 9am-5pm. Closed bank holidays. Bus: Any to Market St. Cable car: California St. line. BART: Montgomery St.

Yerba Buena Gardens Unless you're at Yerba Buena to catch a performance, you're more likely to visit the 5-acre gardens, a great place to relax in the grass on a sunny day and check out several artworks. The most dramatic outdoor piece is an emotional mixed-media memorial to Martin Luther King, Jr. Created by sculptor Houston Conwill, poet Estella Majozo, and architect Joseph de Pace, it features 12 panels, each inscribed with quotations from King, sheltered behind a 50-foot-high waterfall. There are also several actual garden areas here, including a Butterfly Garden, the Sister Cities Garden (highlighting flowers from the city's 13 sister cities), and the East Garden, blending Eastern and Western styles. May through October, Yerba Buena Arts & Events puts on a series of free outdoor festivals featuring dance, music, poetry, and more by the San Francisco Ballet, Opera, Symphony, and others.

Located on 2 square city blocks bounded by Mission, Folsom, Third, and Fourth sts. www.yerbabuenagardens.com. Daily 6am-10pm. Free admission. Contact Yerba Buena Arts & Events: ✆ 415/543-1718 or www.ybgf.org for details about the free outdoor festivals. Bus: 5, 9, 14, 15, 30.

SOMETIMES FREE

All praise to the concept of "free days" at museums! That is, most of these institutions, which have a regular admission fee that can run over $20 (like the California Academy of Sciences), have 1 day a month in which you can enter gratis (or for a "suggested donation"). So mark your calendars for the money-saving times, and check out the box on p. 102, which lists the institutions and their free days.

Asian Art Museum Previously in Golden Gate Park and reopened in what was once the Civic Center's Beaux Arts–style central library, San Francisco's Asian Art Museum is one of the Western world's largest museums devoted to Asian art. Its collection boasts more than 15,000 art objects, such as world-class sculptures, paintings, bronzes, ceramics, and jade items, spanning 6,000 years of history and regions of south Asia, west Asia, Southeast Asia, the Himalayas, China, Korea, and Japan. Inside you'll find 40,000 square feet of gallery space showcasing 2,500 objects at any given time. Add temporary exhibitions, live demonstrations, learning activities, Cafe Asia, and a store, and you've got one very good reason to head to the Civic Center. **Free admission the first Sunday of each month.**

200 Larkin St. (btw Fulton and McAllister sts.). ✆ **415/581-3500.** www.asianart.org. Admission $12 adults, $8 seniors 65 and over, $7 youths 13–17 and college students with ID, free for children 12 and under, $5 flat rate for all (except children 11 and under, who are free) after 5pm Thurs. Tues–Wed and Fri–Sun 10am–5pm; Thurs 10am–9pm. Bus: All Market St. buses. Streetcar: Civic Center.

★ **California Academy of Sciences** San Francisco's California Academy of Sciences has been entertaining locals and tourists for more than 150 years, and with the grand opening of the all-new Academy in September 2008, it's going stronger than ever. Four years and $500 million in the making, it's now the only institution in the world to combine an aquarium, a planetarium, a natural history museum, and a scientific research program under one roof, and so vastly entertaining that the entire family could easily spend a whole day here. In fact, the spectacular new complex has literally reinvented the role of science museums in the 21st century, where visitors interact with animals, educators, and biologists at hands-on exhibits such as a four-story living rainforest dome and the world's deepest living coral reef display. Even the Academy's 2.5-acre undulating garden roof is an exhibit, planted with 1.7 million native California plants, including thousands of flowers (all that's missing are the Teletubbies).

More than 38,000 live animals fill the new Academy's aquarium and natural history exhibits, making it one of the most diverse collections of live animals at any museum or aquarium in the world. Highlights include the **Morrison Planetarium,** the world's largest all-digital planetarium that takes you on a guided tour of the solar system and beyond using current data from NASA to produce the most accurate

Morbid Landmarks

For those who enjoy excursions to the dark side, here are a few points of interest that will never make it into San Francisco Visitors Bureau brochures. And it doesn't cost a thing to look.

- **The People's Temple:** At 1859 Geary St. is where Jim Jones gathered disciples before leading them to their eventual death at a mass suicide in Guyana. The building itself still stands; it's now a Korean Presbyterian church.
- **The Manson Manor:** It's hard to believe that Charles Manson recruited some of his deadliest "family" members—including Susan Atkins and Squeaky Fromme—during the peak of Haight-Ashbury's peace-and-love scene, but he lived at 636 Cole St. for a few months in 1967 before heading to Southern California to organize his killing spree.
- **San Quentin State Prison:** The "Q" has hosted some of California's most notorious criminals, including the aforementioned Mr. Manson, Sirhan Sirhan, and William Harris (one of Patty Hearst's kidnappers). They don't give tours of death row or anything, but you can take a ferry to Larkspur (**http://goldengate ferry.org/schedules/Larkspur.php**) and hoof it to the prison, where there is a small museum (gas chamber mementos and

and interactive digital universe ever created; the **Philippine Coral Reef,** the world's deepest living coral reef tank where 4,000 sharks, rays, sea turtles, giant clams, and other aquatic creatures live in a Technicolor forest of coral; and the **Rainforests of the World,** a living rainforest filled with mahogany and palm trees, croaking frogs, chirping birds, leaf cutter ants, bat caves, chameleons, and hundreds of tropical butterflies. You can climb into the treetops of Costa Rica, descend in a glass elevator into the Amazonian flooded forest, and walk along an acrylic tunnel beneath the Amazonian river fish that swim overhead. Pretty cool, eh?

Even the dining options here are first-rate, as both the **Academy Café** and **Moss Room** restaurant are run by two of the city's top chefs, such) and a gift shop that sells items made by prisoners (no license plates). If you're headed there by car, take Hwy. 101 north across the Golden Gate Bridge. After about 10 miles take the Sir Francis Drake Blvd. exit and turn right (heading east). The prison entrance is about one mile east on E. Sir Francis Drake Blvd.

- **The Westin Saint Francis:** It's a grande dame and one of the city's most famous hotels, but like some old dames, she's had her wild times. It was the site of President Ford's assassination attempt (Sept 23, 1975) and Fatty Arbuckle's lost weekend (Labor Day weekend, 1921). President Ford was leaving the hotel when Sara Jane Moore whipped out a gun and fired at him from across the street, but an ex-Marine standing next to her grabbed her arm, redirecting the bullet (it was the second assassination attempt in one 2-week trip to California). Fatty Arbuckle was celebrating a multimillion-dollar movie contract inside the hotel at what has often been described as a drunken orgy when a young female guest was found unconscious in Room 1219. She died a few days later, and Arbuckle was tried three times for her murder before finally being acquitted.

Charles Phan and Loretta Keller, and feature local, organic, sustainable foods. The only thing you won't enjoy here is the entrance fee—a whopping $25 per adult—but it includes access to all the Academy exhibits *and* the Planetarium shows, and if you arrive by public transportation they'll knock $3 off the fee (how very green). Combined with a visit to the spectacular de Young museum across the Concourse, it makes for a very entertaining and educational day in Golden Gate Park. However you can skip the high price to get in if you plan ahead: **Free admission the third Wednesday of each month.**

55 Concourse Dr., Golden Gate Park. ✆ **415/379-8000.** www.calacademy.org. Admission $25 adults, $20 seniors 65 and over, $20 youths 12-17, $15 children

7-11, free for children 6 and under. Mon-Sat 9:30am-5pm; Sun 11am-5pm. Closed Thanksgiving and Christmas. Bus: 5, 16AX, 16BX, 21, 44, or 71.

Cartoon Art Museum When Pogo would make a more entertaining afternoon companion than Picasso, it's time to quit the cathedrals of culture and head for smaller houses of object worship, like the Cartoon Art Museum. It's the only museum in the United States dedicated to the preservation and exhibition of cartoon art in all its forms, housing thousands of pieces in its collection within five galleries. Exhibits trace the history of cartoon art from political jabs to underground comics. Temporary shows highlight individual artists, such as Bill Watterson and Edward Gorey, and specific forms, such as television cartoon animation. Most of the comic strips are geared to adults, such as the original Krazy Kat watercolors and Pogo comic strips. Given the inviting name of the museum, kids may be disappointed, but perhaps they'll appreciate the collection of Disney cels and backgrounds that were actually used to make classics such as Fantasia and Snow White. Contact the museum for information on cartooning classes and 1-day workshops for kids. **Regular admission ($6 for adults) becomes a "suggested donation" the first Tuesday of each month.**

655 Mission St. ✆ 415/227-8666. www.cartoonart.org. Admission $6 adults, $4 students and seniors, $2 kids 6-12. Tues-Sun 11am-5pm. 1st Tues of the month is "pay what you wish" day. Closed Mon and major holidays. Bus: 14, 15, 30, or 45. Muni: Any streetcar to Montgomery St.

The Chinese Historical Society of America This is a good place to develop an appreciation of the Chinese experience in California, and also worth a quick drop-in to add a little gravity to your day before digging into that dim sum. A museum and research center, the Historical Society documents the fascinating history of the Chinese in California through photographs, art, and changing exhibits. Its bookstore stocks children's titles as well as fiction and nonfiction on Chinese themes. The center also hosts occasional tours during the year, such as a "Ghosts of Chinatown" tour before Halloween, at additional cost. **Free admission is the first Thursday of each month.**

965 Clay St. ✆ 415/391-1188. www.chsa.org. Admission $3 adults, $2 seniors and college students, $1 children 6-17, free for children 5 and under. Tues-Fri noon-5pm; Sat-Sun noon-4pm.

de Young Museum After closing for renovation for several years, San Francisco's oldest museum (founded in 1895) reopened in late 2005 in its new state-of-the-art Golden Gate Park facility. Its vast holdings include one of the finest collections of American paintings in the United States from Colonial times through the 20th century, as well as decorative arts and crafts; Western and non-Western textiles; and arts from Africa, Oceania, and the Americas. Along with superb revolving exhibitions, the de Young has long been beloved for its educational arts programs for both children and adults, and now it's equally enjoyed for its stunning architecture and sculpture-graced surroundings. The striking facade consists of 950,000 pounds of textured and perforated copper that's intended to patinate with age, while the northeast corner of the building features a 144-foot tower that slowly spirals from the ground floor and culminates with an observation floor offering panoramic views of the entire Bay Area (from a distance it has the surreal look of a rusty aircraft carrier cruising through the park).

FREE ALERT: Access to the top of the de Young tower is free of charge (see box below). In fact, that complimentary access is another feature that sets the de Young apart: While visitors must pay an entrance fee to visit the museum galleries, vast swaths of common space are open to everyone. On a stroll through the park, you can step into the de Young, take in the impressive painting by Gerhard Richter that watches over the main lobby, head to the tower room and contemplate ethereal wire creations by renowned local sculptor Ruth Asawa, pop up to the top floor to take in the priceless view, and then walk out to the sculpture garden to appreciate works by such well-known artists as Joan Miro and Henry Moore—all for free. (One must-see sculpture in the garden is the *Three Gems* structure by James Turrell—if you stand in the middle of the unusual orb and talk, you can feel your vocal vibrations.)

The de Young's surrounding sculpture gardens and lush, grassy expanses are perfect for picnicking. Adding to the allure is surprisingly good and healthy organic fare at the grab-and-go or order-and-wait cafe/restaurant. You'll enjoy browsing through the museum's interesting gift shop as well. ***Note:*** Underground parking is accessed at 10th Avenue and Fulton Street. Also, admission tickets to the de Young may be used on the same day for free entrance to The Legion of Honor (see below). **Admission to the entire complex is free the first Tuesday of each month.**

50 Hagiwara Tea Garden Dr. (inside Golden Gate Park, 2 blocks from the park entrance at Eighth Ave. and Fulton). ✆ **415/863-3330.** www.thinker.org. Admission $10 adults, $7 seniors, $6 youths 13–17 and college students with ID, free for children 12 and under. $2 discount for Muni riders with Fast Pass or transfer receipt. AE, MC, V. Tues–Sun 9:30am–5:15pm. Closed Jan 1, Thanksgiving Day, and Dec 25. Bus: 5, 16AX, 16BX, 21, 44, or 71.

FREE Views from the Top of the de Young

One of the best free views in town is from the top of the 144-foot-tall tower at the **de Young Museum.** It's open to all visitors, even if they haven't paid to enter the museum. You'll see fabulous views of northwestern San Francisco, from where you can see Golden Gate Park, the Presidio, Lincoln Park, even the Pacific Ocean and the Marin Headlands beyond. Plus, the tower houses a massive aerial map of San Francisco, so detailed that you can probably work out which building on it is your hotel. In fact, the map has proved so popular that the museum put a gift shop in the tower so visitors could take home their own poster-sized version of it.

★ **The Exploratorium** *Scientific American* magazine rated The Exploratorium "the best science museum in the world"—and I couldn't agree more. Inside you'll find hundreds of exhibits that explore everything from giant-bubble blowing to Einstein's theory of relativity. It's like a mad scientist's penny arcade, an educational fun house, and an experimental laboratory all rolled into one. Touch a tornado, shape a glowing electrical current, or take a sensory journey in total darkness in the **Tactile Dome** ($3 extra, and call ✆ **415/561-0362** to make advance reservations)—even if you spent all day here you couldn't experience everything. Every exhibit at The Exploratorium is designed to be interactive, educational, safe, and, most important, fun. And don't think it's just for kids; parents inevitably end up being the most reluctant to leave. I went here recently and spent 3 hours in just one small section of the museum, marveling like a little kid at all the mind-blowing hands-on exhibits related to light and eyesight. On the way out, be sure to stop in the wonderful gift store, which is chock-full of affordable brain candy.

The museum is in the Marina District at the beautiful **Palace of Fine Arts,** the only building left standing from the Panama-Pacific Exposition of 1915. The adjoining park with lagoon—the perfect place for an afternoon picnic—is home to ducks, swans, sea gulls, and grouchy geese, so bring bread. **Free admission the first Wednesday of each month.**

3601 Lyon St., in the Palace of Fine Arts (at Marina Blvd.). ✆ **415/EXPLORE** (397-5673), or 415/561-0360 (recorded information). www.exploratorium.edu. Admission $14 adults; $11 seniors, youth 13–17, visitors with disabilities, and college students with ID; $9 children 4–12; free for children 3 and under. AE, MC, V. Tues–Sun 10am–5pm. Closed Mon except Martin Luther King Day, Presidents' Day, Memorial Day, and Labor Day. Free parking. Bus: 28, 30, or Golden Gate Transit.

The Legion of Honor Designed as a memorial to California's World War I casualties, this neoclassical structure is an exact replica of The Legion of Honor Palace in Paris, right down to the inscription *HONNEUR ET PATRIE* above the portal. The exterior's grassy expanses, cliffside paths, and incredible view of the Golden Gate and downtown make this an absolute must-visit attraction before you even get in the door. The inside is equally impressive: The museum's permanent collection covers 4,000 years of art and includes paintings, sculpture, and decorative arts from Europe, as well as international tapestries, prints, and drawings. The chronological display of 4,000 years of ancient and European art includes one of the world's finest collections of Rodin sculptures. The sunlit Legion Cafe offers indoor and outdoor seating at moderate prices. Plan to spend 2 or 3 hours here. **Free admission the first Tuesday of each month.**

In Lincoln Park (34th Ave. and Clement St.). ✆ **415/750-3600,** or 415/863-3330 (recorded information). www.thinker.org. Admission $10 adults, $7 seniors 65 and over, $6 youths 13–17 and college students with ID, free for children 12 and under. Fees may be higher for special exhibitions. Tues–Sun 9:30am–5:15pm. Bus: 18.

San Francisco Museum of Modern Art (SFMOMA) Swiss architect Mario Botta, in association with Hellmuth, Obata, and Kassabaum, designed this $65-million museum, which has made SFMOMA one of the more popular areas to visit for tourists and residents alike. The museum's permanent collection houses the West

Coast's most comprehensive collection of 20th-century art, including painting, sculpture, photography, architecture, design, and media arts. The collection features master works by Ansel Adams, Bruce Conner, Joseph Cornell, Salvador Dali, Richard Diebenkorn, Eva Hesse, Frida Kahlo, Ellsworth Kelly, Yves Klein, Sherrie Levine, Gordon Matta-Clark, Henri Matisse, Piet Mondrian, Pablo Picasso, Robert Rauschenberg, Diego Rivera, Cindy Sherman, Alfred Stieglitz, Clyfford Still, and Edward Weston, among many others, as well as an ever-changing program of special exhibits. Unfortunately, few works are on display at one time, and for the money (if you're paying full price!) the experience can be disappointing—especially compared to the finer museums of New York. However, this is about as good as it gets in our boutique city, so take it or leave it. Docent-led tours take place daily. Times are posted at the admission desk. Phone or check SFMOMA's website for current details of upcoming special events and exhibitions.

The **Caffè Museo,** to the right of the museum entrance, offers very good-quality fresh soups, sandwiches, and salads. Be sure to visit the **MuseumStore,** which carries a wonderful array of modern and contemporary art books, innovative design objects and furniture, jewelry and apparel, educational children's books and toys, posters, and stationery: It's one of the best shops in town and always carries their famed "FogDome"—a snow globe with a mini MOMA that gets foggy rather than snowy when you shake it. **Free admission the first Tuesday of each month.**

151 Third St. (2 blocks south of Market St., across from Yerba Buena Gardens). ✆ 415/357-4000. www.sfmoma.org. Admission $13 adults, $8 seniors, $7 students over 12 with ID, free for children 12 and under. Half-price for all Thurs 6-9pm. Thurs 11am-8:45pm; Fri-Tues 11am-5:45pm. Closed Wed and major holidays. Bus: 15, 30, or 45. Streetcar: J, K, L, or M to Montgomery.

San Francisco Zoo Located between the Pacific Ocean and Lake Merced in the southwest corner of the city, the San Francisco Zoo, which once had a reputation for being a bit shoddy and out-of-date, has come a long way in recent years (that is, until the tiger vs. teen incident). Though grown-ups who are into wildlife will enjoy the visit, it's an especially fun trip with kids because they'll really get a kick out of the hands-on Children's Zoo, along with the many other animal attractions (the flock of shockingly pink flamingos near the entrance is especially appealing).

Founded at its present site near the ocean in 1929, the zoo is spread over 100 acres and houses more than 930 animals, including some 245 species of mammals, birds, reptiles, amphibians, and invertebrates. Exhibit highlights include the Lipman Family Lemur Forest, a forest setting for five endangered species of lemurs from Madagascar that features interactive components for the visitor; Jones Family Gorilla World, a tranquil setting for a family group of western lowland gorillas; Koala Crossing, which connects to the Australian Walkabout exhibit with its kangaroos, wallaroos, and emu; Penguin Island, home to a large breeding colony of Magellanic Penguins (join them for lunch at 2:30pm daily); and the Primate Discovery Center, home to rare and endangered monkeys. In the South American Tropical Forest building, a large green anaconda can be found, as well as other South American reptile and bird species. Puente al Sur (Bridge to the South) has a pair of giant anteaters and some capybaras. The Lion House is home to rare Sumatran and Siberian tigers and African lions. You can see the big cats fed every day at 2pm (except Mon, when you are less likely to see them since when they're not eating they like to hang out in secluded areas). African Savanna is a 3-acre mixed-species habitat with giraffes, zebras, antelope, and birds.

The 6-acre Children's Zoo offers kids and their families opportunities for close-up encounters with domestic rare breeds of goats, sheep, ponies, and horses in the Family Farm. Touch and feel small mammals, reptiles, and amphibians along the Nature Trail and gaze at eagles and hawks stationed on Hawk Hill. Visitors can see the inner workings of the Koret Animal Resource Center, a thriving facility that houses the animals used in the educational outreach programs, and visit the incredible Insect Zoo. One of the Children's Zoo's most popular exhibits is the Meerkat and Prairie Dog exhibit, where kids can crawl through tunnels and play in sand, just like these two amazing burrowing species.

Don't miss the Little Puffer miniature steam train, which takes passengers around a ⅓-mile track, and the historic Dentzel Carousel (both $2 per ride). There's a coffee cart by the entrance as well as two decent cafes inside, definitely good enough for a bite with the kids (though the lines can be long and slightly confusing if you're handling food and kid duty at the same time). **Free admission the first Wednesday of each month.**

FREE If It's Free, It's for Me!

To beef up attendance and give indigent folk like us travel writers a break, many of San Francisco's public attractions and museums are open free to the public 1 day of the month (as mentioned earlier). Use the following list to plan your week around the museums' free-day schedules, then turn to the individual attraction listings earlier for more information on each museum.

First Tuesday

- California Palace of the Legion of Honor (p. 99)
- Cartoon Art Museum (p. 96)
- Center for the Arts at Yerba Buena Gardens (p. 92)
- de Young Museum (p. 97)
- San Francisco Museum of Modern Art (p. 99)

First Wednesday

- The Exploratorium (p. 98)
- San Francisco Zoo (p. 100)

First Thursday

- The Chinese Historical Society of America (p. 96)

First Sunday

- Asian Art Museum (p. 93)

Third Wednesday

- California Academy of Sciences (p. 93)

Great Highway btw Sloat Blvd. and Skyline Blvd. ✆ **415/753-7080.** www.sfzoo.org. Admission $11 adults, $8 seniors 65 and over and youth 12–17, $5 children 3–11, free for children 2 and under. Free to all 1st Wed of each month, except $2 fee for Children's Zoo. Carousel $2. Daily 10am–5pm, 365 days a year. Bus: 23 or 18. Streetcar: L from downtown Market St. to the end of the line.

DIRT CHEAP (OR THEREABOUTS)

AT&T Park If you're a baseball fan, you'll definitely want to schedule a visit to the magnificent AT&T Park, home of the San Francisco Giants and hailed as one of the finest ballparks in America. From April to October, a sellout crowd of 40,800 fans packs the $319-million ballpark for nearly every game—which has a smaller, more intimate feel than Monster Park (where the 49ers play) and prime views of San Francisco Bay—and root for their National League Giants.

DIRT-CHEAP ALERT! During the Major League season, tickets to the games are usually hard to come by (and expensive when you find them), but you can try to join the Bleacher Bums by purchasing one of the 500 bleacher-seat tickets sold every day before the game. FINE PRINT To get one of these tickets, you have to show up at the ballpark 4 hours early to get a lottery number, then come back 2 hours before the game to get your tickets (maximum four per person). The upside is that the tickets are only $8.50 to $10.

FREE ALERT: If you can't get bleacher seats, you can always join the "knothole gang" at the Portwalk (located behind right field) to catch a free glimpse of the game through cut-out portholes into the ballpark. In the spirit of sharing, Portwalk peekers are encouraged to take in only an inning or two before giving way to fellow fans.

One guaranteed way to get into the ballpark is to take a **guided tour of AT&T Park** and go behind the scenes, where you'll see the press box, the dugout, the visitor's clubhouse, a luxury suite, and more. All tours run daily at 10:30am and 12:30pm. Ticket prices are $10 for adults, $8 for seniors over 55, and $6 for kids 12 and under. There are no tours on game days, and limited tours on the day of night games. To buy tickets online log onto **www.sfgiants.com**, then click on "AT&T Park" and "Ballpark Tours" from the drop-down list. You can also buy tour tickets at any Giants Dugout Store or Tickets.com outlet. For more tour information call ✆ **415/972-2400.**

At the southeast corner of SoMa at the south end of the Embarcadero (bounded by King, 2nd, and 3rd sts.). ✆ **415/972-2000.** www.sfgiants.com. Metro: N line. Bus: 10, 15, 30, 45, and 47.

★ **Cable Cars** There is one surefire perfect way to spend your first afternoon in San Francisco—take $5 out of your pocket, stand in line at the Powell/Market cable car turntable at the intersection of Powell and Market streets, and hop on the Powell–Hyde cable car. Don't even *think* about not doing it because it seems too touristy—locals have been known to invite out-of-town guests purely for an excuse to take this ride.

The Powell–Hyde line is my favorite (as opposed to the Powell–Mason line, a route that's a bit less exciting) because it ends up just steps away from the **Buena Vista Cafe** at 2765 Hyde St., a National Historic Landmark where a post–cable car Irish coffee is an esteemed tradition, especially on a foggy afternoon. The Powell–Hyde line twists through the city, climbing "halfway to the stars" atop Nob Hill, then plummeting back down on a breathtaking roller coaster ride—did you notice the brakes are made of wood?—that levels out around the famous crooked section of **Lombard Street** (p. 78) before coasting down to the bay. No postcard can capture what it feels like the first moment you glimpse those million-dollar views of the bay.

Tip: If the lines at Powell/Market or Fisherman's Wharf turntables are unbearable, you'll rarely have to wait long for the California Street line, which runs east-west from the Financial District, through Chinatown, over Nob Hill, and stops at Van Ness Avenue. It's not as thrilling as the Powell–Hyde line, but the line sure is shorter.

Waiting in Line Is for Tourists

Here's the secret to catching a ride on a cable car without waiting in line for hours: Don't wait at the turnaround stops at the beginning and end of the lines. Walk several blocks up the line (follow the tracks) and do as the locals do: Hop on when the car stops, hang on to a pole, and have your $5 ready to hand to the brakeman (hoping, of course, that he'll never ask). On a really busy weekend, however, the cable cars often don't stop to pick up passengers en route because they're full, so you might have to stand in line at the turnarounds with the other peons.

Mission Dolores San Francisco's oldest standing structure, the *Mission San Francisco de Asís* (also known as Mission Dolores), has withstood the test of time, as well as two major earthquakes, relatively intact. In 1776, at the behest of Franciscan missionary Junípero Serra, Father Francisco Palou came to the Bay Area to found the sixth in a series of missions that dotted the California coastline. From these humble beginnings grew what was to become the city of San Francisco. The mission's small, simple chapel, built solidly by Native

Americans who were converted to Christianity, is a curious mixture of native construction methods and Spanish-colonial style. A statue of Father Serra stands in the mission garden, although the portrait looks somewhat more contemplative, and less energetic, than he must have been in real life. A 45-minute self-guided tour costs $5; otherwise, admission is $3 for adults and $2 for children.

16th St. (at Dolores St.). ✆ 415/621-8203. www.missiondolores.org. Admission $3 adults, $2 children. Daily 9am-5pm summer; 9am-4pm winter; 9am-4:30pm spring; 9am-noon Good Friday. Closed Thanksgiving, Easter, and Dec 25. Bus: 14, 26, or 33 to Church and 16th sts. Streetcar: J.

WORTH THE SPLURGE

★ **Alcatraz Island** Alcatraz is by far the best tourist attraction in the city, and worth every penny of the admission price. Nearly every souvenir stand in the city sells a variety of tacky T-shirts proclaiming the wearer to be an inmate, escapee, or survivor of the notorious island prison, once home to folks like Al Capone, Machine Gun Kelly, and Robert Stroud, the Birdman of Alcatraz. It cost a fortune to keep them imprisoned here because all supplies, including water, had to be shipped in. In 1963, after an apparent escape in which no bodies were recovered, the government closed the prison, and in 1972 the island became part of the Golden Gate National Recreation Area.

But far from being yet another tourist trap, Alcatraz Island is more like a set for a nightmarish Fellini movie co-authored by Stephen King—part bucolic Mediterranean island, part claustrophobic cell-block nightmare. Aside from morbid and/or historical fascination, the jagged island, 135 feet above the bay, is a surprisingly nice spot for walking, with views of the city's skyline and the Golden Gate Bridge. Tours, including an audio tour of the prison block and a slide show, are given by the park's rangers, who entertain guests with interesting anecdotes.

Allow about 2½ hours for the round-trip boat ride and the tour. Wear comfortable shoes (the National Park Service notes that there are a lot of hills to climb on the tour) and take a heavy sweater or windbreaker, because even when the sun's out, it's cold there. You should also bring snacks and drinks with you if you think you'll want them. Although there is a beverage-and-snack bar on the ferry, the options are limited and expensive, and only water is available on the island. The excursion to Alcatraz is very popular and space is limited,

The "Only in San Francisco" list of Rare & Strange (free) Sightings

As your broke or cheap self wanders around town, look for the people and objects listed below. Some are easier to find than others, but if you check off more than half, you've really gotten around.

- **A Chinatown Funeral Procession:** Look for a fancy convertible decorated with pictures of the deceased followed by the Green Street Band playing Western pop tunes. Funeral corteges generally tour North Beach and Chinatown.
- **The Doorman at the Sir Francis Drake:** For nearly 3 decades Tom Sweeney has greeted guests of the Sir Francis Drake in a traditional beefeater outfit.
- **The Rock Balancer:** Bill Dan rides his bike to Crissy Field many afternoons and promptly draws huge crowds by balancing large rocks on top of each other in apparently gravity-defying ways. He uses no glue, yet his towers miraculously withstand the afternoon breezes.
- **Critical Mass:** On the last Friday of every month at 5:30pm, a huge group of bicyclists takes over the city streets to celebrate cycling and to assert cyclists' right to the road.
- **The Twins:** Nob Hill residents Vivian and Marian Brown, blond, coiffed, 70-something identical twin sisters, are local celebrities simply for dressing exactly alike (fabulously so) and never being seen without one another. Spotting them is said to be good luck.

so purchase tickets as far in advance as possible (up to 90 days) via the **Alcatraz Cruises** website at **www.alcatrazcruises.com**. You can also purchase tickets in person by visiting the Hornblower Alcatraz Landing ticket office at Pier 33. The first departure, called the "Early Bird," leaves at 9am, and ferries depart about every half-hour afterward until 2pm. Night tours (highly recommended) are also available

- **The Wild Parrots of Telegraph Hill:** A famous flock of wild green parrots, descendants of escapee pets, roosts in the trees around the Filbert Steps. Listen for the noise of their cawing and then see if you can spot these cherry-headed birds.
- **Robin Williams:** The actor/comedian lives near Baker Beach and is said to jog along Crissy Field. Occasionally he shows up unannounced at local comedy clubs.
- **Bush Man:** I had the bejesus scared out of me by this guy once. He hides behind a bushy branch on the sidewalk at Fisherman's Wharf, then jumps out at unsuspecting passersby. It's quite entertaining watching the reaction from tourists as they soil their shorts.
- **The Sisters of Perpetual Indulgence:** This wildly cross-dressed gaggle of queer "21st century nuns" is often seen at some of the city's saucier events, such as the Folsom Street Fair. The San Francisco Order of these "absolutely fabulous" artists and activists is the largest and oldest in the world.
- **Art Cars:** Keep your eyes peeled for weird and wonderful autos. You'll know one when you see it. There's a GI Joe–covered station wagon and other cars painted in weird and wacky colors, traveling canvases of public art. The end of September brings the ArtCar Fest to the Bay Area (**www.artcarfest.com**), a gathering of these wildly decorated vehicles and the people who love them.

Thursday through Monday and are a more intimate and wonderfully spooky experience.

Pier 41, near Fisherman's Wharf. ✆ **415/981-7625.** www.alcatrazcruises.com or www.nps.gov/alcatraz. Admission (includes ferry trip and audio tour) $25 adults, $23 seniors 62 and older, $15 children 5–11. Night tours cost $32 adults, $29 seniors 62 and older, $19 children 5–11. Arrive at least 20 min. before departure time.

3 Neighborhoods Worth Exploring

To really get to know San Francisco, break out of the downtown and Fisherman's Wharf areas to explore the ethnically and culturally diverse neighborhoods. Walk the streets, browse the shops, grab a bite at a local restaurant—you'll find that San Francisco's beauty and charm are around every corner, not just at the popular tourist destinations (that, and it don't cost you nuthin'). We suggest several neighborhood-based itineraries in chapter 8.

NOB HILL

When the cable car started operating in 1873, this hill became the city's exclusive residential area. Newly wealthy residents who had struck it rich in the gold rush (and were known by names such as the "Big Four" and the "Comstock Bonanza kings") built their mansions here, but they were almost all destroyed by the 1906 earthquake and fire. The only two surviving buildings are the Flood Mansion, which serves today as the **Pacific Union Club,** and **The Fairmont Hotel,** which was under construction when the earthquake struck and was damaged but not destroyed. Today, the burned-out sites of former mansions hold the city's luxury hotels—the InterContinental **Mark Hopkins,** the **Stanford Court, The Huntington Hotel,** and spectacular **Grace Cathedral,** which stands on the Crocker mansion site. Nob Hill is worth a visit if only to stroll around **Huntington Park,** attend a Sunday service at the cathedral, or *ooh* and *aah* your way around the Fairmont's spectacular lobby.

SOUTH OF MARKET (SoMa)

From Market Street to Townsend Street and the Embarcadero to Division Street, SoMa has become the city's newest cultural and multimedia center. The process started when alternative clubs began opening in the old warehouses in the area nearly a decade ago. A wave of entrepreneurs followed, seeking to start new businesses in what was once an extremely low-rent area compared to the neighboring Financial District. Today, gentrification and high rents hold sway, spurred by a building boom that started with the **Moscone Convention Center** and continued with the **Yerba Buena Center for the Arts and Yerba Buena Gardens,** the **San Francisco Museum of Modern Art, Four Seasons Hotel, W Hotel, St. Regis Hotel,** and the **Metreon Entertainment**

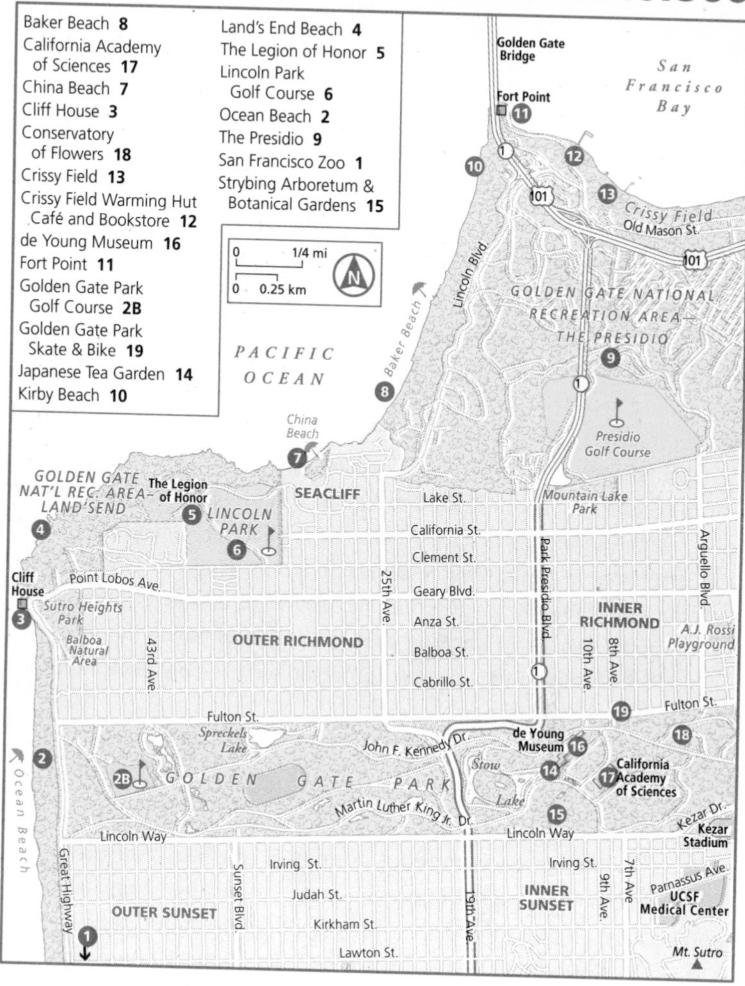

Center. Other institutions, businesses, and museums move into the area on an ongoing basis. A substantial portion of the city's nightlife takes place in warehouse spaces throughout the district.

NORTH BEACH

In the late 1800s, an enormous influx of Italian immigrants to North Beach firmly established this aromatic area as San Francisco's "Little Italy." Dozens of Italian restaurants and coffeehouses continue to

Exploring the Birthplace of the Beats

Bohemian-history buffs can pay homage to some of the hallowed grounds that have made San Francisco a capital of late-20th-century counterculture. The Beat movement, for instance, was sired here in 1953 when Allen Ginsberg moved to San Francisco and Lawrence Ferlinghetti opened **City Lights bookstore** (p. 214) at 261 Columbus Ave. Already in residence were Neal Cassady and Jack Kerouac, who resided at 29 Russell St., a small alley off Hyde Street between Union and Grand streets.

Stoned to the gills one weekend in 1955, Ginsberg wrote his magnum opus, *Howl*, in his apartment at 1214 Polk St. (btw Bush and Sutter sts.), and read it for the first time 2 weeks later to a spellbound audience at the tiny **Six Gallery** at 3119 Fillmore St. (btw Filbert and Greenwich sts.). City Lights published the poem in 1956, and the police immediately declared it obscene, focusing national attention on North Beach. *Chronicle* columnist Herb Caen coined the term "beatnik" to describe the disheveled literati—Kerouac, Ferlinghetti, Ginsberg—who dug poetry and jazz at places like **Vesuvio** (255 Columbus Ave.), on the corner of what is now Jack Kerouac

flourish in what is still the center of the city's Italian community. Walk down **Columbus Avenue** on any given morning and you're bound to be bombarded by the wonderful aromas of roasting coffee and savory pasta sauces. Although there are some interesting shops and bookstores in the area, it's the dozens of eclectic little cafes, delis, bakeries, and coffee shops that give North Beach its Italian-Bohemian character. Below is a short history and geography of some of the places that beget the movement that became known as "Beat." We've also put a walking tour of North Beach in on p. 234.

CHINATOWN

The first of the Chinese immigrants came to San Francisco in the early 1800s to work as servants. By 1851, 25,000 Chinese people were working in California, and most had settled in San Francisco's Chinatown. Fleeing famine and the Opium Wars, they had come seeking the good fortune promised by the "Gold Mountain" of California, and

Alley; **The Place** (1546 Grant Ave.), which Jack Kerouac described in *The Dharma Bums* as "the favorite bar of the hepcats around the Beach"; **the Cellar** (576 Green St.); and funky ol' **Specs'** (12 Saroyan Place), my favorite North Beach dive.

In 1958, after Kerouac's *On the Road* became a bestseller and Hollywood producers came up with the watered-down TV series *Route 66* to exploit the theme, tour-bus gawkers descended on North Beach to stare at the "angelheaded hipsters burning for the ancient heavenly connection to the starry dynamo in the machinery of night," making popular hangouts like **Caffe Trieste** (601 Vallejo St.; p. 173), the now defunct Co-Existence Bagel Shop (1398 Grant Ave.), and **Enrico's** (504 Broadway) feel like zoos for the caged poets.

If all this walking sounds like way too much work, may I suggest a compromise? Buy a copy of *Howl* at City Lights (or bring your own dog-eared copy . . .), walk over to Vesuvio, and softly read the poem aloud while nursing a Jack Kerouac cocktail—a deadly combo of tequila, rum, fruit juice, and lime that goes down a little too easy.

hoped to return with wealth to their families in China. For the majority, the reality of life in California did not live up to the promise. First employed as workers in the gold mines during the gold rush, they later built the railroads, working as little more than slaves and facing constant prejudice. Yet the community, segregated in the Chinatown ghetto, thrived. Growing prejudice led to the Chinese Exclusion Act of 1882, which halted all Chinese immigration for 10 years and severely limited it thereafter (the Chinese Exclusion Act was not repealed until 1943). Chinese people were also denied the opportunity to buy homes outside the Chinatown ghetto until the 1950s.

Today, San Francisco has one of the largest communities of Chinese people in the United States. More than 80,000 people live in Chinatown, but the majority of Chinese people have moved out into newer areas like the Richmond and Sunset districts. Although frequented by tourists, the area continues to cater to Chinese shoppers, who crowd the vegetable and herb markets, restaurants, and shops. Tradition runs deep here, and if you're lucky, through an open window you might hear women mixing mah-jongg tiles as they play the centuries-old game. (***Be warned:*** You're likely to hear lots of spitting around here, too—it's part of local tradition.)

The gateway at Grant Avenue and Bush Street marks the entry to Chinatown. The heart of the neighborhood is Portsmouth Square, where you'll find locals playing board games or just sitting quietly.

On the newly beautified and renovated Waverly Place, a street where the Chinese celebratory colors of red, yellow, and green are much in evidence, you'll find three **Chinese temples:** Jeng Sen (Buddhist and Taoist) at no. 146, Tien Hou (Buddhist) at no. 125, and Norras (Buddhist) at no. 109. If you enter, do so quietly so that you do not disturb those in prayer.

A block west of Grant Avenue, **Stockton Street,** from 1000 to 1200, is the community's main shopping street, lined with grocers, fishmongers, tea sellers, herbalists, noodle parlors, and restaurants. Here, too, is the Buddhist Kong Chow Temple, at no. 855, above the Chinatown post office.

Lord, Byron of Beers for Me

If you're strolling through North Beach, be sure to poke your head into **O'Reilly's Irish Pub** (622 Green St. off Columbus Ave.) to admire the mural of Irish writers and poets peering out from the back wall (how many can you name?). This homey watering hole dishes out heaping plates of hearty Irish food and a fine selection of beers (including Guinness, of course) that are best enjoyed at one of the sidewalk tables. Happy Hour is Monday through Friday from 2 to 7pm and there's free Wi-Fi.

JAPANTOWN

More than 12,000 citizens of Japanese descent (1.4% of the city's population) live in San Francisco, or ***Soko,*** as the Japanese who first emigrated here often called it. Initially, they settled in Chinatown and south of Market along Stevenson and Jessie streets from Fourth to Seventh streets. After the earthquake in 1906, SoMa became a light industrial and warehouse area, and the largest Japanese concentration took root in the Western Addition between Van Ness Avenue and Fillmore

Street, the site of today's Japantown, now 100 years old. By 1940, it covered 30 blocks.

In 1913, the Alien Land Law was passed, depriving Japanese Americans of the right to buy land. From 1924 to 1952, the United States banned Japanese immigration. During World War II, the U.S. government froze Japanese bank accounts, interned community leaders, and removed 112,000 Japanese Americans—two-thirds of them citizens—to camps in California, Utah, and Idaho. Japantown was emptied of Japanese people, and war workers took their place. Upon their release in 1945, the Japanese found their old neighborhood occupied. Most of them resettled in the Richmond and Sunset districts; some returned to Japantown, but it had shrunk to a mere 6 or so blocks.

Today, the community's notable sights include the **Buddhist Church of San Francisco,** 1881 Pine St. (at Octavia St.), www.bcsfweb.org; the **Konko Church of San Francisco,** 1909 Bush St. (at Laguna St.); the **Sokoji–Soto Zen Buddhist Temple,** 1691 Laguna St. (at Sutter St.); **Nihonmachi Mall,** 1700 block of Buchanan Street between Sutter and Post streets, which contains two steel fountains by Ruth Asawa; and the **Japan Center,** an Asian-oriented shopping mall occupying 3 square blocks bounded by Post, Geary, Laguna, and Fillmore streets. At its center stands the five-tiered **Peace Pagoda,** designed by world-famous Japanese architect Yoshiro Taniguchi "to

FREE Free Fortune Cookie Factory Tour

At 56 Ross Alley is the **Golden Gate Fortune Cookie Factory,** a tiny Chinatown storefront where, since 1962, three women sit at a conveyer belt, folding messages into thousands of fortune cookies as the manager invariably calls out to tourists, beckoning them to stroll in, watch the cookies being made, and buy a bag of 40 for about $3. Sure, there are other fortune cookie bakeries in the city, but this is the only one left where the cookies are still made by hand the old-fashioned way. You can purchase regular fortunes or unfolded flat cookies without fortunes, or, if you bring your own fortunes, they can create custom cookies (great for dinner parties) at around $6 for 50 cookies—a very cheap way to impress your friends. The factory is open daily 9am to 8:30pm and admission is always free; ✆ **415/781-3956.**

convey the friendship and goodwill of the Japanese to the people of the United States." Surrounding the pagoda, through a network of arcades, squares, and bridges, you can explore dozens of shops and showrooms featuring everything from TVs and tansu chests to pearls, bonsai, and kimonos. **Kabuki Springs & Spa** (p. 197) is the center's most famous tenant. But locals also head to its numerous restaurants, teahouses, shops, and multiplex movie theater.

There is often live entertainment in this neighborhood on summer weekends, including Japanese music and dance performances, tea ceremonies, flower-arranging demonstrations, martial arts presentations, and other cultural events. **The Japan Center** (**© 415/922-6776**) is open daily from 10am to midnight, although most shops close much earlier. To get there, take bus no. 2, 3, or 4 (exit at Buchanan and Sutter sts.) or no. 22 or 38 (exit at the northeast corner of Geary Blvd. and Fillmore St.).

HAIGHT-ASHBURY

Few of San Francisco's neighborhoods are as varied—or as famous—as Haight-Ashbury. Walk along Haight Street, and you'll encounter everything from drug-dazed drifters begging for change to an armada of the city's funky-trendy shops, clubs, and cafes. Turn anywhere off Haight, and instantly you're among the clean-cut, young urban professionals who can afford the steep rents in this hip 'hood. The result is an interesting mix of well-to-do and well-screw-you aging flower children, former Deadheads, homeless people, and throngs of tourists who try not to stare as they wander through this most human of zoos. Some find it depressing, others find it fascinating, but everyone agrees that it ain't what it was in the free-lovin' psychedelic Summer of Love. Is it still worth a visit? Not if you are here for a day or two, but it's certainly worth an excursion on longer trips, if only to enjoy a cone of Cherry Garcia at the now-famous Ben & Jerry's Ice Cream Store on the corner of Haight and Ashbury streets, and then to wander and gawk at the area's intentional freaks.

THE CASTRO

Castro Street, between Market and 18th streets, is the center of the city's gay community as well as a lovely neighborhood teeming with shops, restaurants, bars, and other institutions that cater to the area's colorful residents. Among the landmarks are **Harvey Milk Plaza** and the **Castro Theatre** (www.castrotheatre.com), a 1930s movie palace with a Wurlitzer organ. The gay community began to move here in the late 1960s and early 1970s from a neighborhood called Polk Gulch, which still has a number of gay-oriented bars and stores. Castro is one of the liveliest streets in the city and the perfect place to shop for gifts and revel in free-spiritedness. Check **www.castroonline.com** for more info.

THE MISSION DISTRICT

Once inhabited almost entirely by Irish immigrants, the Mission District is now the center of the city's Latino community as well as a mecca for young, hip residents. It's an oblong area stretching roughly from 14th to 30th streets between Potrero Avenue on the east and Dolores on the west. In the outer areas, many of the city's finest Victorians still stand, although they seem strangely out of place in the mostly lower-income neighborhoods. The heart of the community lies along 24th Street between Van Ness and Potrero, where dozens of excellent ethnic restaurants, bakeries, bars, and specialty stores attract people from all over the city. The area surrounding 16th Street and Valencia is a hotbed for impressive—and often impressively cheap—restaurants and bars catering to the city's hip crowd. The Mission District at night doesn't feel like the safest place (although in terms of creepiness, the Tenderloin, a few blocks off Union Sq., beats The Mission by far), and walking around the area should be done with caution; but it's usually quite safe during the day and is highly recommended.

Other signs of cultural life in the neighborhood are progressive theaters such as **Theatre Rhinoceros** (www.therhino.org) and Theater Artaud (www.artaud.org). At 16th Street and Dolores is the Mission San Francisco de Asís, better known as **Mission Dolores** (p. 104). It's the city's oldest surviving building and the district's namesake.

4 Parks & Gardens

GOLDEN GATE PARK

Golden Gate Park covers 1,017 acres stretching from the Panhandle to the beach. Besides various major attractions covered in the Entertainment chapter, it has 11 lakes, 2 waterfalls, 21 tennis courts, horseshoe pits (off Conservatory Way near Grove St.; bring your own

Cheap Skate Sundays (Get It?)

Always good for a giggle is a Sunday spent skating through Golden Gate Park (particularly if your skating skills are rusty). Although people skate in Golden Gate Park all week long, Sundays are best because John F. Kennedy Drive between Kezar Drive and Transverse Road is closed to cars. **Golden Gate Park Skate & Bike** on Fulton Street between 6th and 7th avenues (✆ **415/668-1117;** www.goldengateparkbikeandskate.com) rents skates for about $5 an hour or $20 per day, and safety equipment is included in the rental. Also on Sundays from noon to 5pm in Golden Gate Park, really good skaters congregate at a small paved lot near 6th Avenue and Fulton Street for a hugely entertaining skate dance party to show off their skills on wheels.

horseshoes), a nine-hole golf course, fly-casting pools, a miniature yacht club, a 5-acre Japanese tea garden, a primitive garden featuring plants from the dinosaur era, and the very same polo grounds where Allen Ginsberg and Timothy Leary ushered in the Summer of Love at the first "Human Be-In" in 1967.

The city's reigning playground, Golden Gate Park has been home to the 49ers football team and all the city's major hippie happenings (including Jerry Garcia's memorial service in 1995); it's still home to Sunday strollers, skaters, and joggers; museums; free operas; and even a herd of buffalo.

Attractions in Golden Gate Park

Conservatory of Flowers

Opened to the public in 1879, this glorious Victorian glass structure is the oldest existing public conservatory in the Western Hemisphere. After a bad storm in 1995 and delayed renovations, the conservatory was closed and visitors were only able to imagine what wondrous displays existed within the striking glass assemblage. Thankfully, a $25-million renovation, including a $4-million exhibit upgrade, was completed a few years ago, and now the Conservatory is a cutting-edge horticultural destination with more than 1,700 species of plants. Here you can check out the rare tropical flora of the Congo, Philippines, and beyond within the stunning structure. As one of only four public institutions in the U.S. to house a highland tropics exhibit, its five galleries also include the lowland tropics, aquatic plants, the largest Dracula orchid collection in the world, and special exhibits. It doesn't take long to visit, but make a point of staying awhile; outside there are good sunny spots for people-watching as well as paths leading to impressive gardens begging to be explored. If you're around during summer and fall, don't miss the Dahlia Garden to the right of the entrance in the center of what was once a carriage roundabout—it's an explosion of colorful Dr. Seuss–like blooms. The conservatory is open Tuesday through Sunday from 9am to 5pm, closed Mondays. FINE PRINT Admission is $5 for adults; $3 for youth 12 to 17 years of age, seniors, and students with ID; $1.50 for children 5 to 11; and **free for children 4 and under and for all visitors the first Tuesday of the month.** For more information, visit www.conservatoryofflowers.org or call © **415/666-7001.**

Japanese Tea Garden The 5-acre Japanese Tea Garden is the oldest in America. When you enter through the hand-carved gate, you really feel as though you're in Japan. The bamboo-lined footpaths and bridges pass ponds full of koi fish, tiny Bonsai trees, stone lanterns, Shinto shrines, and a serene 18th-century Buddha. In early spring, the garden is ablaze with cherry blossoms. (Go early in the morning to avoid crowds.) Cap your visit with a rest stop at the tea pavilion for a fortune cookie and a relaxing cup of green tea served by women in traditional Japanese costume (it's included with the $4 entrance fee). The garden is open daily November through February from 8:30am to 5pm (teahouse 10am–4:30pm), March through October from 8:30am to 6pm (teahouse 10am–5:30pm). For information on admission, call © **415/752-4227.** For the **teahouse,** call © **415/752-1171.**

FREE Free Golden Gate Park Walking Tours

The **San Francisco Park Trust** offers free docent-led walking tours of Golden Gate Park. Rich in history and enlightening anecdotes, these behind-the-scenes tours cover a range of park highlights, everything from AIDS Grove to the Japanese Tea Garden and Stow Lake. Tour dates and times vary seasonally, so call the 24-hour hotline for schedule details at © **415/263-0991** or log onto their website at www.sfpt.org.

The Presidio FREE In October 1994, the Presidio passed from the U.S. Army to the National Park Service and became one of a handful of urban national parks that combines historical, architectural, and natural elements in one giant arboreal expanse. (It also contains a previously private golf course and a home for George Lucas's production company.) The 1,491-acre area incorporates a variety of terrain—coastal scrub, dunes, and prairie grasslands—that shelter many rare plants and more than 200 species of birds, some of which nest here. The area encompasses more than 470 historic buildings, a scenic golf course, a national cemetery, 22 hiking trails (to be doubled over the next decade), and a variety of terrain and natural habitats. The National Park Service offers walking and biking tours around the Presidio (reservations are suggested), as well as a free shuttle "PresidioGo." For more information, call the **Presidio Visitors Center** at ✆ **415/561-4323,** or visit www.nps.gov/prsf. FINE PRINT Admission to the park is free, but some educational and interpretive programs require reservations. To make reservations, call the Visitors Center.

FREE Sweating the Stairs

You don't need to join a gym to stay in shape in San Francisco—you only need to go outside. There are dozens of steep public staircases in the city that will give you a good workout, but the most popular sweat-inducing steps are the **Lyon Street Steps** between Green Street and Broadway. Built in 1916, this historic stairway street contains four steep sets of stairs totaling 288 steps. Begin at Green Street and climb all the way up, past manicured hedges and flower gardens, to an iron gate that opens into the Presidio. A block east, on Baker Street, another set of 369 steps descends to Green Street.

Strybing Arboretum & Botanical Gardens FREE More than 7,000 plant species grow here, among them some ancient plants in a special "primitive garden," rare species, and a grove of California redwoods. Docent tours begin at 1:30pm daily, with an additional 10:20am tour on weekends. Strybing is open Monday through Friday from 8am to 4:30pm, and Saturday, Sunday, and holidays from 10am to 5pm. Admission is free. For more information, call ✆ **415/661-1316** or visit www.strybing.org.

GOLDEN GATE NATIONAL RECREATION AREA

The largest urban park in the world, GGNRA makes New York's Central Park look like a putting green, covering three counties along 28 miles of stunning, condo-free shoreline. Run by the National Park Service, the Recreation Area wraps around the northern and western edges of the city, and just about all of it is open to the public with no access fees (except for overnight camping at Kirby Cove, visiting Alcatraz Island, and Muir Woods National Monument). The Muni bus system provides transportation to the more popular sites, including Aquatic Park, Cliff House, Fort Mason, and Ocean Beach. For more information, contact the **National Park Service** (✆ **415/561-4700;** www.nps.gov/goga).

Here is a brief rundown of the salient features of the park's peninsula section, starting at the northern section and moving westward around the coastline:

Aquatic Park, adjacent to the Hyde Street Pier, has a small swimming beach, although it's not that appealing (and darned cold). Far more entertaining is a visit to the **San Francisco Maritime National Historical Park's Visitor Center** a few blocks away (see p. 91 for more information).

FREE Listen to the H2Organ

Now here's an interesting form of free entertainment that even most locals don't know about: Head over to the Marina Green at the foot of Lyon Street and walk past the Golden Gate Yacht Club to the end the jetty, where you'll see a bizarre assortment of carved chunks of granite and marble. This is the **Wave Organ,** an acoustic art sculpture consisting of a series of different lengths of pipes that extend into the bay and resonate to the motion of the waves, making subtle sounds—mostly gurgles, swooshes, and sloshes—depending on which little cubby you're sitting in. It's a bit of a spooky experience at night, especially if you know that it's made from stone salvaged from the demolition of a cemetery.

Go Fly a Kite in Marina Green!

If you're short on cash but loaded with free time in San Francisco, here's a suggestion that might just make your day. Head over to the **Chinatown Kite Shop** (p. 229) and plunk down $10 on a groovy cobra snake kite (handmade with silk and bamboo!). Then take the Powell-Hyde cable car to Fisherman's Wharf and walk over to the Marina Green, one of the best places on the planet to fly a kite. Get your kite airborne and *voilà!*—an afternoon of free quality entertainment, complemented by gorgeous Golden Gate Bridge views. Plus you get a cool souvenir.

Fort Mason Center, from Bay Street to the shoreline, consists of several buildings and piers used during World War II. Today they hold a variety of museums, theaters, shops, and organizations, and Greens vegetarian restaurant (p. 72), which affords views of the Golden Gate Bridge. For information about Fort Mason events, call ✆ **415/441-3400** or visit www.fortmason.org. The park headquarters is also at Fort Mason.

Farther west along the bay at the northern end of Laguna Street is **Marina Green,** a favorite local spot for kite flying, jogging, and walking along the Promenade. The St. Francis Yacht Club is also here.

Next comes the 3½-mile paved **Golden Gate Promenade,** San Francisco's best and most scenic biking, jogging, and walking path. It runs along the shore past **Crissy Field** (✆ **415/561-7690;** www.crissyfield.org) and ends at Fort Point under the Golden Gate Bridge (be sure to stop and watch the gonzo windsurfers and kite surfers, who catch major wind here, and admire the newly restored marshlands). The **Crissy Field Warming Hut Café and Bookstore**—developed with input from renowned chef Alice Waters of Berkeley's Chez Panisse—is open from 9am to 5pm Wednesday through Sunday and offers organic soups, salads, sandwiches, coffee drinks, and a decent selection of outdoor-themed books and cards.

Just west of Crissy Field is **Fort Point** (✆ **415/556-1693;** www.nps.gov/fopo), built in 1853 to 1861 to protect the narrow entrance to the harbor. It was designed to house 500 soldiers manning 126 muzzle-loading cannons. By 1900, the fort's soldiers and obsolete guns had been removed, but the formidable brick edifice remains. Fort

Point is open Friday through Sunday only from 10am to 5pm, and free guided tours and cannon demonstrations are given at the site once or twice a day on open days, depending on the time of year.

5 Free & Dirt-Cheap Tours

SELF-GUIDED WALKING TOURS

Hills, schmills! Don't let a few steep slopes deter you from one of San Francisco's greatest pleasures—walking around the neighborhoods and exploring the city for yourself. Before you set out to explore the city, pick up some free walking-tour guides from the **San Francisco Visitor Information Center** (Hallidie Plaza, 900 Market St. at Powell St.; © **415/391-2000**). For more walking tours of the city see chapter 8.

FREE ALERT! The **San Francisco Convention and Visitors Bureau** also has a Web page—**www.sfcvb.org/travel_media/podcasts.asp**—that offers links to more than a dozen city-related **podcasts** that you can download for free or a small fee. For example, the Barbary Coast Trail MP3 audio tour offers highlights of 20 of San Francisco's most important historic sites, and offers period music, sound effects, historic reenactments, and even maps. Another example is the de Young Museum podcast, which includes monthly information about current and upcoming exhibitions, as well as interviews with artists and curators.

Barbary Coast Trail Walking Tour San Francisco's reputation as a rollicking place where anything goes dates from the Barbary Coast days when gang warfare, prostitution, gambling, and drinking were major city pursuits, and citizens took law and order into their own hands. If you can believe it, there's actually a trail that commemorates these wild times. Called the Barbary Coast Trail, it's a 3.8-mile trail within the city that's marked by 170 bronze medallions and arrows embedded in the sidewalk. It starts at the Old U.S. Mint in Downtown, then heads north through the city's historic neighborhoods before ending near Aquatic Park.

Historical highlights along the way range from the birthplace of the Gold Rush to the western terminus of the Pony Express, the Tong War battles in Chinatown, and several museum stops such as the Wells Fargo History Museum that showcase Gold Rush–era relics. The **San Francisco Museum and Historical Society** (© **415/537-1105**) sponsors the walk. If you log onto their website at www.sfhistory.org, you can purchase a nifty Barbary Coast Trail Official Guide for $9 (makes a great souvenir), or better yet just download and print a free map from their website. Also listed on their website is a schedule of free guided walking tours of the Barbary Coast Trail, which usually depart on Saturday and last about 2 hours.

★ **City Guides Walking Tours** FREE The San Francisco Public Library offers about 20 free 1½- to 2-hour walking tours of San Francisco through a program called **City Guides,** hosted by a group of volunteers who have completed an exhaustive training program in San Franciscan history, art, and architecture. In fact, there's hardly a section of the city that isn't covered by a City Guides walking tour. All you have to do is pick the tour that interests you and show up at the proper corner on time. You can get an insider's view of Chinatown, admire San Francisco's collection of beautifully restored Victorian homes on the Landmark Victorians of Alamo Square tour, or explore the haunts of the original 49ers on the Gold Rush City walk. It's a superb way to get to know the city's varied neighborhoods and it's free (although donations are gladly accepted). Reservations aren't even necessary—just show up at the designated meeting point. The starting locations vary. For more information, call ✆ **415/557-4266** or visit www.sfcityguides.org.

Golden Gate Promenade FREE Some of the most beautiful—and least hilly—places to walk or jog in San Francisco are its promenades, which trace the shoreline of the bay. The best and most popular is the Golden Gate Promenade because of the beautiful views and decided lack of automobile traffic. It starts at Aquatic Park/Fort Mason at the western edge of Fisherman's Wharf—the 28 Muni bus route runs near the trail, so you can go one-way or round-trip, or stop anywhere along the way. The Promenade, which is marked by blue-and-white signs, passes through Crissy Field (p. 120) before ending at Fort Point (p. 120), where steps lead up to the Golden Gate Bridge's pedestrian walkway. The entire route is less than 4 miles long (not counting the walk across the bridge).

SFMHS Walking Tours FREE The San Francisco Museum and Historical Society (SFMHS) offers numerous free history walks throughout the city. The most popular is the Barbary Coast Trail (see earlier), but they also offer other interesting walking tours such as **High On The Haight,** which details how this famous neighborhood became a mecca for the hippies and the counterculture; the **Victorian**

Alliance Fall House Tour, a stroll through the Presidio Heights neighborhood renowned for its rich architectural heritage; and the **Financial District Walking Tour,** which covers the architectural highlights of downtown San Francisco and its history as one of the financial centers of the U.S. For more information call ✆ **415/537-1105** or log onto their website at www.sfhistory.org.

TOURS BY CAR AND PUBLIC TRANSIT

Bay Area BART Tour One of the world's most complex commuter systems, Bay Area Rapid Transit (BART) links San Francisco with other cities and communities throughout the East and South bays. The air-conditioned train cars run along more than 100 miles of mostly elevated rail, including one of the longest underwater transit tubes in the world (don't let those earthquakes make you nervous). The trains can hit a top speed of 80 mph; a computerized control system monitors and adjusts their speed. If you have some time and want to take a tour of the Bay Area, BART sells a $4.65 "Excursion Ticket," which allows you, in effect, to "sightsee" the entire BART system, but you must exit at the station where you entered (if you get out anywhere along the line, the gate instantly computes the normal fare). For more information, call ✆ **415/989-BART** (989-2278) or visit www.bart.gov, where you can also download trip plans directly to your iPod, PDA, or wireless.

The 49-mile Scenic Drive FREE The self-guided, 49-mile drive is an easy way to orient yourself and to grasp the beauty of San Francisco and its extraordinary location. It's also a flat-out stunning and very worthy excursion. Beginning in the city, it follows a rough circle around the bay and passes virtually all the best-known sights, from Chinatown to the Golden Gate Bridge, Ocean Beach, Seal Rocks, Golden Gate Park, and Twin Peaks. Originally designed for the benefit of visitors to San Francisco's 1939 and 1940 Golden Gate International Exposition, the route is marked by blue-and-white sea gull signs. Although it makes an excellent half-day tour, this miniexcursion can easily take longer if you decide, for example, to stop to walk across the Golden Gate Bridge or to have tea in Golden Gate Park's Japanese Tea Garden. The **San Francisco Visitor Information Center** (Hallidie Plaza, 900 Market St. at Powell St.; ✆ **415/391-2000**) distributes free route maps, which are handy since a few of the Scenic Drive marker signs are missing. ***Tip:*** Try to avoid the downtown area during the weekday rush hours from 7 to 9am and 4 to 6pm. FINE PRINT You really do need a car (or a friend with a car) for this tour, as it's not doable by bike or on foot.

★ **Sausalito Boat Tour** There are plenty of bay cruises that troll for tourist dollars at Fisherman's Wharf and PIER 39, but it's far more fun (and cheaper at just $7.50 one-way) to go to the Ferry Building at the foot of Market Street and ride with the locals on an afternoon Golden Gate Ferry to the seaside village of Sausalito. The 30-minute trip across San Francisco Bay features the same fabulous views of Alcatraz and the Golden Gate Bridge you'll see on the tourist tugs, and—wait for it—there's even a full bar onboard.

You can do a 90-minute round-tripper, but why not make a day of it and spend the afternoon exploring Sausalito. There's really just one main street—Bridgeway—so it's easy to walk around the yuppie/nautical/ex-bohemian enclave and find a perfect spot to watch the sun set behind the San Francisco skyline. If sunsets aren't your thing, and you'd sooner toss back a pint at a rowdy tavern full of live music and boisterous baby boomers, try the **No Name Bar** (757 Bridgeway; ✆ **415/332-1392**), but don't drink too many happy hour specials unless you intend to spend the night—the last ferry departs for San Francisco at 7:20pm.

6 Awesome Art & Architecture

MISSION DISTRICT MURALS

For a total immersion into the mural art scene on the gritty streets of San Francisco—hundreds of colorful murals painted on the walls, fences, and sides of buildings in the Mission District—take BART to the 24th Street station and head up 24th toward Potrero Hill (you'll see it looming in front of you) until you come to Balmy Alley, nestled between Treat Avenue and Harrison Street. This 1-block lane is inundated with murals: Practically every inch of every fence, wall, and garage door is covered with color. Many of the alley's most cherished murals were defaced or destroyed by vandals in the past, but local muralists have painted new images and restored old ones. After you've perused Balmy Alley, go back out to 24th Street and head farther toward the hill until you reach York Street, about 4 blocks away. Again you will be treated to a marvelous assortment of brilliantly colored murals.

Sorting Through the SF Art Scene

The best place to find out what's going on in the San Francisco art scene is **SFARTS.org.** Their website's "SFARTS Search" feature is a fast and easy way to help you find the San Francisco arts events that interest you. They also have a "Visiting San Francisco" wizard where (1) you select the date you arrive in San Francisco and the number of days you'll be here, (2) you pick the type of arts events that interest you most, and (3) *voila!* a whole list of art events to choose from is generated.

Another excellent resource for learning about contemporary art and culture goings-on in the city is **FECAL FACE DOT COM** (yes, Fecalface.com). The site features artist interviews, studio visits, blogs by prominent artists and personalities, and an hourly updated news section and coverage of current art openings. It even has its own FECAL FACE DOT GALLERY—"the physical destination for Fecalface.com"—at 66 Gough St. at Market Street, open Thursday and Friday from 4 to 8pm and Saturday and Sunday from noon to 6pm.

If you still haven't gotten your mural fix, walk over to the **Precita Eyes Mural Arts Center,** 2981 24th St. at Harrison St. (✆ **415/285-2287;** www.precitaeyes.org). This community resource center hosts "Mural Walk" tours of the area that cover at least 60 Mission District murals in one 8-block stretch. FINE PRINT The tours cost about $10 to $12 dollars, but you can save yourself about $8 by buying a $3 Mural Map at the center and taking a self-guided tour.

ART GALLERIES

Art galleries are one of San Francisco's best free culture resources. Not only do these minimuseums provide us with works of inspiration, but they also give us free booze and snacks at their openings (see the "First Thursdays" sidebar later). Don't be shy about barging into a show with million-dollar pieces—galley owners are almost as happy raising the profiles of their artists as they are closing a sale, and both are essential for upping the prices they charge.

The majority of fine-art dealers in the city are at **Union Square,** from Grant Avenue to Mason Street and Geary to Post Street. Some of the most popular include these:

Catharine Clark Gallery Catharine Clark's is a different kind of gallery experience. Although many galleries focus on established artists and out-of-this-world prices, Catharine's exhibits works by up-and-coming contemporary as well as established artists (mainly from California). It nurtures beginning collectors by offering a purchasing plan that's almost unheard of in the art business. You can buy a piece on layaway and take up to a year to pay for it—interest free! Prices here make art a realistic purchase for almost everyone for a change, but serious collectors also frequent the shows because Clark has such a keen eye for talent. Shows change every 6 weeks.

150 Minna St., ground floor (btw Third and New Montgomery sts.). ✆ **415/399-1439.** www.cclarkgallery.com. Tues–Fri 10:30am–5:30pm and Sat 11am–5:30pm. Closed Sun–Mon.

Fraenkel Gallery This photography gallery features works by contemporary American and European artists. Excellent shows change every 2 months.

49 Geary St. (btw Grant Ave. and Kearny St.), 4th floor. ✆ **415/981-2661.** www.fraenkelgallery.com. Tues–Fri 10:30am–5:30pm and Sat 11am–5pm. Closed Sun–Mon.

Hang This is an amazingly affordable gallery for attractive pieces by yet-to-be-discovered Bay Area artists. The staff is friendly and helpful, and the gallery is designed to cater to new and seasoned collectors who appreciate original art at down-to-earth prices. Hours vary, depending on what's on display. See the website for the latest info.

556 Sutter St. ✆ **415/434-4264.** www.hangart.com.

Images of the North The highlight here is one of the most extensive collections of Canadian and Alaskan Inuit art in the United States. There's also a small collection of Native American masks and jewelry.

2036 Union St. (at Buchanan St.). ✆ **415/673-1273.** www.imagesnorth.com. Tues–Sat 11am–5:30pm and by appointment.

Meyerovich Gallery Paintings, sculptures, and works on paper here are by modern and contemporary masters, including Chagall, Matisse, Miró, and Picasso. Meyerovich's new Contemporary Gallery, across the hall, features works by Lichtenstein, Stella, Frankenthaler, Dine, and Hockney.

FREE First Thursdays Art Event at Union Square

The first Thursday of every month, from 5:30 to 7:30pm, the San Francisco Art Dealers Association sponsors a program to stimulate interest in the art galleries in and around Union Square. And it works: People from all over the Bay Area show up for a chance to meet with artists and gallery owners while sipping free wine (and the occasional Cosmo) and nibbling on cheese. It's a fun way to spend a Thursday evening, pretending you're a wealthy art buyer while double-fisting some 2-buck Chuck. For a list of participating galleries, call ✆ **415/921-1600,** or just show up at Union Square around 5:30pm and join the party.

251 Post St. (at Stockton St.), 4th floor. ✆ **415/421-7171.** www.meyerovich.com. Mon–Fri 10am–6pm and Sat 10am–5pm. Closed Sun.

CHECKING OUT THE ARCHITECTURE

Exploring SF's Victorian Homes

Some 14,000 Victorian buildings—mostly private homes—are scattered throughout San Francisco, but the ones you usually see on the postcards (The **Painted Ladies** along the 700 block of Steiner St.) are lined up around Alamo Square, the center of a small, wealthy neighborhood bordered by Golden Gate Avenue on the north, Fell Street on the south, Webster Street on the east, and Divisadero Street on the west. These ornate wooden homes range from gracious to almost garish, depending upon how much gingerbread is involved and who has been choosing the color scheme, but most of them have been meticulously restored.

If picture-pretty private residences are less intriguing to you than timeworn structures in a working-class neighborhood, head over to the inner Mission District, where several types of the city's oldest Victorians—stick, Italianate, and Queen Anne—can be found on or near Liberty Street, a small side street between 20th and 21st streets. These structures survived the 1906 earthquake because the fires stopped at 20th Street. An 1878 stick-style building, characterized by square bay windows with flat wooden "sticks" that have carved scrolls, leaves, and flowers, stands at 956 Valencia St., on the corner of Liberty.

Head north on Liberty, and you'll see rows of Victorians built between 1870 and 1894. At least five of them (19, 23, 35, 43, and 77) are Italianate-style, distinguished by ornate porticos, facades above the rooflines, and slanted bay windows designed to bring in more light on foggy San Francisco days. The house at 27 Liberty is a local adaptation of a Queen Anne, identifiable primarily because of the shingled walls (most Queen Annes have rounded corner towers, but there are many variations on this theme). Some of the most interesting houses in the Mission District combined several architectural styles to get just the right amount of gewgaw and curlicues—the house at 827 Guerrero St. (corner of Liberty St.) has a Queen Anne tower, a Gothic front window, and a Moorish doorway. The Mission is full of wonderful houses; walk around and explore for yourself.

More Architectural Highlights

San Francisco is a center of many architecturally striking sights, all of which are free to visit (or at least peer at).

Built between 1913 and 1915, **City Hall,** located in the Civic Center District, is part of this "City Beautiful" complex done in the Beaux Arts style. The dome rises to a height of 306 feet on the exterior and is ornamented with oculi and topped by a lantern. The interior rotunda soars 112 feet and is finished in oak, marble, and limestone, with a monumental marble staircase leading to the second floor. With a major renovation completed in the late 1990s, the building was returned to its former splendor. No doubt you saw it on TV during early 2004, when much of the hoopla surrounding the short-lived and controversial gay marriage proceedings was depicted on the front steps. (Remember Rosie O'Donnell emerging from this very building after getting married to her girlfriend?) Free public tours are given Monday through Friday at 10am, noon, and 2pm. Call ✆ **415/554-4933** for details.

The Union Square and Financial District areas also have a number of buildings worth checking out. One is the former **Circle Gallery,** 140 Maiden Lane. Now a gallery housing Folk Art International, Xanadu Tribal Arts, and Boretti Amber & Design, it's the only building in the city designed by Frank Lloyd Wright (in 1948). The gallery was the prototype for the Guggenheim's seashell-shaped circular gallery space, even though it was meant to serve as a retail space for V. C. Morris, a purveyor of glass and crystal. Note the arresting exterior, a solid wall with a circular entryway to the left. Maiden Lane is just off Union Square between Geary and Post streets.

The **Hallidie Building,** 130–150 Sutter St., designed by Willis Polk in 1917, is an ideal example of a glass-curtain building. The vast glass facade is miraculously suspended between the two cast-iron cornices. The fire escapes that course down each side of the building complete the proscenium-like theatrical effect.

Two prominent pieces of San Francisco's skyline are in the Financial District. The **Transamerica Pyramid,** 600 Montgomery St., between Clay and Washington streets, is one of the tallest structures in San Francisco. This corporate headquarters was completed in 1972, stands 48 stories tall, and is capped by a 212-foot spire. The former **Bank of America World Headquarters,** 555 California St., was designed by Wurster, Bernardi, and Emmons with Skidmore, Owings, and Merrill. This carnelian-marble-covered building dates from 1969. Its 52 stories are topped by a panoramic restaurant and bar, the Carnelian Room. The focal point of the building's formal plaza is an abstract black granite sculpture, known locally as the "Banker's Heart," designed by Japanese architect Masayuki Nagare.

The **Medical Dental Building,** 450 Sutter St., is a steel-frame structure beautifully clad in terra cotta. It was designed by Miller and Pflueger in 1929. The entrance and the window frames are elaborately ornamented with Mayan relief work; the lobby ceiling is similarly decorated with gilding. Note the ornate elevators.

At the foot of Market Street you will find the **Ferry Building.** Built between 1895 and 1903, it served as the city's major transportation hub before the Golden Gate and Bay bridges were built; some 170 ferries docked here daily unloading Bay Area commuters until the 1930s. The tower that soars above the building was inspired by the Campanile of Venice and the Cathedral Tower in Seville. In 2003, a 4-year renovation was completed and the building is now a spectacular mixed-use landmark building featuring a 660-foot-long, sky-lit nave, which had been partially filled in and destroyed in the 1950s. If you stop by the Ferry Building, you might also want to go to **Rincon Center,** 99 Mission St., to see the WPA murals painted by the Russian artist Refregier in the post office.

Several important buildings are on or near Nob Hill. The **Flood Mansion,** 1000 California St., at Mason Street, was built between 1885 and 1886 for James Clair Flood. Thanks to the Comstock Lode, Flood rose from being a bartender to one of the city's wealthiest men. He established the Nevada bank that later merged with Wells Fargo. The house cost $1.5 million to build at the time; the fence alone cost $30,000. It was designed by Augustus Laver and modified by Willis Polk after the 1906 earthquake to accommodate the Pacific Union Club. Unfortunately, you can't go inside: The building is now a private school.

Built by George Applegarth in 1913 for sugar magnate Adolph Spreckels, the **Spreckels Mansion,** 2080 Washington St., is currently home to romance novelist Danielle Steel (don't even try to get in to see her!). The extraordinary building has rounded-arch French doors on the first and second floors and curved balconies on the second floor. Inside, the original house featured an indoor pool in the basement, Adamesque fireplaces, and a circular Pompeian room with a fountain.

Finally, one of San Francisco's most ingenious architectural accomplishments is the **San Francisco–Oakland Bay Bridge.** Although it's visually less appealing than the nearby Golden Gate Bridge (except at night when it's lit up), the Bay Bridge is in many ways more spectacular. The silvery giant that links San Francisco with Oakland is one of the world's longest steel bridges (8¼ miles). It opened in 1936, 6 months before the Golden Gate. Each of its two decks contains five automobile lanes. The Bay Bridge is not a single bridge at all, but a superbly dovetailed series of spans joined midbay, at Yerba Buena Island, by one of the world's largest (in diameter) tunnels. To the west of Yerba Buena, the bridge is actually two separate suspension bridges, joined at a central anchorage. East of the island is a 1,400-foot cantilever span, followed by a succession of truss bridges. This east span of the bridge is finally being replaced after being damaged in the 1989 Loma Prieta earthquake and a years-long fight between city residents, planners, and designers. And it looks even more complex than it sounds. You can drive across the bridge (the toll is $3, paid westbound), or you can catch a bus at the Transbay Terminal (Mission at First St.) and ride to downtown Oakland.

7 Beaches, Biking, Golf & Hiking

BEACHES

Here's a news flash: Northern California ain't anything like Malibu. The water is usually as cold as ice, the wind can be fierce enough to blow your tuna sandwich into the next person's picnic basket, and the summer sky is generally overcast—though it will still give you a dreadful sunburn if you don't wear sunblock. So don't look for swaying palms and white-sand beaches. That's a different California. The rugged, cliffside beaches here are some of the most spectacular in the world. Huge waves crash against sheer walls of rock, but a treacherous undertow and unpredictable surf conditions make them dangerous for swimming. You go here for the beautiful scenery and onshore activities, not the chance to make like Michael Phelps.

Ocean Beach (at the end of Golden Gate Park, near the Cliff House) is the most dramatic seaside vista in the city—at least the sea lions that gather on Seal Rocks seem to think so—but it is forbidden to swim there. You can enjoy sunbathing, beachcombing, hiking, and sipping a drink at the **Cliff House** (1090 Point Lobos Ave.; ✆ **415/386-3330**), but don't even think about dipping your little toe in the water. Swimming is also prohibited at **Land's End Beach** (north of the Cliff House), **Kirby Beach** (below the northern end of the Golden Gate Bridge), **Rodeo Beach** (at Fort Cronkite, Marin Headlands), and **Tennessee Beach** (north of Rodeo Beach), though beachcombing can be fun if you stay a safe distance from the water.

There are safe swimming beaches in the city, if you can stand the cold water: **China Beach** (28th Ave. and Sea Cliff Dr.) and **Aquatic Park** (end of Hyde St.). Both are sandy coves where lifeguards are on duty during the summer; they're open April 15 to October 15 from 7am to dusk. More popular with adventurous locals is **Baker Beach,** where nude sunbathing is fashionable for gay and straight sunbathers. Officially designated clothing-optional by the city, it's easily reached by public transportation. The truly gay men's section is beyond the large rock formations, which are most easily navigated at low tide. That part of the beach is definitely a cruise scene. The rest of the beach, however, has a predominant atmosphere of comfortable indifference to the fact that many people are not wearing clothes. Swimming is not prohibited but is definitely very dangerous and should be avoided. No lifeguards are on duty; there are changing rooms, which seem rather pointless when no one's wearing clothes anyway. The beach is open April 15 to October 15 from 7am to 9pm.

BIKING

Because of the numerous steep hills and insane drivers, San Francisco isn't much of a biking town, particularly for visitors who just want a scenic ride. There are, however, a few areas that are conducive to a pleasant day of pedaling around, such as Golden Gate Park, the Golden Gate Bridge, and Ocean Beach. The San Francisco Parks and Recreation Department maintains two city-designated bike routes. One winds 7.5 miles through Golden Gate Park to Lake Merced; the other traverses the city, starting in the south, and continues over the Golden Gate Bridge. These routes are not dedicated to bicyclists, who must exercise caution to avoid crashing into pedestrians. Helmets are recommended for adults and required by law for kids 17 and under. A bike map is available from the **San Francisco Visitor Information Center** (Hallidie Plaza, 900 Market St. at Powell St.; © **415/391-2000**) for $3 and from bicycle shops all around town. You can also download a free PDF of the San Francisco Bicycle Coalition's **SF Bike Map & Walking Guide** at **www.sfbike.org/maps**.

Ocean Beach has a public walk- and bikeway that stretches along 5 waterfront blocks of the Great Highway between Noriega and Santiago streets. It's an easy ride from Cliff House or Golden Gate Park. For cruising Fisherman's Wharf and the Golden Gate Bridge, your best bet is to rent a bike from **Blazing Saddles** (© **415/202-8888;** www.blazingsaddles.com), which has five locations around Fisherman's Wharf. Bikes rent for about $28 per day, including maps, locks, and helmets; tandem bikes are available as well.

For the Golden Gate Park area, head to **Golden Gate Park Skate & Bike** on Fulton Street between 6th and 7th avenues (© **415/668-1117;** www.goldengateparkbikeandskate.com), which rents mountain bikes and tandem bikes starting at $5 an hour.

GOLF

San Francisco has several public golf courses, but only two that are reasonably cheap. The 9-hole **Golden Gate Park Course,** 47th Avenue and Fulton Street (© **415/751-8987;** www.goldengateparkgolf.com), charges greens fees of $14 per person Monday through Thursday, $18 Friday through Sunday. The 1,357-yard course is par 27. All holes are par 3, and this course is appropriate for all levels. The course is a little weathered in spots, but it's casual, fun, and inexpensive. It's open daily from sunup to sundown.

The 18-hole **Lincoln Park Golf Course,** 34th Avenue and Clement Street (© **415/221-9911;** www.parks.sfgov.org), charges greens fees of $31 per person Monday through Thursday, $36 Friday through

Sunday, with rates decreasing after 4pm in summer, 2pm in winter. They'll also rent you a set of clubs for $25. It's San Francisco's prettiest municipal course, with terrific views and fairways lined with Monterey cypress and pine trees. The 5,181-yard layout plays to par 68, and the 17th hole has a glistening ocean view. This is the oldest course in the city and one of the oldest in the West. It's open daily at daybreak.

A good place to tune up your game is the **Mission Bay Golf Center,** Sixth Street at Channel Street (✆ **415/431-7888**). San Francisco's most popular driving range is an impeccably maintained 7-acre facility that consists of a double-decker steel and concrete arc containing 66 covered practice bays. The grass landing area extends 300 yards, has nine target greens, and is lit for evening use. There's a putting green and a chipping and bunker practice area. The center is open Monday from 11:30am to 11pm, Tuesday through Sunday from 7am to 11pm. A bucket of balls costs $8, and the last bucket is sold at 10pm. To get there from downtown San Francisco, take Fourth Street south to Channel Street and turn right.

If you need golfing info, call the **Automated Tee Time and Golf Information Line** (✆ **415/750-4653**), with a menu of information on San Francisco's five public courses—tee times, fees, directions, and more. You can reserve a tee time, get directions to the courses, and obtain information on the hours of operation, greens fees, cart and club rentals, and lessons.

For more information on where to play around that won't bust your budget, see the box "Tee Time on the Cheap" on p. 204 in chapter 6.

HIKING

The **Golden Gate National Recreation Area** at the west end of the city offers plenty of hiking opportunities. The most popular hike in the city is the **Coastal Trail,** which runs all the way from the Fort Point area to Land's End and the Cliff House (a good place to refuel with a Bloody Mary). The cliff-top walk passes though shaded cypress groves with numerous scenic overlooks and access to several shoreline pocket beaches. Your best bet is to pick up a trail map of the Golden Gate National Recreation Area at the **park service headquarters** at Building 201 at Fort Mason; enter on Franklin Street at Bay Street (✆ **415/561-4700;** www.nps.gov/goga). Or, better yet, download a free trail map at the GGNRA's website at www.nps.gov/goga/planyourvisit/maps.htm.

Cocktails and dancing (and live grooves) are just some of your after-dark options in San Francisco.

5 ENTERTAINMENT & NIGHTLIFE

For a city with fewer than a million inhabitants, San Francisco boasts an impressive entertainment scene. In fact, San Francisco claims to sell more theater tickets per capita than any major city in America. Most people would be shocked to hear that little trivia gem, given the fact that so many of the high-profile productions in town are recycled Broadway musicals that appeal mostly to out-of-towners. San Francisco leaves the monumental cost of producing mainstream shows to Broadway, concentrating its own money and effort on unconventional creations. Sure, you can spend your money on tickets on the touring company of last year's Tony winner, but your hard-earned entertainment dollar would be more wisely spent on some of the most innovative, dynamic stage productions in the country—written, produced, directed, and performed by our top local talent (see "Enjoying the Indie SF Theater Scene" box p. 152).

As for the club and music scene, San Francisco's is phenomenal. Dozens of über-hip lounges are augmented by one of the best dance-club cultures this side of New York, and skyscraper lounges offer some of the most dazzling city views in the world. In short, there's always something going on in the city and, unlike in Los Angeles or New York, you don't have to pay outrageous cover charges or be "chosen" to be a part of the scene. But keep in mind that the town isn't up all night: Bars close at 2am, so get an early start if you want a full night on the town in San Francisco.

The 411 on San Francisco Nightlife

For up-to-date nightlife information in the city, the *San Francisco Weekly* (www.sfweekly.com) and the *San Francisco Bay Guardian* (www.sfbg.com) both run comprehensive listings. They're available free at bars and restaurants and from street-corner boxes all around the city. Also, the Sunday edition of the *San Francisco Chronicle* features a "Datebook" section, printed on pink paper, with information on and listings of the week's events. If you have Internet access, check out www.citysearch.com, www.sfgate.com, or www.sfstation.com for the latest in bars, clubs, and events.

CALENDAR OF EVENTS

From the crowning of Japantown's Cherry Blossom Queen to Chinese New Year and Día de los Muertos, San Francisco's extraordinary diversity is celebrated in one festival after another. All year long we find reasons to drink beer outside, fry some corn dogs, and celebrate that we don't live in Detroit. Most of the events listed are free or, if not, easy to sneak into (but that's another book for another day). The dates move around a lot, so call or log on to make sure you're in the right free place at the right free time. For more local event listings, log onto **www.sfgate.com/events.**

January

Anniversary of the Sea Lions' Arrival, PIER 39 FREE. It was on a chilly day in January 1990 that they first starting arriving, those lovable barking beasts. *OORT OORT OORT!* They came for the herring (who wouldn't?) and decided they liked their new PIER 39 digs. Toward the middle of the month, PIER 39 throws a free fête for the pinnipeds with special guests from the Marine Mammal Center to answer all your sea lion queries. For dates and information, log onto **www.pier39.com.**

February

Chinese New Year, Chinatown FREE. Around this time of year (late January to mid February), public celebrations spill onto every street in Chinatown. Festivities begin with the "Miss Chinatown USA" pageant parade, and climax a week later with a celebratory parade of marching bands, rolling floats, barrages of fireworks, and a block-long dragon writhing in and out of the crowds. The revelry runs for several weeks and wraps up with a memorable parade through Chinatown that starts at Market and Second streets and ends at Kearny Street. Arrive early for a good viewing spot on Kearny Street. You can purchase bleacher seats online starting in December. Make your hotel reservations early. For dates and information, call ✆ **415/982-3000** or visit www.chineseparade.com. In 2009 it's the Year of the Ox, and as of February 14, 2010, it will be the Year of the Tiger.

March

St. Patrick's Day Parade, Union Square and Civic Center FREE. Everyone's an honorary Irish person at this festive affair, which starts at 11:30am at Market and Second streets and continues to City Hall. But the party doesn't stop there. Head down to the Civic Center for the postparty, or venture to the Embarcadero's Harrington's bar (245 Front St.) and celebrate with hundreds of the Irish-for-a-day yuppies as they gallivant around the closed-off streets and numerous pubs. For information, call ✆ **415/675-9885;** www.sfstpatricksdayparade.com. Sunday before March 17.

April

Cherry Blossom Festival, Japantown FREE. Meander through the arts-and-crafts and food booths lining the blocked-off streets around Japan Center and watch traditional drumming, flower arranging, origami making, or a parade celebrating the cherry blossom and Japanese culture. Call ✆ **415/563-2313** for information. Mid- to late April.

San Francisco International Film Festival, around San Francisco with screenings at the AMC Kabuki 8 Cinemas (Fillmore and Post sts.), and at many other locations. Begun in 1957, this is America's oldest film festival. It features close to 200 films and videos from more than 50 countries. Tickets are relatively inexpensive, and screenings are accessible to the public. Entries include new films by beginning and established directors. For a schedule or information, call © **415/561-5000** or visit www.sffs.org. Mid-April to early May.

May

Cinco de Mayo Festival, Mission District FREE. This is when the Latino community celebrates the victory of the Mexicans over the French at Puebla in 1862; mariachi bands, dancers, food, and a parade fill the streets of the Mission. The festival usually takes place at Mission Dolores Park on Dolores Street at 18th Street, while the parade typically starts at 10am at 24th and Bryant streets and ends at the Civic Center. Both venues are subject to change, so log on to **www.sfcincodemayo.com** to confirm the schedule or contact the Mission Neighborhood Center for more information at © **415/206-0577.** First Sunday in May.

Bay to Breakers Foot Race, the Embarcadero through Golden Gate Park to Ocean Beach FREE. Even if you don't participate, you can't avoid this run from downtown to Ocean Beach, which stops morning traffic throughout the city. More than 75,000 entrants gather—many dressed in wacky, innovative, and sometimes X-rated costumes—for the approximately 7.5-mile run. Although you're expected to pay an entrance fee to participate, there are plenty of folks who don't bother. Of course, you get a T-shirt and a photo of yourself crossing the finish line if you do register. If you don't want to run, join the throng of spectators who line the route. Sidewalk parties, bands, and cheerleaders of all ages provide a good dose of true San Francisco fun. For recorded information, call © **415/359-2800,** or check their website, www.baytobreakers.com. Third Sunday of May.

Carnaval Festival, Harrison Street between 16th and 23rd streets FREE. The Mission District's largest annual event, held from 9:30am to 6pm, is a day of festivities that includes food, music, dance, arts and crafts, and a parade that's as sultry and energetic as the Latin American and Caribbean people behind it. For one of San Franciscans' favorite events, more than half a million spectators line the parade route, and samba musicians and dancers continue to entertain on 14th Street, near Harrison, at the end of the march, where you'll find food and craft booths, music, and more revelry. Call the hot line at ✆ **415/920-0125** for information. Celebrations are held Saturday and Sunday of Memorial Day weekend, but the parade is on Sunday morning only. See **www.carnavalsf.com** for more information.

KFOG KaBoom, China Basin FREE. This is probably the best fireworks show you will ever see. Held in May when the fog is at bay (smart), it's both an annual all-day outdoor concert held by San Francisco's KFOG radio station (tickets required), and a free nighttime fireworks show that's synchronized to a KFOG soundtrack (cool) and watched by more than 350,000 people. Log onto **www.kfog.com/Kaboom** for information. Mid-May.

June

Union Street Art Festival, Pacific Heights, along Union Street from Steiner to Gough streets FREE. This outdoor fair celebrates San Francisco with themes, gourmet food booths, music, entertainment, and a juried art show featuring works by more than 250 artists. It's a great time and a chance to see the city's young well-to-dos partying it up. Call the **Union Street Association** (✆ **415/441-7055**) for more information or see www.unionstreetfestival.com. First weekend of June.

Haight-Ashbury Street Fair, Haight-Ashbury FREE. A far cry from the froufrou Union Street Fair, this grittier fair features alternative crafts, ethnic foods, rock bands, and a healthy number of hippies and street kids whooping it up and slamming beers in front of the blaring rock-'n'-roll stage. The fair usually extends along Haight between Stanyan and Ashbury streets. For details and the exact date, call ✆ **415/863-3489** or visit www.haightstreetfair.org.

North Beach Festival, Grant Avenue, North Beach FREE. In 2006, this party celebrated its 52nd anniversary; organizers claim it's the oldest urban street fair in the country. Close to 100,000 city folk meander along Grant Avenue, between Vallejo and Union streets, to eat, drink, and browse the arts-and-crafts booths, poetry readings, swing-dancing venue, and *arte di gesso* (sidewalk chalk art). But the most enjoyable parts of the event are listening to music and people-watching. Call ✆ **415/989-2220** or visit www.northbeachfestival.com for details. Usually Father's Day weekend, but call to confirm.

Stern Grove Music Festival, Sunset District FREE. Pack a picnic and head out early to join the thousands who come here to lie in the grass and enjoy classical, jazz, and ethnic music and dance in the grove, at 19th Avenue and Sloat Boulevard. The free concerts take place every Sunday at 2pm between mid-June and August. Show up with a lawn chair or blanket, but savvy locals know to show up early to claim the best spots on the lawn. The lineup usually includes the San Francisco Symphony, San Francisco Ballet, jazz artists, and students from the San Francisco Opera's Merola Program. There are food booths if you forget snacks, but you'll be dying to leave if you don't bring warm clothes—the Sunset District can be one of the coldest parts of the city. Call ✆ **415/252-6252** for listings; www.sterngrove.org. Sundays, mid-June through August.

San Francisco Lesbian, Gay, Bisexual, Transgender Pride Parade & Celebration, downtown's Market Street FREE. This prideful event draws up to one million participants who celebrate all of the above—and then some. The parade proceeds west on Market Street until it gets to the Civic Center, where hundreds of food, art, and information booths are set up around several soundstages. Call ✆ **415/864-3733** or visit www.sfpride.org for information. Usually the third or last weekend of June.

July

Fillmore Jazz Festival, Pacific Heights FREE. Say hello to the largest FREE jazz festival on the West Coast. July starts with a bang, when the upscale portion of Fillmore closes to traffic and the blocks between Jackson and Eddy are filled with arts and crafts, gourmet food, and live jazz from 10am to 6pm. Call ✆ **510/970-3217** for more information; www.fillmorejazzfestival.com. First weekend in July.

Fourth of July Celebration & Fireworks, Fisherman's Wharf FREE. This event can be something of a joke—more often than not, fog comes into the city, like everyone else, to join in the festivities. Sometimes it's almost impossible to view the million-dollar pyrotechnics from PIER 39 on the northern waterfront. Still, it's a party, and if the skies are clear, it's a darn good show. Visit **www.pier39.com/Events/events.htm** for more info.

North Beach Jazz Festival, North Beach. This popular North Beach jazz fest has ballooned to a 7-day lineup. It has purposely maintained a distinctly grassroots, homegrown feel by consistently featuring local talent, and incorporating the neighborhood's unique jazz culture into the festivities. Log onto **www.sunsettickets.com/images/nbjazz** for more information. Third week in July.

San Francisco Marathon, San Francisco and beyond. This is one of the largest marathons in the world. It starts and ends at the Ferry Building at the base of Market Street, winds 26-plus miles through virtually every neighborhood in the City, and crosses the Golden Gate Bridge. For entry information, visit **www.runsfm.com.** Usually the last weekend in July.

August

Nihonmachi Street Fair, Japantown. This celebration of the Bay Area's diverse Asian and Pacific American communities occurs on 1 Saturday and Sunday each August in Japantown, on Post Street between Laguna and Fillmore streets. Asian-American artisans show their creations, and the "Food Fest" features the cooking of Asia and the Pacific Islands. A children's area includes games and the opportunity to learn traditional arts and crafts. Call ✆ **415/771-9861** or visit www.nihonmachistreetfair.org. Second week of August.

September

Ghirardelli Square Chocolate Festival, Fisherman's Wharf FREE. This annual benefit is for Open Hand, a worthy local charity that delivers food to homebound AIDS patients. Chocoholics wander from one tasting to another, provided by local shops and restaurants. Serious eaters can enter the sundae-eating contest. The prize is the winner's weight in chocolate! Call ✆ **415/775-5500** or visit www.ghirardellisq.com. Second week of September.

FREE Forsooth! 'Tis the Bard in the Park!

On every weekend from late August to September, the San Francisco Shakespeare Festival presents Shakespeare in the Park, a series of free performances of popular plays such as *The Tempest, Twelfth Night,* and *Much Ado About Nothing.* Bring your blankets, flasks, and picnic baskets and show up at the Presidio's Main Post Parade Ground Lawn at 7:30pm on Saturdays and 2:30pm on Sundays. For more info call ✆ 415/558-0888 or log onto www.sfshakes.org.

San Francisco Comedy Day Celebration, Golden Gate Park FREE. Some of the best comics in the U.S. come together in Golden Gate Park's Sharon Meadow for a Sunday afternoon full of laughter. At least 30 comedians participate in this free event. Visit **www.comedyday.com.** Late September.

Sausalito Art Festival, Sausalito FREE. A juried exhibit of more than 20,000 original works of art, this festival includes music—provided by jazz, rock, and blues performers from the Bay Area and beyond—and international cuisine, enhanced by wines from some 50 Napa and Sonoma producers. Parking is impossible; take the **Blue & Gold Fleet ferry** (✆ **415/705-5555**) from Fisherman's Wharf to the festival site. For more information, call ✆ **415/332-3555** or log onto www.sausalitoartfestival.org. Labor Day weekend.

Opera in the Park, usually in Sharon Meadow, Golden Gate Park FREE. Each year the San Francisco Opera launches its season with a free concert featuring a selection of arias. Call ✆ **415/861-4008** to confirm the location and date. Usually the Sunday after Labor Day.

Sandcastle Classic, Ocean Beach FREE. This annual fundraiser for Leap, an artists-in-residence program, turns Ocean Beach into a fantastical canvas for sand castles, pyramids, wild animals, and flights of fancy. Admission is free, but donations are appreciated. Call ✆ **415/512-1899** or visit www.leap4kids.org. It usually takes place at the end of the month, but sometimes occurs in October.

San Francisco Blues Festival, on the grounds of Fort Mason, the Marina. The largest outdoor blues music event on the West Coast will be 35 years old in 2007 and continues to feature local and national musicians performing back-to-back during the 3-day extravaganza. You can charge tickets by phone at ✆ **415/421-8497** or online at www.ticketmaster.com. For information, call ✆ **415/979-5588** or visit www.sfblues.com. Usually in late September.

FREE Opera in the Park

Since 1971, San Francisco Opera has presented Opera in the Park, an annual free concert in Golden Gate Park held on the Sunday following opening night of the opera's fall season (typically the second week of Sept). The hugely popular event traditionally features artists from the opening weekend, performing in full dress with the San Francisco Opera Orchestra. Although it draws some 20,000 listeners, it never fills up, but you'll want to arrive early for a good seat. Be sure to bring a blanket, a picnic basket, and a jacket in case the fog rolls in.

Folsom Street Fair, along Folsom Street between 7th and 12th streets, SoMa, from 11am to 6pm FREE. This is a local favorite for its kinky, outrageous, leather-and-skin gay-centric blowout celebration. It's hardcore, so only open-minded and adventurous types need head into the leather-clad and partially dressed crowds. For info call ✆ **415/861-3247** or visit www.folsomstreetfair.org. Last Sunday of September.

October

Fleet Week, Marina and Fisherman's Wharf FREE. Residents gather along the Marina Green, the Embarcadero, Fisherman's Wharf, and other vantage points to watch incredible (and loud!) aerial performances by the Blue Angels, flown in tribute to our nation's marines. Call ✆ **650/599-5057** or visit www.fleetweek.us/fleetweek for details and dates.

Artspan Open Studios, various San Francisco locations FREE. Find an original piece of art to commemorate your trip, or just see what local artists are up to by grabbing a map to more than 800 artists' studios that are open to the public during weekends in October. Call ✆ **415/861-9838** or visit www.artspan.org for more information.

Castro Street Fair, the Castro FREE. Celebrate life in the city's most famous gay neighborhood. Call ✆ **415/841-1824** or visit www.castrostreetfair.org for information. First Sunday in October, from 11am to 6pm.

Italian Heritage Parade, North Beach and Fisherman's Wharf FREE. The city's Italian community leads the festivities around Fisherman's Wharf, celebrating Columbus's landing in America. The year 2008 marked the festival's 140th, and as usual included a parade along Columbus Avenue. But for the most part, it's a great excuse to hang out in North Beach and people-watch. For information, call ✆ **415/587-8282** or visit www.sfcolumbusday.org. Observed the Sunday before Columbus Day.

San Francisco Jazz Festival, various San Francisco locations. This festival presents eclectic programming in an array of fabulous jazz venues throughout the city. With close to 3 weeks of nightly entertainment and dozens of performers, the jazz festival is a hot ticket. Past events have featured Herbie Hancock, Dave Brubeck, the Modern Jazz Quartet, Wayne Shorter, and Bill Frisell. For information, call ✆ **800/850-SFJF** (850-7353) or 415/788-7353, or visit www.sfjazz.org. Also check the website for other events throughout the year. Late October and early November.

FREE Ushering your way to free shows

If you can't figure out a way to sneak into a performance for free (the practice aka "second acting"), there's an alternative that will let you see the whole play for free: Volunteer as an usher. I did this often during my college days and I never had a bad night (the Steve Miller concert was fantastic). It's often the best way to see a show at a major theater when the tickets head upward of the $50 mark. First you find out what shows you want to see, then call the venue or check their website at least 10 days in advance. The volunteer ushering programs differ from venue to venue but here's the gist of it:

You give them your name, phone number, age (usually 18 and over only), and what night/shifts you want to work. If they call you back and you agree to work a shift, you need to show up on time wearing black pants and a white shirt, and appear reasonably kempt. You'll seat people before the show, and depending on the venue, and guide latecomers to their seats. Some venues ask for help cleaning up after. Here are a few major venues that offer ushering opportunities (you can always call other venues and see if they're doing the same):

- **American Conservatory Theater** (ACT) volunteer hotline: ✆ 415/439-2349
- **Cal Performances:** http://cpinfo.berkeley.edu/information/job/volunteer.php
- **Herbst Theater:** http://sfwmpac.org/herbst/ht_popups/volunteerinfo.html
- **Marines Memorial Theatre:** ✆ 415/441-7444; www.marinesmemorialtheatre.com
- **San Francisco Symphony:** ✆ 415/864-6000; www.sfsymphony.org
- **Yerba Buena Center for the Arts:** ✆ 415/978-2787; www.ybca.org

November

The **Embarcadero Center Lighting Ceremony and Celebration,** Justin Herman Plaza **FREE**. You can get into the Christmas spirit for the Embarcadero building lighting (the four towers gleam during the holiday season). There are also performances taking place on the seasonal ice-skating rink, which is open for public skating until after the New Year. Skates can be rented at the ticket booth. Friday before Thanksgiving.

December

Christmas at Sea, Fisherman's Wharf **FREE**. Bring the little ones for a special day of singing, cider, and stories onboard the historic ships docked at the Hyde Street Pier. Call ✆ **415/561-6662** or visit www.maritime.org. Mid-December.

The Nutcracker, War Memorial Opera House, Civic Center. The **San Francisco Ballet** (✆ **415/865-2000**) performs this Tchaikovsky classic annually. Order tickets to this holiday tradition well in advance. Visit www.sfballet.org.

FREE Power to the Pedalers

On the last Friday of every month at 5:30pm, a huge group of gonzo bicyclists takes over the city streets for a hugely popular event called **Critical Mass.** The point of it all is to celebrate cycling and to assert cyclists' right to the road, but it's mainly a really fun and free thing to do on a Friday evening. Also entertaining are the frustrated looks of all the bike-hating drivers who get caught unaware and have to wait out the loooong procession. The launchpad is at Justin Herman Plaza between Embarcadero BART and the Ferry Building. All you need to do to participate is show up with a bike and start pedaling.

1 Cheap Opera (Chopera?)

Pocket Opera Impresario Donald Pippin has been bringing his own, true-to-the-intentions-of-the-composer versions of opera to appreciative audiences for over 3 decades. The majority is sung in

SAN FRANCISCO AFTER DARK

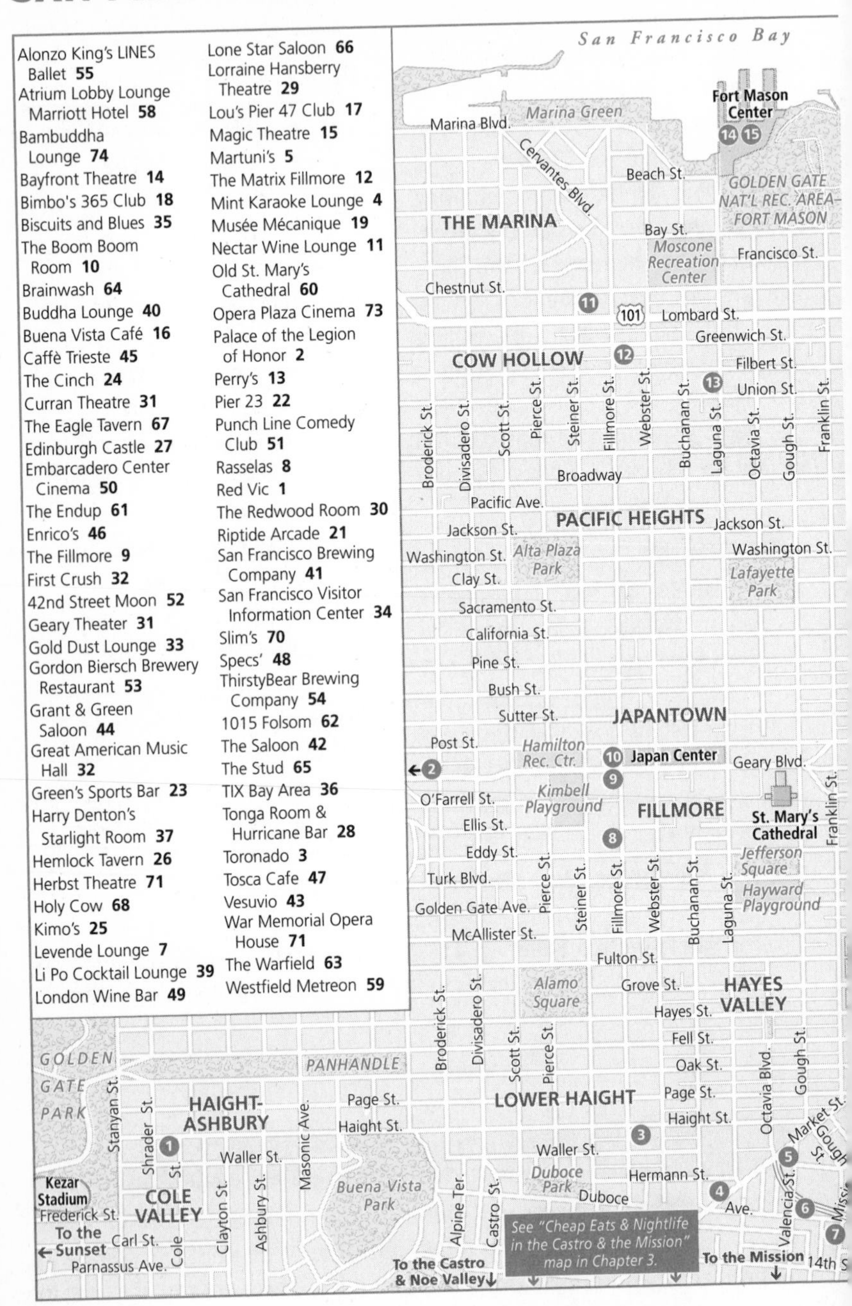

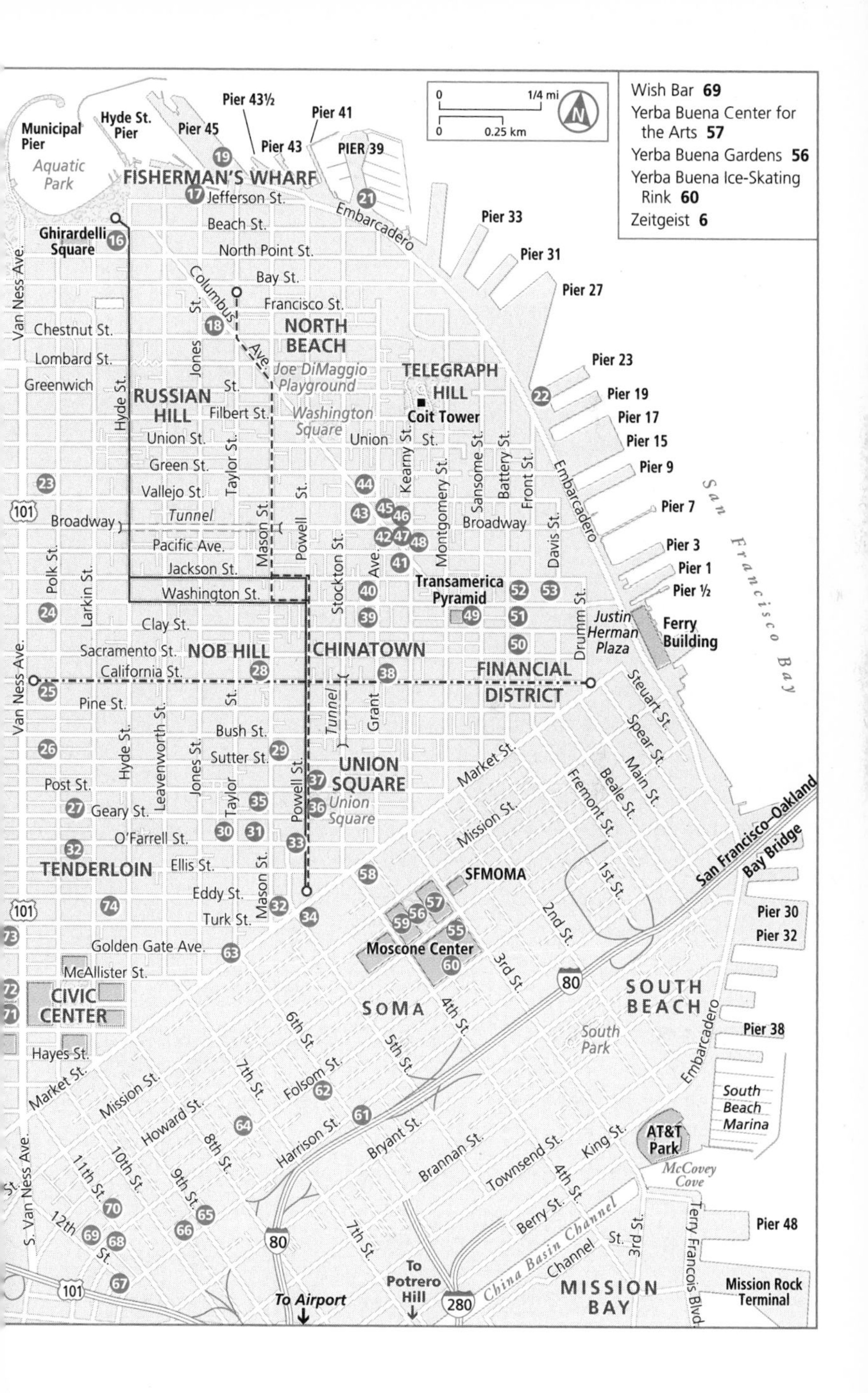

Wish Bar 69
Yerba Buena Center for the Arts 57
Yerba Buena Gardens 56
Yerba Buena Ice-Skating Rink 60
Zeitgeist 6
0 1/4 mi
0 0.25 km
N
Municipal Pier
Hyde St. Pier
Pier 45
Pier 43½
Pier 43
Pier 41
PIER 39
Aquatic Park
FISHERMAN'S WHARF
Jefferson St.
Beach St.
North Point St.
Bay St.
Francisco St.
Embarcadero
Pier 33
Pier 31
Pier 27
Pier 23
Pier 19
Pier 17
Pier 15
Pier 9
Pier 7
Pier 3
Pier 1
Pier ½
Ghirardelli Square
Van Ness Ave.
Chestnut St.
Lombard St.
Greenwich St.
Columbus Ave.
NORTH BEACH
Joe DiMaggio Playground
Washington Square
TELEGRAPH HILL
Coit Tower
RUSSIAN HILL
Filbert St.
Union St.
Green St.
Vallejo St.
Broadway
Tunnel
Pacific Ave.
Jackson St.
Washington St.
Clay St.
Sacramento St.
California St.
Pine St.
Bush St.
Sutter St.
Post St.
Geary St.
O'Farrell St.
Ellis St.
Eddy St.
Turk St.
Golden Gate Ave.
McAllister St.
Hayes St.
Hyde St.
Jones St.
Taylor St.
Mason St.
Powell St.
Stockton St.
Grant Ave.
Kearny St.
Montgomery St.
Sansome St.
Battery St.
Front St.
Davis St.
Drumm St.
Polk St.
Larkin St.
Leavenworth St.
Transamerica Pyramid
Justin Herman Plaza
Ferry Building
San Francisco Bay
NOB HILL
CHINATOWN
FINANCIAL DISTRICT
UNION SQUARE
Union Square
TENDERLOIN
CIVIC CENTER
Steuart St.
Spear St.
Main St.
Beale St.
Fremont St.
1st St.
2nd St.
3rd St.
4th St.
5th St.
6th St.
7th St.
8th St.
9th St.
10th St.
11th St.
12th St.
Market St.
Mission St.
Howard St.
Folsom St.
Harrison St.
Bryant St.
Brannan St.
Townsend St.
King St.
Berry St.
Channel St.
SFMOMA
Moscone Center
SOMA
San Francisco–Oakland Bay Bridge
Pier 30
Pier 32
SOUTH BEACH
South Park
Pier 38
South Beach Marina
AT&T Park
McCovey Cove
Pier 48
Terry Francois Blvd.
China Basin Channel
MISSION BAY
Mission Rock Terminal
S. Van Ness Ave.
To Airport
To Potrero Hill
101
80
280
16 17 18 19 21 22 23 24 25 26 27 28 29 30 31 32 33 34 35 36 37 38 39 40 41 42 43 44 45 46 47 48 49 50 51 52 53 55 56 57 58 59 60 61 62 63 64 65 66 67 68 69 70 71 72 73 74

Go Nuts for Doughnuts (& Classical Music!)

If you're a morning person of meager funds with a love for doughnuts and classical music, boy howdy are *you* in for a treat. The open rehearsals have a seat with your name on it. Before most concerts, the San Francisco Symphony allows the public to attend open rehearsals at Davies Symphony Hall for the bargain price of $20, *including* FREE DOUGHNUTS!!! In fact, many aficionados prefer these rehearsals because the music is equally exquisite and you get to see and hear the performers and conductors in a relaxed, intimate circumstance. Most open rehearsals take place Wednesday mornings, 9am to noon (they break the doughnuts out at 8:30am). Tickets sell out quickly for popular international performers, so call the Symphony box office (✆ **415/864-6000**) and order them in advance if possible. ***Note:*** The symphony season starts in September, takes a break for a few months, and then picks up again in June and July.

English by professional opera singers accompanied by the Pocket Philharmonic with minimal costumes and virtually no sets, but Pippin gets the point across and makes opera alive and understandable to everyone. He's done more to nurture new audiences for opera than anyone else around. Productions in San Francisco are held Fridays to Sundays at the Florence Gould Theater, Palace of the Legion of Honor. There are $20 student rush tickets sold 30 minutes before the show, and regular admission is $34 in advance, $37 at the door (with discounts for students and seniors). ✆ **415/972-8934** (box office). www.pocketopera.org.

San Francisco Opera Yes, the opera, because if you don't mind standing for a few hours you can buy standing-section tickets for only ten bucks. Yes, $10. The San Francisco Opera was the second municipal opera in the United States and is one of the city's cultural icons. Brilliantly balanced casts may feature celebrated stars like Frederica Von Stade and Plácido Domingo along with promising newcomers and regular members in productions that range from traditional to avant-garde. All productions have English supertitles. The season starts in September, lasts 14 weeks, takes a break for a few months, and then picks up again in June and July. During the interim winter period, future opera stars are featured in showcases and recitals. Performances are held most evenings, except Monday, with matinees on Sunday. Tickets start at $24 and go on sale in August. Unless Domingo is in town, some less coveted seats are usually available until curtain time. War Memorial Opera House, 301 Van Ness Ave. (at Grove St.). ✆ **415/864-3330** (box office). www.sfopera.com.

FREE Concerts in the Park

Hard to believe, but for more than 125 years the Golden Gate Park Band—one of America's oldest professional concert bands—has presented free concerts every Sunday from April to October in Golden Gate Park (duh) at 1pm. The concerts last about 2 hours and range from opera, marches, and Broadway show tunes to orchestral transcriptions, novelty tunes, folk music, and big-band swing. The concerts take place at the Spreckles Temple of Music in the park's Music Concourse.

2 Theater

Note: Be sure to check with **TIX Bay Area** (✆ **415/433-7827;** www.tixbayarea.org) to see if they offer half-price tickets to a local show.

American Conservatory Theater (A.C.T.) The Tony Award–winning American Conservatory Theater made its debut in 1967 and established itself as the city's premier resident theater group and one of the nation's best. The A.C.T. season runs September through July and features both classic and experimental works.

FREE Free Night of Theater

For 3 weeks in October of 2008, TIX Bay Area gave away free theater tickets to more than 100 shows throughout the Bay Area to help promote the nationwide Free Night of Theater event. Log onto www.tixbayarea.org or www.freenightoftheater.net to see if you can score some free tickets. It's an annual event . . . look for it each autumn!

★ Half-Price Theater Tickets

You have a friend in the theater business: TIX Bay Area. TIX sells half-price tickets on the day of performance to select Bay Area cultural and sporting events. Half-price tickets are primarily sold at their Union Square kiosk, while some are available only online (and some are available both places). To find out which shows have half-price tickets, call the TIX info line or check out their website, then either purchase the tickets online or go to their kiosk at the southwest corner of Union Square on Powell Street between Geary and Post streets (you can't miss it). A service charge, ranging from $1.75 to $6, is levied on each ticket depending on its full price. You can pay with cash, traveler's checks, Visa, MasterCard, American Express, or Discover Card with photo ID. TIX is open Tuesday through Thursday from 11am to 6pm, Friday from 11am to 7pm, Saturday from 10am to 7pm, and Sunday from 10am to 3pm. ***Note:*** Half-price tickets go on sale at 11am every day except Mondays (when the office is closed). For more information call ✆ **415/ 433-7827** or log onto www.tixbayarea.org.

Its home is the fabulous **Geary Theater,** a national historic landmark that is regarded as one of America's finest performance spaces. Performing at the Geary Theater, 415 Geary St. (at Mason St.). ✆ **415/ 749-2ACT** (749-2228). www.act-sf.org.

Curran Theatre The Curran opened in 1922 with the goal of hosting American and European productions in San Francisco. Its "Best of Broadway" series has featured hits like *Les Misérables,* and 2009 will see *August: Osage County* and the pre-Broadway tryout of the musical *Ever After.* Its partner theaters, the Orpheum and Golden Gate, also hold big-name shows such as *Wicked* and *The Lion King*. Shows run anywhere from 2 to 6 weeks. 445 Geary St. (btw Mason and Taylor sts.). ✆ **415/551-2000.** www.shnsf.com.

Fort Mason Center At first glance, this complex, a former military base between Aquatic Park and the Marina Green, looks like a large group of abandoned warehouse buildings. In fact, on any given day the activity level inside is impressive. Besides its museums, galleries, and nonprofit organizations, Fort Mason supports the **Cowell Theater,** the **Herbst Pavilion,** the **Magic Theater,** and the **Bayfront Theater**. The 437-seat Cowell Theater is the site of performances by local artistic companies such as the Smuin Ballet/SF and the New Pickle Circus. The Magic Theater produces new works by playwrights such as Sam Shepard, and the Bayfront Theater is the site of Bay Area Theatresports, an improvisational group. You can find out what's happening at Fort Mason on its website, or by calling the information line at © **415/345-7544.** Tickets may be purchased through its box office. Marina Blvd., at Buchanan St. © **415/345-7575** (box office). www.fortmason.org.

FREE Yerba Buena Gardens Festival

Between May and October the Yerba Buena Gardens Festival presents nearly 100 programs—music, theater, dance, cultural events, children's programs—in the SoMa District's Yerba Buena Gardens, and every one of them is free and open to the public. Annual highlights include the world-renowned San Francisco Mime Troupe, and the San Francisco Theater Festival, featuring 100 theater companies and solo artists on 14 stages. For more info log onto **www.ybgf.org.**

42nd Street Moon If you're fond of "lost" musicals and early-20th-century songwriters—Rogers and Hart, Cole Porter, the Gershwins, Oscar Hammerstein II—the staged concert versions of shows from the 1920s on up will entertain you. 42nd Street Moon productions have no sets, minimal staging, and few costume changes, but the music shines brightly. Most shows take place at the Eureka Theater. 215 Jackson St. © **415/255-8207.** www.42ndstmoon.org.

Lamplighters Music Theatre Since 1952, the Lamplighters have brought the works of Gilbert and Sullivan and other comic operas to stages around the Bay Area. The shows are great fun, and an excellent way to introduce light opera to the plebes. The season encompasses three productions scattered throughout the year, staged at the theater at Yerba Buena Gardens or Herbst Theatre. Tickets are sold through Yerba Buena Center for the Arts; © **415/978-2787.** Herbst Theatre tickets are sold through City Box Office; © **415/392-4400.** www.lamplighters.org.

Enjoying the Indie SF Theater Scene

Melissa Hillman, artistic director of Impact Theater, did a quick Q&A with us on the Bay Area independent theater scene, recommended companies, and where to find out more info.

Q: Is the theater scene in SF centered anywhere in particular?

A: The Bay Area is very spread out geographically and you can find plenty of theatre in all 9 counties, but it tends to be concentrated in the cities of San Francisco, Berkeley, and San Jose.

Q: Is there a website where people can find out what is going on specifically in the indie theater scene?

A: Absolutely! Theatre Bay Area! Head for **www.theatrebayarea.org** and click on "What's Playing."

Q: What are the best/most interesting/most unusual companies (yours, of course, included)?

A: There are 400 theatre and dance companies in the SF Bay Area, and they range from Tony Award-winning LORT house Berkeley Rep to the tiniest experimental theatres. Here are a few highlights:

- **Theatre Rhinoceros:** www.therhino.org. Helmed by John Fisher, who grew up in the Bay Area, Theatre Rhino is the oldest continuously running GLBT theatre company in the US. Theatre Rhino is located in San Francisco's Mission district.
- **Impact Theatre:** www.impacttheatre.com. Impact Theatre focuses on new plays by emerging playwrights, with an annual classic play staged in a fast-paced, action-packed manner. Impact Theatre is located in the basement of La Val's Pizza, just north of the UC Berkeley campus. Patrons are encouraged to bring their pizza and beer down into the theatre.
- **Shotgun Players:** www.shotgunplayers.org. Shotgun works overtime at bringing imaginative, relevant stagings to classics and new works alike. Shotgun Players can be found at The Ashby Stage, located directly across the street from the Ashby BART station.
- **Golden Thread Productions:** www.goldenthread.org. Golden Thread is one of the only companies in the nation that focuses

exclusively on theatre that explores Middle Eastern cultures and identities as represented throughout the globe. Golden Thread performs in a variety of locations in and around the city of San Francisco.

- **Active Arts Theatre for Young Audiences:** www.activearts theatre.org. Active Arts is fun, high-quality children's theatre at affordable prices. They perform in the historic Julia Morgan Theatre in Berkeley and at the Bay Area Discovery Museum in Sausalito. Often their productions are based on award-winning children's books.
- **Traveling Jewish Theatre:** www.atjt.com. Traveling Jewish Theatre presents theatre that shares the Jewish vision of *tikkun olam*, repair or healing of the world. They do both new plays and Jewish classics. Their plays range from hard-hitting political dramas to fun-filled, crazy satires. TJT performs in venues in San Francisco.
- **Teatro Vision:** www.teatrovision.org. Teatro Vision is the Bay Area's leading Chicano theatre. They perform plays in English and in Spanish with English supertitles. Teatro Vision does a wide range of plays about the Chicano experience, ranging from the tragic to the wildly comic. Teatro Vision performs in San Jose.
- **City Lights Theatre Company of San Jose:** www.cltc.org. City Lights does a wide variety of new and classic plays in their intimate, 108-seat venue in downtown San Jose. They do six shows a year, ranging from lighthearted musicals to thought-provoking dramas. City Lights also does a New Play Reading Series and a Jazz Showcase.
- **African-American Shakespeare Company:** www.african-american shakes.org. African-American Shakespeare Company produces multicultural stagings of classic plays. Of particular note is their annual holiday show, Cinderella, which is designed for all ages to enjoy. True to their name, they also stage contemporary, relevant productions of Shakespeare. Af-Am Shakes performs in San Francisco.

- **Woman's Will:** www.womanswill.org. Woman's Will produces all-female stagings of classic plays. They do free plays in local parks throughout the Bay Area during the summer, and shows in more traditional venues throughout the year. In addition to Shakespeare, they have also done works by Brecht, Mac Wellman, and other prominent playwrights. Woman's Will performs in Oakland and throughout the Bay Area.
- **Dandelion Dancetheater:** www.dandeliondancetheater.org. Dandelion Dancetheater produces work that lives at the crossroads of dance and theatre. Their work includes dancers, actors, singers and musicians of varied sizes, shapes, and physical abilities, sometimes including performers in wheelchairs. Their highly innovative, engaging work has received enthusiastic national attention, including a Princess Grace Award for founder and choreographer Eric Kupers. They primarily perform in San Francisco, but have performed all over the Bay Area and often tour other areas as well.

Q: About what do ticket prices run for companies like this?

A: Alternative theatre pricing ranges from mid-level ($20s and $30s) to very inexpensive ($10 to $15).

Q: Do these theaters let people volunteer usher or have I Pay What I Can nights?

A: Many do; visit individual websites for more information.

Lorraine Hansberry Theatre San Francisco's top African-American theater group performs in a 300-seat state-of-the-art theater. It mounts special adaptations from literature along with contemporary dramas, classics, and music. Phone for dates and programs. Performing at 620 Sutter St. (at Mason St.). ✆ **415/345-3980.** www.lhtsf.org.

★ **The Magic Theatre** The highly acclaimed Magic Theatre is a major West Coast company dedicated to presenting the works of new plays; over the years it has nurtured the talents of such luminaries as Sam Shepard and David Mamet. Shepard's Pulitzer Prize–winning play *Buried Child* had its premiere here, as did Mamet's *Dr. Faustus*. The season usually runs from October to June; performances are held Tuesday through Sunday. Performing at Bldg. D, Fort Mason Center, Marina

Boulevard (at Buchanan St.). ✆ **415/441-8822.** www.magictheatre.org.

The Marsh Dubbing itself as "a breeding ground for new performance," this venerable Valencia Street performance house consists of a complex of theaters hosting definitely-off-Broadway works by a wide range of artists and performers. With most tickets starting at $15 it could be a bargain if the show's a winner. 1062 Valencia St. ✆ **800/838-3006** or 415/826-5750. www.themarsh.org.

It's Magic! Cheap Theater

The Magic Theatre sets aside a limited number of tickets for "Sliding Scale Wednesdays." Sliding scale tickets are available only at the door, starting at 7pm. Prices range from $5 to $25 and reservations aren't accepted; so it's a good idea to call the box office ahead of time to determine availability.

3 Dance

Alonzo King's LINES Ballet Founded by ballet master Alonzo King, LINES blends classical and contemporary ballet accompanied by music from the world's greatest living composers. This is a touring ballet company based in San Francisco that performs at the Yerba Buena Center for the Arts. Student tickets at some performances are available for as little as $15 and full-price tickets begin at $25. 700 Howard St. (btw 3rd and 4th sts.). ✆ **415/978-2787.** www.linesballet.org.

San Francisco Ballet One of the country's finest ballet companies, the San Francisco Ballet officially begins its season in February and ends in May. **Dirt-Cheap Alert:** Tickets to the ballet

Friday Night Ballroom Dancing

Relive your closet Ginger Rogers fantasies with a Friday night at Cheryl Burke Dance, where for as little as $14 you can learn the proper footwork for ballroom, salsa, tango, fox trot, rumba, cha-cha, and so on. Lessons start at 7pm, and the dance parties start at 8pm and last until midnight. I've been to a few of these back when it was called the Metronome Ballroom, and my date and I had a blast. Check out their website at **www.cherylburkedance.com** to see what's on the dance ticket.

can be purchased for as little as $10 for the standing room section and can be purchased at the box office, but only on performance days. War Memorial Opera House, 301 Van Ness Ave. (at Grove St.). © **415/865-2000.** www.sfballet.org.

Cheap Classical at Lunch

If you're in the city at lunchtime on a Tuesday with nothing better to do, head to the Old St. Mary's Cathedral at 660 California St. at Grant Street for a dose of highbrow culture. At 12:30pm sharp a company called Noontime Concerts (© **415/777-3211;** www.noontimeconcerts.org) hosts classical chamber music concerts, with a mission to "enrich the cultural life of San Francisco during the lunch hour with easily accessible, affordable, live classical music concerts performed by professional Bay Area and international touring artists." A donation of $5 is all they ask for in return, and it's even tax-deductible.

Smuin Ballet/SF Smuin Ballet performances draw less on classical movements and more on theatricality, using music by composers like Elton John and the Beatles that give the pieces a modern spin. Smuin Ballet appears at the Yerba Buena Center for the Arts. Tickets may be purchased through either the Yerba Buena box office or **http://tickets.com.** Ask about half-price "rush" tickets and "two-fer" offers. 700 Howard St. (btw 3rd and 4th sts.). © **415/978-2787.** www.smuinballet.org.

4 Comedy Clubs

BATS Improv Combining improvisation with competition, BATS (Bay Area Theatre Sports) performs hilarious improvisational tournaments in which teams of actors compete against each other in scenes, songs, and games, based on suggestions from the audience. When they're on you'll actually hurt from laughing so hard. There are also long-form shows throughout the year with improvisations of movies, musicals, and even Shakespeare; audience members supply suggestions for titles and plot points, and characters and dialogue are then made up and performed immediately onstage. Reservations and discount tickets available through their website; remaining tickets are sold at the box office the night of the show. Tickets range from $5–$15. Performing at Bayfront Theatre at the Fort Mason Center, Bldg. B no. 350, 3rd floor. ✆ **415/474-8935.** www.improv.org.

Punch Line Comedy Club Adjacent to the Embarcadero One office building, this is the largest comedy nightclub in the city. Three-person shows with top national and local talent are featured here Tuesday through Saturday. Sundays and Monday are the cheap nights: Showcase night is Sunday, when 15 comics take the mic, and there's an all-star showcase or a special event on Monday (beware of the two-drink minimum, however). 444 Battery St. (btw Washington and Clay sts.), plaza level. ✆ **415/397-4337** or 415/397-7573 for recorded information. www.punchlinecomedyclub.com.

FREE Stern Grove Music Festival

Pack a picnic and head out early to join the thousands who come to the foggy Sunset District to attend the always-free Stern Grove Music Festival and listen to top-quality classical, jazz, and ethnic music groups. The concerts take place at 19th Avenue and Sloat Boulevard every Sunday at 2pm between mid-June and August. Show up with a lawn chair or blanket and a cooler (there are food booths if you forget snacks), but you'll be dying to leave if you don't bring warm clothes—the Sunset District can be one of the coldest parts of the city in the summer. Call ✆ **415/252-6252** or log onto www.sterngrove.org for more information.

5 Retro & Indie Movie Theatres

★ **Castro Theatre** Built in 1922 by renowned Bay Area architect Timothy Pflueger, and listed as a City of San Francisco registered landmark, the beautiful Castro Theatre is known for its screenings of classics and for its FABulous Wurlitzer organ, which is usually played before each evening show. There's a different feature almost nightly, and more often than not it's a double feature. Bargain matinees are usually offered on Wednesday, Saturday, Sunday, and holidays. They also play host to a number of festivals throughout the year. Phone or visit their website for schedules, prices, and show times. 429 Castro St. (near Market St.). ✆ **415/621-6120.** www.castrotheatre.com.

Embarcadero Center Cinema This is a great spot for stellar foreign language films like Pedro Almadvar's *Volver,* first-rate indie films, and award-winning documentaries. 1 Embarcadero Center (at Battery and Sacramento sts.). ✆ **415/267-4893.** www.landmarktheatres.com.

Opera Plaza Cinema Belonging to the same theater group as the Embarcadero Center, this small cineplex offers an alternative to Hollywood fare, with excellent foreign and independent films. You'll want to take a cab here in the evenings, but at least it's close to Union Square. 601 Van Ness Ave. (btw Golden Gate and Turk sts.). ✆ **415/267-4893.** www.landmarktheatres.com.

Red Vic The worker-owned Red Vic movie collective originated in the neighboring Victorian building that gave it its name. The theater specializes in independent releases and premieres and contemporary cult hits, and situates its patrons among an array of couches. Prices are $8.50 but the matinees are just $6.50. Tickets go on sale 20 minutes before each show. Phone for schedules and showtimes or log onto their website. 1727 Haight St. (btw Cole and Shrader sts.). ✆ **415/668-3994.** www.redvicmoviehouse.com.

The Roxie Film Center Founded in 1909, the Roxie is the oldest continually running theater in San Francisco, and so when it almost went under in 2005, a private donor saved it with a huge donation and a great idea; the theater merged with the New College of California and is now a nonprofit film center serving both students and the general public. Management has promised that the programming will stay the same and that they will continue to screen the best new alternative films anywhere, as well as host filmmakers like Akira Kurosawa and Werner Herzog. The low-budget contemporary features are largely devoid of Hollywood candy coating; many are West Coast premieres. Tickets prices start at $5 for the weekend matinee. Log onto their

FREE Dolores Park Movie Night

Every second Thursday of the month you can watch free movies—*Fast Times at Ridgemont High, Jaws, The Muppet Movie,* and so forth—at Dolores Park, located at 20th and Dolores streets. Bring a blanket and even your dog if you'd like, as well as a little cash to buy the world's best tamales from the Tamale Lady (**www.doloresparkmovie.org**).

website for schedules and show times. 3117 16th St. (at Valencia St.). ✆ **415/863-1087.** www.roxie.com.

6 Concert Venues

★ **Bimbo's 365 Club** Originally located on Market Street when it opened in 1931, this North Beach destination is a fabulous spot to catch outstanding live rock and jazz (think Chris Isaak and the Brian Setzer Orchestra) and dance amid glamorous surroundings. Grab tickets in advance at the box office, which is open Monday through Friday, 10am to 4pm. 1025 Columbus Ave. (at Chestnut St.). ✆ **415/474-0365.** www.bimbos365club.com.

The Fillmore Anyone who was listening to rock 'n' roll in the 1960s undoubtedly knows of the Fillmore. The late Bill Graham made his reputation here as a concert producer and promoter, and iconic musicians from Janis Joplin to Frank Zappa to Jerry Garcia played the former dance hall. Today, the Fillmore continues to rock with acts such as Los Lobos, Tom Jones, and Wilco. Seating is limited, so either prepare to stand in a crowded room (and be grateful for California's no-smoking laws) or head up to the balcony, where you'll also need to stand to see the show, but which is usually not too crowded. ***Tip:*** Forget Ticketmaster's surcharge—buy your tix at the box office instead. 1805 Geary Blvd. (at Fillmore St.). ✆ **415/346-6000.** www.livenation.com.

FREE Fillmore Jazz Festival

Say hello to the largest FREE jazz festival on the West Coast. The first weekend in July starts with a bang in the Fillmore District, when the upscale portion of Fillmore Street closes to traffic and the blocks between Jackson and Eddy are filled with arts and crafts, gourmet food, and live jazz from 10am to 6pm. Call ✆ **510/970-3217** or log onto www.fillmorejazzfestival.com for more information.

Great American Music Hall If there's ever a music hall worth splurging on a ticket for, this is it. Built in 1907 as a restaurant/bordello, the Great American Music Hall is likely one of the most gorgeous rock venues you'll encounter. With ornately carved balconies, frescoed

FREE Show 'em Your Double Axel!

Every Wednesday from 7:30 to 9pm is free skate-rental night for anyone 18 or over at the Yerba Buena Ice Skating Rink. The rink's located at 750 Folsom St., between Third and Fourth streets (© **415/820-3532**; www.skatebowl.com).

ceilings, marble columns, and huge hanging light fixtures, you won't know whether to marvel at the structure or watch the acts, which have ranged from Duke Ellington and Sarah Vaughan to Arctic Monkeys, The Radiators, and She Wants Revenge. All shows are all ages (6 and up) so you can bring your family, too. You can buy a complete dinner before the show, but it's a lot cheaper to order bar snacks (such as nachos, black bean and cheese flautas, burgers, and sandwiches). You can buy tickets at Tickets.com, but it's a lot cheaper to buy tickets at the box office. 859 O'Farrell (btw Polk and Larkin sts.). © **415/885-0750.** www.musichallsf.com.

The Warfield The venerable Market Street venue has seen better days, but it provides plenty of elbow room for non-moshers. Bands who recently played at the Warfield include Cake, Queen of the Stone Age, and Alice in Chains. For those who are happier sitting down, the theater balcony has reserved seating. 982 Market St. (at 6th St.). © **415/775-7722.** www.livenation.com.

Yerba Buena Center for the Arts and Yerba Buena Gardens FREE It's a rare weekend that you can't find something going on at this amazing city cultural center. Better yet, events in the gardens are free. From May through October in the Esplanade, the Yerba Buena Gardens Festival features outdoor classical, jazz, blues, and gospel music; dance recitals; and lunchtime concerts. 701 Mission St. (at 3rd St.). © **415/978-2787** (box office). www.ybae.org.

7 Clubs

Note: The club and music scene is always changing, often outdating recommendations before the ink can dry on a page. Most of the venues below are promoted as different clubs on various nights of the week, each with its own look, sound, and style. Discount passes and club announcements are often available at clothing stores and other shops along upper Haight Street.

★ **Biscuits and Blues** One of the best downtown club deals in the city is B&B's Friday and Saturday "Happy Hour Jam Sessions" where, from 3:30 to 6:30pm, you can swill cheap drinks and listen to great blues bands for free. From 7pm on, they serve drink specials along with their signature fried chicken; namesake moist, flaky biscuits; and some new small-plate entrees dubbed "Southern tapas." With a crisp, blow-your-eardrums-out sound system, New Orleans–speak-easy (albeit commercial) appeal, and a nightly lineup of live acts, there's no better place to muse the blues than this basement-cum-nightclub. 401 Mason (at Geary St.). ✆ **415/292-2583.** www.biscuitsandblues.com. Cover (during performances) $10–$20.

The Boom Boom Room The late John Lee Hooker and his partner Alex Andreas bought this Western Addition club several years back and used Hooker's star power to pull in some of the best blues bands in the country (even the Stones showed up for an unannounced jam session). Though it changed focus and is now a roots music oriented club, it's still a fun, dark, small, cramped, and steamy joint where you can hear good live tunes—ranging from New Orleans funk, soul, and new wave, to trance jazz, live drum 'n' bass, electronica, house, and more—Tuesday through Sunday until 2am. Cover varies from free to about $15, so call ahead to check. If you're going to the Fillmore (see later) to see a band, stop by here first for a drink and come back after your show for more great music. The neighborhood's a bit rough, so be sure to park in the underground lot across the street. 1601 Fillmore St. (at Geary Blvd.). ✆ **415/673-8000.** www.boomboomblues.com.

Scope-a-Scene

The local newspapers won't direct you to the city's underground club scene, nor will they advise you which of the dozens of clubs are truly hot. To get dialed in, check out reviews from the ravers themselves at **www.sfstation.com/clubs**. The far more commercial **Club Line** (✆ **415/339-8686;** www.sfclubs.com) offers up-to-date schedules for the city's larger dance venues.

Bottom of the Hill Voted one of the best places to hear live rock in the city by the *San Francisco Bay Guardian,* this popular neighborhood club attracts a diverse crowd ranging from rockers to real-estate salespeople; it also offers tons of all-ages shows. The main attraction is an eclectic range of live music almost every night (focusing on indie punk with the occasional country band thrown in), but the club also offers pretty good burgers, a bar menu, and outdoor seating on the back patio Wednesday through Friday from 4pm to 2am, Saturday through Tuesday 8:30pm to 2am. Happy hour runs Wednesday to Friday from 4 to 7pm. 1233 17th St. (at Missouri St.). ✆ **415/621-4455.** www.bottomofthehill.com. Cover $6–$12.

Cafe du Nord If you like your clubs dim, sexy, and with a heavy dose of old-school ambience, boy howdy will you dig Café du Nord. This subterranean supper club has rightfully self-proclaimed itself as the place for a "slightly lurid indie pop scene set in a beautiful old 1907 speakeasy." It's also where an eclectic crowd gathers to linger at the front room's 40-foot mahogany bar, or dine on the likes of panko-crusted prawns and blackened mahi-mahi. The small stage hosts an eclectic mix of local and visiting artists ranging from Shelby Lynne (country) to the Dickdusters (punk) and local favorite Ledisi (R&B). 2170 Market St. (at Sanchez St.). ✆ **415/861-5016.** www.cafedunord.com. Cover ranges from $5–$20.

Enrico's FREE Enrico's is a sidewalk-restaurant/supper-club destination on North Beach's Broadway strip. Anyone with an appreciation for live jazz (featured

Cheap Boot-Scootin' Lessons

Country and western dancing is far from hip in San Francisco, but nevertheless there are plenty of cowgirls—of both genders—who like to don their cowboy duds and have a little fun. The best place in town (the only place, actually) is the **Sundance Saloon.** Every Thursday and Sunday night you can get dance lessons in the early evening, then two-step your little pea-pickin' heart out until 10:30pm—all for only $5. Where else but in a fabulous gay-lesbian-bisexual-transgender blender dance hall could you learn line dances like the Tush Push, Backstreet Attitude, Circle Jerk, and Dog Bone Boogie? On a good night, you might just hook up with a cowpoke wearing nothing but chaps. It's located at 550 Barneveld Ave. off Industrial Ave. (✆ **415/820-1403;** www.sundancesaloon.org).

nightly with no cover), late-night noshing, and people-watching from the patio will be quite content spending an alfresco evening under the heat lamps here. I tend to drop by for a mojito or two, nosh on their addictive deep-fried olives or pizza Margherita, listen to a bit of live jazz, and stumble on. 504 Broadway (at Kearny St.). ✆ **415/982-6223.** www.enricossidewalkcafe.com.

Grant & Green Saloon FREE Along with The Saloon (see later), this is one of those historic North Beach dive bars that every local has been to but can't remember when. It's always a solid choice for listening to live music with no cover. Mondays feature jazz, Tuesdays are DJ and karaoke, and the local bands on Thursday through Saturday are decent. All in all, the space is an all-around great place to let your hair down. 1371 Grant Ave. (at Green St.). ✆ **415/693-9565.** www.grantandgreen.com.

FREE Salsa Dancing at the Ramp

The Ramp is an indoor/outdoor bar/restaurant serving salads, burgers, and breakfast on the edge of the bay in China Basin. It's always worth a visit on sunny days, particularly between May and October, when you can dance to live music on the weekends; Saturdays feature salsa bands from 5 to 9pm, and Sundays bring world music from 5 to 8pm. And there's no cover charge. It's located at 855 Terry Francois St., off Third Street at Mariposa Street (✆ **415/621-2378;** www.ramprestaurant.com).

Lou's Pier 47 Club You won't find many locals in the place, but Lou's happens to be good, old-fashioned fun. It's a casual spot where you can relax with Cajun seafood (downstairs) and live blues bands (upstairs) nightly. A vacation attitude makes the place one of the more, um, jovial spots near the wharf. There's a $3 to $5 cover for bands that play between 4 and 8pm and a $3 to $10 cover for bands that play between 8 or 9pm and midnight or 1am. 300 Jefferson St. (at Jones St.). ✆ **415/771-5687.** www.louspier47.com.

Pier 23 If there's one good-time destination that's an anchor for San Francisco's party people, it's the Embarcadero's Pier 23. Part ramshackle patio spot and part dance floor with a heavy dash of dive bar, here it's all about fun for a startlingly diverse clientele (including a one-time visit by Bill Clinton!). The well-worn box of a restaurant with tented patio is a prime sunny-day social spot for white collars, but on weekends, it's a straight-up people zoo where every age and persuasion coexist more peacefully than the cast in a McDonald's commercial. Expect to boogie down shoulder-to-shoulder to 1980s hits and leave with a contagious feel-good vibe. There's only a cover of $5–$10 when the band's playing. Pier 23, at the Embarcadero (at Battery St.). ✆ **415/362-5125.** www.pier23cafe.com.

Rasselas Large, casual, and comfortable with couches and small tables, Rasselas is a popular locals spot for jazz, blues, soul, and R&B combos seven days a week. They only charge cover on Friday and Saturday ($10), and if you arrive early you can usually get in for free. The adjacent restaurant serves good and relatively cheap Ethiopian cuisine nightly from 5 to 10pm, which, combined with the live music, makes for quite the cost-cutting cultural evening. 1534 Fillmore St. (at Geary Blvd.). ✆ **415/346-8696.** www.rasselasjazzclub.com. 2-drink minimum.

The Saloon FREE An authentic gold rush survivor, this North Beach dive is the oldest bar in the city. Popular with both bikers and daytime pinstripers, it schedules live "North Beach Blues" nightly and afternoons Friday through Sunday. FINE PRINT On Friday and Sunday nights plan on paying a $5 cover to see Johnny Nitro, whose band has been playing here as long as I can remember. 1232 Grant Ave. (at Columbus St.). ✆ **415/989-7666.**

Slim's Co-owned by musician Boz Scaggs, this glitzy restaurant and bar serves California cuisine and seats 200, but it's usually standing room only during almost nightly shows ranging from performers of homegrown rock, jazz, blues, and alternative music. An added bonus for the musically inclined family: All ages are always welcome. Call or check their website for a schedule; hot bands sell out in advance, but sometime there's no cover at all. 333 11th St. (at Folsom St.). ✆ **415/522-0333.** www.slims-sf.com. Cover free–$30.

8 Bars with DJ Grooves

Bambuddha Lounge With a 20-foot reclining Buddha on the roof it's pretty easy to spot the Bambuddha, a reliably lively restaurant/bar/lounge adjoining the funky-cool Phoenix Hotel. The ultramodern San Francisco–meets–Southeast Asia decor includes floor-to-ceiling waterfalls and indoor/outdoor slate fireplaces in the dining room, and the city's only outdoor poolside cocktail lounge. Affordable and above-average Southeast Asian cuisine is served late into the evening, and a state-of-the-art sound system streams ambient, down-tempo, soul, funk, and house music to a mostly 20-something crowd. 601 Eddy St. (at Larkin St.). ✆ **415/885-5088.** www.bambuddhalounge.com. Cover $5–$10.

The Bliss Bar FREE Surprisingly trendy for sleepy family-oriented Noe Valley, this small, stylish, and friendly bar is a great place to stop for a varied mix of locals, colorful cocktail concoctions, and a DJ spinning at the front window from 9pm to 2am every night except Sunday and Monday. If it's open, take your cocktail into the too-cool back Blue Room. **Dirt-Cheap Alert:** Stop by from 4 to 7pm when martinis, lemon drops, cosmos, watermelon cosmos, and apple martinis are only $4. 4026 24th St. (btw Noe and Castro sts.). ✆ **415/826-6200.** www.blissbarsf.com.

Levende Lounge FREE A fusion of fine dining, cocktailing, and DJ grooves, Levende Lounge is one of the Mission's hottest spots for young singles looking to hook up. **Dirt-Cheap Alert:** Drop in early for happy hour Monday through Friday from 5 to 7pm in a setting amid exposed brick walls and cozy lighting. Later, tables are traded for lounge furnishings for some late-night noshing and flirting. Some nights have cover charges, but you can avoid the fee with a dinner reservation, and food is served until 11pm. 1710 Mission St. (at Duboce St.). ✆ **415/864-5585.** www.levendesf.com.

Wish Bar FREE Swathed in burgundy and black with exposed cinder-block walls, cement floors, and red-shaded sconces aglow with candlelight, even you will look cool at this mellow SoMa bar in the popular night crawler area around 11th and Folsom streets. With a bar in the front, DJ spinning upbeat lounge music in the back, and seating—including cushy leather

FREE Legendary Trivia Quiz

Every Tuesday night at 8:30pm the Edinburgh Castle Pub hosts The Legendary Castle Quiz, a free event that pits your brains against their tough (well, for you maybe) trivia questions. You might even win a cash prize!

couches—in between, it's often packed with a surprisingly diverse (albeit youthful) crowd. Closed Sundays. 1539 Folsom St. (btw 11th and 12th sts.). © **415/278-9474.** www.wishsf.com.

9 Dance Clubs

El Rio FREE This Mission District Latin dance club attracts quite the mixed crowd who really know their salsa moves. Perks include a big backyard that has that sort of Doris Day/Rock Hudson patio party kind of feel. The music schedule varies, so be sure to call ahead or check their website. **Dirt-Cheap Alert:** Happy hour specials range from Monday Dollar Days (well, $2 for well drinks, $1 Pabst) to free oysters on the half shell every Friday at 5:30pm and free BBQ every Friday and Sunday. 3158 Mission St. (at Army St.). © **415/282-3325.** www.elriosf.com.

The Endup This legendary party space with a huge, heated outdoor deck (complete with waterfall and fountain no less), indoor fireplace, and eclectic clientele has always thrown some of the most intense all-nighters in town. In fact, it's practically a second home to the city's DJs. There's a different theme every night: Friday Ghettodisco, Super Soul Sundayz, and so on. The Endup is ever-popular with the sleepless dance-all-day crowd that comes here after the other clubs close, hence the name. It's open Saturday morning 6am to noon and then nonstop from Saturday night around 10pm to Sunday night/Monday morning at 4am. Call or check the website to confirm nights—offerings change from time to time. 401 Sixth St. (at Harrison St.). © **415/357-0827.** www.theendup.com. Cover free–$15.

Air Your Dirty Laundry in Public

You can do your laundry, listen to live music or a poetry reading, dine, and check your stock portfolio online for free at SoMa's **Brainwash,** the hippest laundromat on the planet. It's open Monday through Thursday from 7am to 11pm, Friday and Saturday from 7am to midnight, and Sunday from 8am to 11pm; rates are $3 for 20 minutes. 1122 Folsom St., between Seventh and Eighth streets (© **415/861-FOOD** [861-3663]; www.brainwash.com).

Harry Denton's Starlight Room Perched on the top floor of the Sir Francis Drake Hotel, the Starlight Room is a pantheon to 1930s San Francisco, a throwback to the days when red-velvet banquettes, chandeliers, and fashionable duds were de rigueur. The 360-degree view of the city is worth the cover charge alone (there's actually no cover charge Sunday through Tuesday, and it ranges from $10 to $15 the other nights of the week), but if you arrive before 8:30pm, you only have to pay for the overpriced cocktails. The bar stocks a pricey collection of single-malt Scotches and champagnes, and you can snack from the "Lite" menu. Early evening is more relaxed, but come the weekend this place gets loose. ***Tip:*** Come dressed for success (no casual jeans, open-toed shoes for men, or sneakers), or you'll be turned away at the door. Atop the Sir Francis Drake Hotel, 450 Powell St., 21st floor. ✆ **415/395-8595.** www.harrydenton.com.

"Bus"-ting a Move with El Voladote

Now here's a bright idea: For $38 per person the most gaudy bus you've ever seen—El Voladote—will take you and your amigos on a cruise to three of the spiciest dance clubs in the Mission District. The *autobus de fiesta* rolls every Friday and Saturday night, and the price includes cover charges at three clubs. Call ✆ **415/546-3747** or log onto www.mexicanbus.com for details.

Holy Cow FREE Its motto, "Never a cover, always a party," has been the case since 1987 when this industrial SoMa nightclub opened. The local clubbers rarely come here anymore, but it's still a reliable place for tourists and geezers like me who want to break a sweat on the dance floor to DJs spinning club classics and Top 40. Nightly drink specials make it difficult to leave sober, so plan your transportation accordingly. ***Note:*** The bar is open only Thursday through Saturday from 9pm to 2am. 1535 Folsom St. (btw 11th and 12th sts.). ✆ **415/621-6087.** www.theholycow.com.

1015 Folsom The ginormous party warehouse—total capacity is 2,000 persons—has three levels of dance floors that make for an extensive variety of dancing venues. DJs pound out house, disco, funk, acid-jazz, and more, with lots of groovy lasers and LED lights to stimulate the eye. Each night is a different club that attracts its own crowd, ranging from yuppie to hip-hop. Open Thursday through Saturday 10pm to 2am. 1015 Folsom St. (at Sixth St.). ✆ **415/431-1200.** www.1015.com. Cover varies.

Roccapulco Salsa dancing is all the rage deep within the Mission District, and the place to take a lesson or just sit back watching expert couples heat up the expansive dance floor is Roccapulco. A $10 cover charge gets you a 1-hour salsa lesson on Friday and Saturday nights at 8:30pm, followed by live Latin bands. **FREE ALERT:** Better yet, show up on Monday at 6pm for free salsa lessons. 3140 Mission St. (at Precita St.). ✆ **415/648-6611.** www.roccapulco.com.

10 Bars

Buddha Lounge FREE If you like colorful dive bars you'll love the Buddha Lounge. This heart-of-Chinatown bar is a great glimpse into Chinatown's neighborhood culture. Of course, most tourists shy away from what appears to be yet another dark, seedy watering hole, but it's really just a cheery neighborhood bar. Be brave. Step inside, order a drink, and pretend you're in a Charlie Chan movie. The best part is when the Chinese woman behind the bar answers the phone: "*Hello, Buddha*!" 901 Grant Ave. (at Washington St.). ✆ **415/362-1792.**

Buena Vista Café FREE "Did you have an Irish coffee at the Buena Vista?" The popular myth is that the Irish coffee was invented at the Buena Vista, but the real story is that this wharfside cafe was the first bar in the country to serve Irish coffee after a local journalist came back from a trip and described the drink to the bartender. Since then, the bar has poured more of these addictive pick-me-up drinks than any other bar in the world, and ordering one has become a San Francisco must-do. Heck, it's entertaining just to *watch* the venerable tenders pour up to 10 whiskey-laden coffees at a time (a rather messy event). The cafe is in a prime tourist spot along the wharf, so plan on waiting for a stool or table to free up on weekends. And if you need a snack to soak up the booze, they serve food here as well. 2765 Hyde St. (at Beach St.). ✆ **415/474-5044.** www.thebuenavista.com.

Edinburgh Castle FREE Since 1958, this legendary Scottish pub has been known for having rare British ales on tap and one of the best selections of single-malt Scotches in the city. The homey pub is festively decorated with a mishmash of across-the-pond mementos, including an authentic Ballantine caber (a long wooden pole) used in the annual Scottish games. Fish and chips (served in newspaper of course) and other traditional British foods are available until 11pm. The Edinburgh also features author readings and performances and has hosted such noteworthy writers as Po Bronson, Beth Lisick, and Anthony Swofford. Open 5pm to 2am daily. 950 Geary St. (btw Polk and Larkin sts.). ✆ **415/885-4074.** www.castlenews.com.

It's Not the Fall . . . It's the Sudden Stop

For a cheap thrill in the SoMa district, walk over to the Marriott Hotel at 777 Market St. at Grant Avenue, take the elevator up to the Atrium Lobby Lounge, order a stiff coke at the bar, slowly walk toward the floor-to-ceiling window behind you, peer straight down, and ponder that fact that the only thing between you and the pavement 40 stories below is a single pane of glass.

Gold Dust Lounge FREE If you're staying downtown and want to head to a friendly, festive bar loaded with old-fashioned style and revelry, you needn't wander far off Union Square. This classically cheesy watering hole is all that. The red banquettes, gilded walls, dramatic chandeliers, pro bartenders, and "regulars" are the old-school real deal. Add live music and cheap drinks and you're in for a good ol' time. ***Tip:*** It's cash only, so come with some greenbacks. 247 Powell St. (at Geary St.). ✆ **415/397-1695.**

Green's Sports Bar FREE If you think San Francisco sports fans aren't as enthusiastic as those on the East Coast, well, you're right. These days it's pretty easy to find an empty seat at Green's during a 49ers or Giants game. The city's de facto sports bar is a classic, cozy hangout with lots of dark wood, polished brass, windows that open onto the street, and an array of elevated TVs showing various sporting events via satellite. Highlights include 18 beers on tap, a pool table, and a boisterous happy hour scene every Monday through Friday from 4 to 7pm. Food isn't served, but you can place an order from the various restaurants along Polk Street and eat at the bar (they even provide a selection of menus). 2239 Polk St. (at Green St.). ✆ **415/775-4287.**

Hemlock Tavern FREE This former gay dance club is now one of the most popular bars on Polk Street and always packed on weekends. There's lots of dark wood, warm colors, a line for the bathroom, and an enclosed backroom that's dedicated just to smokers. The crowd is a bit younger than the Edinburgh Castle crew, but there's a similar mix of locals, hipsters, musicians, and visitors who would never think of themselves as tourists. The jukebox is sweet, and you can chow down on warm peanuts (toss the shells on the floor) and wash 'em down with a good selection of beers on tap. 1131 Polk St. (at Sutter St.). ✆ **415/923-0923.** www.hemlocktavern.com.

Li Po Cocktail Lounge FREE A dim, divey, and slightly spooky Chinese bar that was once an opium den, Li Po's alluring character stems from its mishmash clutter of dusty Asian furnishings and mementos, including an unbelievably huge ancient rice-paper lantern hanging from the ceiling and a glittery golden shrine to Buddha behind the bar. The bartenders, who pour a mean Li Po Special Mai Tai, love to creep out patrons with tales of opium junkies haunting the joint. Bands and DJs occasionally whip up a sweaty dance scene in the basement, but it's a hit-and-miss schedule. 916 Grant Ave. (btw Washington and Jackson sts.). ✆ **415/982-0072.**

Martuni's FREE San Francisco has plenty of bars with pianos in them, but for the real singalong piano bar experience you'll want to head to Martuni's. After a couple of stiff martinis, you'll loosen up enough to join the eclectic crowd in rousing renditions of everything from Cole Porter to Elton John. If you're not up for singing, you can cuddle with your date in the dark alcoves and watch the fun; otherwise, sidle up to the piano and

Mmmm, Kielbasa Thursdays

If you want to find me (the author, Pooley) on Thursday nights, I'll probably be at Gestalt Haus, my favorite bar in the Mission that does nothing but beers and $5 sausage sandwiches (brilliant). Really good beer and $5 sausage sandwiches. Great eclectic crowd, friendly bartenders, funky decor, and the kind of disgusting bathroom that keeps the fussier types at bay. It's at 3159 16th St. between Valencia and Guerrero; ✆ 415/560-0137.

let 'er rip. 4 Valencia St. (at Market St.). ✆ **415/241-0205.**

Matrix Fillmore FREE The Matrix represents the best and worst of the Marina/Cow Hollow young-n-yuppie scene: It attracts some of the city's top eye candy, but also has L.A.-style attitude in abundance (I was once asked to give up my fireplace loveseat to someone more important). Dress in black, order a mojito, say "like" a lot, and you'll do just fine. The slick lounge atmosphere is further enhanced by dyed concrete floors, flatscreen TVs, and a free-standing centerpiece fireplace with its "Zen minimalist" mantel. One plus: The bar offers 10 wines by the glass and a large by-the-bottle selection including cult classics like Dalla Valle. Valet parking is available at the nearby Balboa Café (Fillmore and Greenwich sts.). 3138 Fillmore St. (btw Greenwich and Filbert sts.). ✆ **415/563-4180.** www.matrixfillmore.com.

Drinking and Writing and Reading

One of our favorite reading series (because it takes place in a bar!) is Charlie Jane Anders's "Writers With Drinks" (**www.writerswithdrinks.com**), a popular long-running monthly series at the Make-Out Room, 3225 22nd St. (✆ **415/647-2888;** www.makeoutroom.com). Admission is $3 to $5 (sliding scale) and proceeds go to area nonprofits. Another "don't miss" is Michelle Tea's (free) "Radar Reading and Salon Series," held monthly at the main branch of the San Francisco Public Library, on 100 Larkin St. (**www.myspace.com/radarreading**).

Perry's FREE If you've read *Tales of the City,* you may remember that this bar and restaurant has a colorful history as a pickup place for Pacific Heights and Marina singles. Although the times are not as wild today, locals still come to check out the happenings at the dark mahogany bar. A separate dining room offers breakfast, lunch, dinner, and weekend brunch. It's a good place for hamburgers, simple fish dishes, and pasta. Menu items range from $6 to $22. 1944 Union St. (at Laguna St.). ✆ **415/922-9022.**

The Redwood Room FREE Best known for its gorgeous redwood paneling made from a single 2,000-year-old tree, the Clift Hotel's Redwood Room bar and lounge has a plush, modern feel that's illuminated by beautiful original Deco sconces. If you know who Ian

Best Place to Get Drunk & Nailed

Shell out $10 for one of Beauty Bar's specialty cocktails and get a free manicure at the national chain's Mission District outpost. If you have six or more girls together, call ahead and give them a heads-up. 2299 Mission St. ✆ **415/285-0323.** www.beautybar.com.

Schrager and Philippe Starck are, then you know their scene: AMEX Platinum posers and randy businessmen who mix, mingle, and never balk at the high drink prices ($9–$25). But even if that's not your scene, it's worth poking your head in to admire the classy decor. In the Clift Hotel, 495 Geary St. ✆ **415/775-4700.** www.clifthotel.com.

Specs' FREE The location of Specs'—look for a tiny nook on the east side of Columbus Avenue just south of Broadway—makes it a bit tough to find but well worth the search. Specs' historically eclectic decor—maritime flags hang from the ceiling while dusty posters, photos, and oddities like dried whale penises line the walls—offers plenty of visual entertainment while you toss back a cold Bud (sans glass of course). A "museum" displayed under glass contains memorabilia and items brought back by long-dead seamen who dropped in between voyages. There are plenty of salty and slightly pickled regulars to match the motif, so you may not want to order a Cosmo while doing your nails at the bar. 12 Saroyan Place (at 250 Columbus Ave.). ✆ **415/421-4112.**

The Tonga Room & Hurricane Bar It's kitschy as all get-out, but there's no denying the goofy Polynesian pleasures of the Fairmont Hotel's tropical oasis. Drop in and join the crowds for an umbrella drink, a simulated thunderstorm and downpour, and a heavy dose of whimsy that escapes most San Francisco establishments. If you're on a budget, you'll definitely want to stop by for the weekday happy hour from 5 to 7pm, when you can stuff your face at the all-you-can-eat bar-grub buffet (baby back ribs, chow mein, pot stickers) for $9.50 and the cost of one drink. Settle in and you'll catch live Top-40 music after 8pm Wednesday through Sunday, when there's a $3 to $5 cover. In the Fairmont Hotel, 950 Mason St. (at California St.). ✆ **415/772-5278.** www.tongaroom.com.

Toronado FREE Gritty Lower Haight isn't exactly a charming street, but there's plenty of nightlife here, catering to an artistic/grungy/skateboarding 20-something crowd. While Toronado definitely draws in the young'uns, its 50-plus microbrews on tap and 100 bottled beers also entice a more eclectic clientele in search of beer heaven. The brooding atmosphere matches the surroundings: an aluminum bar, a few tall tables, minimal lighting, and a backroom packed with tables and chairs. Happy hour runs 11:30am to 6pm every day for $1 off pints. 547 Haight St. (at Fillmore St.). ✆ **415/863-2276.** www.toronado.com.

Tosca Cafe FREE Open Tuesday through Saturday from 5pm to 2am, Sunday 7pm to 2am, Tosca is a low-key and large popular watering hole for local politicos, writers, media types, incognito celebrities such as Johnny Depp or Nicholas Cage, and similar cognoscenti of unassuming classic characters. Equipped with dim lights, red-leather booths, and high ceilings, it's everything you'd expect an old North Beach legend to be. No credit cards. 242 Columbus Ave. (btw Broadway and Pacific Ave.). ✆ **415/986-9651.**

Vesuvio FREE Situated along Jack Kerouac Alley, across from the famed City Lights bookstore, this renowned literary beatnik hangout is packed to the second-floor rafters with neighborhood

FREE Italian-Style Saturday Singalong

Show up at **Caffe Trieste** in the North Beach on most Saturdays between 1 and 5pm. That's when the stringed instruments are tuned up, the chairs are scooted against the walls, and the Caffe Trieste Musical Family entertains the crowd with their lively version of classic Italian operas and heartwarming folk songs. Everybody's so high on caffeine that it quickly becomes one big happy party and the highlight of everyone's vacation. (Even lifelong locals still get a kick out of it.) This family-owned corner institution is one of San Francisco's most beloved cafes—a Beat Generation hang-out that's been around since 1956 serving locally roasted Italian coffee. You'll find it at 601 Vallejo St. at Grant Avenue (✆ **415/392-6739;** www.caffetrieste.com), next to the row of motorcycles.

writers, artists, songsters, wannabes, and everyone else ranging from longshoremen and cab drivers to businesspeople, all of whom come for the laid-back atmosphere. The convivial space consists of two stories of cocktail tables, complemented by changing exhibitions of local art. In addition to drinks, Vesuvio features an espresso machine. 255 Columbus Ave. (at Broadway). © **415/362-3370.** www.vesuvio.com.

Zeitgeist FREE The front door is black, the back door is adorned with a skeleton Playboy bunny, and inside is packed to the rafters with tattooed, pierced, and hard-core-looking partiers. But forge on. Zeitgeist is such a friendly and fun punk-rock-cum-biker-bar beer garden that even the occasional yuppie can be spotted mingling around the slammin' jukebox featuring tons of local bands and huge back patio filled with picnic tables. (There tend to be cute girls here, too.) Along with fantastic dive-bar environs, you'll find 30 beers on draft, a pool table, and pinball machines. The regular crowd, mostly locals and bike messengers, come here to kick back with a pitcher, and welcome anyone else interested in the same pursuit. And if your night turns out, um, better than expected, there's a hotel upstairs. Cash only. 199 Valencia St. (at Duboce). © **415/255-7505.**

11 Brewpubs

Gordon Biersch Brewery Restaurant Gordon Biersch Brewery is San Francisco's largest brew restaurant, serving decent food and tasty beer to an attractive crowd of mingling professionals. There are always several house-made beers to choose from, ranging from light to dark. Menu items run $9.50 to $26. 2 Harrison St. (on the Embarcadero). © **415/243-8246.** www.gordonbiersch.com.

San Francisco Brewing Company The best reason to come here is the happy hour special: an 8-½ ounce microbrew beer for $1.50 (or a pint for $2.75) is offered daily from 4 to 6pm and midnight to 1am. Surprisingly low-key for an alehouse, this cozy brewpub serves its creations with burgers, fries, grilled chicken breast, and the like. The bar is one of the city's few remaining old saloons (ca. 1907), aglow with stained-glass windows, tile floors, sky-lit ceiling, beveled glass, and mahogany bar. A massive overhead fan runs the full length of the bar—a bizarre contraption crafted from brass and palm fronds. The handmade copper brew kettle is visible from the street. Most evenings the place is packed with everyday folks enjoying music, darts, chess, backgammon, cards, dice, and, of course, beer. Menu items range from $4.15—curiously, for edamame (soybeans)—to $21 for a full rack of baby back ribs with all the fixings. 155 Columbus Ave. (at Pacific St.). ✆ **415/434-3344.** www.sfbrewing.com.

12 Wine Bars

First Crush If you're staying downtown and in the mood for a glass of fine wine, take a stroll to this popular restaurant and wine lounge. Amid a stylish and dimly lit interior, an eclectic mix of visitors and locals nosh on reasonably priced "progressive American cuisine" that's paired, if desired, with a large selection of all-California wines served by the glass. But plenty of folks also drop in just to sample flights of wine and talk shop with the wine-savvy staff. This also is a good late-night-bite spot, as it's open until midnight Thursday through Saturday. 101 Cyril Magnin St. (also known as Fifth St., just north of Market St., at Ellis St.). ✆ **415/982-7874.** www.firstcrush.com.

London Wine Bar This British-style wine bar and store is a popular after-work hangout for Financial District suits. It's more of a place to drink and chat, however, than one in which to savor an array of premium wines (though they do offer a sampler). Usually 40 to 50 wines, mostly from California, are open at any given time, and about 800 are available by the bottle. It's a great venue for sampling local Napa Valley wines before you buy, and the pours are reasonably priced. 415 Sansome St. (btw Sacramento and Clay sts.). ✆ **415/788-4811.** www.londonwinesf.com.

Nectar Wine Lounge Catering to the Marina's young and beautiful, this hip place to sip pours about 50 globally diverse wines by the glass (plus 800 choices by the bottle) along with creative small plates; pairings are optional. Soothing shades of browns lend a relaxing ambience to the lounge's industrial-slick decor that includes lots of polished woods and hexagonal highlights. 3330 Steiner St. (at Chestnut St.). ✆ **415/345-1377.** www.nectarwinelounge.com.

13 Gay & Lesbian Bars & Clubs

The Café FREE When this place first opened, it was the only predominantly lesbian dance club on Saturday nights in the city. Once the guys found out how much fun the girls were having, they joined the party.

Today, it's a hugely popular mixed gay and lesbian scene with three bars; two pool tables; a steamy, free-spirited dance floor; and a small, heated patio and balcony where smoking and schmoozing are allowed. A perk: They open at 4pm weekdays and 3pm weekends (2pm on Sun). 2369 Market St. (at Castro St.). © **415/861-3846.** www.cafesf.com.

The Cinch FREE Part cruisy neighborhood bar, part modern-day penny arcade, The Cinch Saloon features free Wi-Fi, two pool tables, five TVs, video games, an Internet jukebox, pinball, and an outdoor smoking patio. They even have their own softball team, the Renegades. With happy hour Monday through Friday 4 to 8pm (all night on Mon), progressive music by DJs on Thursday and Friday nights, and a host of other fun theme nights, the bar attracts a mixed crowd of gays, lesbians, and gay-friendly straights. 1723 Polk St. (near Washington St.). © **415/776-4162.** www.thecinch.com.

The Eagle Tavern FREE One of the city's most established Levi's-'n'-leather bars, The Eagle boasts a heated outdoor patio (where smoking is permitted), a happy hour (Mon–Fri 4–8pm), live bands every Thursday at 9pm, and the occasional mud-wrestling tournament. Straight or gay, it's worth stopping in just to order a bottle of Queer Beer (although the one time I did this, the guy sitting next to me at the bar was completely naked). 398 12th St. (at Harrison St.). © **415/626-0880.** www.sfeagle.com.

The Endup It's a different nightclub every night of the week, but regardless of who's throwing the party, the place is always throbbing with DJ beats and sweaty bodies. There are two pool tables, a fireplace, an outdoor patio, and, on the dance floor, a mob of gyrating souls—particularly on Friday nights. Some nights are straight or mixed, so call ahead if you care. 401 Sixth St. (at Harrison St.). © **415/357-0827.** www.theendup.com.

Esta Noche One of the most interesting neighborhood drag bars is Esta Noche, a small Latin gay bar in the Mission District where the drag queens are more likely to be at the bar or on the dance floor than on stage. (Esta Noche does host drag shows, but not on a regular basis.) The disc jockeys play mostly salsa music—with some disco thrown in—and the dance floor is always jammed. The bartenders are friendly, as are most of the customers, but this is definitely a gay club and not recommended for curious heteros wondering what drag queens do in their spare time. It is also in a kind of seedy section of

16th Street, where there have been a few isolated gay-bashing incidents in the past, so take a cab to the door. 3079 16th St. (at Valencia St.). © **415/861-5757.** www.estanochebar.com.

Kimo's This gay-owned and -operated neighborhood bar in the seedier gay section of town is a friendly oasis, decorated with plastic plants and random pictures on the walls. The bar provides a relaxing venue for chatting, drinking, and quiet cruising, and livens up with indie, punk rock, and jazz bands nightly at Kimo's Penthouse upstairs. 1351 Polk St. (at Pine St.). © **415/885-4535.** Cover $5–$10 for live music.

Lexington Club FREE "Your friendly neighborhood dyke bar" has everything a city girl needs to survive: cheap drinks, a pool table, and a killer jukebox with everything from the Replacements to Edith Piaf. They really know how to have a good time at this bar, and it's friendly to men and straight women as well. They also offer great drink specials throughout the week, such as "All Day Free Pool & $1 PBRs & $3 Shots of Jim Beam" every Monday. 3464 19th St. (btw Valencia and Mission sts.). © **415/863-2052.** www.lexingtonclub.com.

Lone Star Saloon FREE Expect lesbians and a heavier, furrier motorcycle crowd (both men and women) here most every night. The Thursday night and Saturday and Sunday afternoon beer busts on the patio are especially popular and cost $7 to $9 per person. 1354 Harrison St. (btw 9th and 10th sts.). © **415/863-9999.** www.lonestarsaloon.com.

Metro FREE This bar provides the gay community with high-energy music and the best view of the Castro District from its large balcony. The bar seems to attract people of all ages who enjoy the friendliness of the bartenders and the highly charged, cruising atmosphere. There's a Spanish restaurant on the premises if you get hungry. 3600 16th St. (at Market St.). © **415/703-9751.**

The Mint Karaoke Lounge FREE This is a gay and lesbian karaoke bar—sprinkled with a heavy dash of straight folks on weekends—where you can get up and sing your heart out every night. Along with song, you'll encounter a mixed 20- to 40-something crowd that combines cocktails with do-it-yourself cabaret. Want to eat and listen at the same time? Feel free to bring in the Japanese food from the attached restaurant. Sashimi goes for about $7, main entrees $8, and sushi combo plates about $11. 1942 Market St. (at Laguna St.). © **415/626-4726.** www.themint.net. 2-drink minimum.

> **Underground Entertainment**
>
> **If you'd rather slit your wrists than visit hokey tourist attractions like PIER 39, log onto www.LaughingSquid.com and see what the city's Burning Man types are up to. Since 1995 Laughing Squid's "Squid List" has been the Bay Area's *sine qua non* online resource for art, culture, and technology. Along with links to local art and culture events, the Laughing Squid also hosts the Squid List, a daily event announcements list. There's some really freaky fringe stuff on this Web page, with plenty of garbage-level entertainment among several gems. Either way, it makes for entertaining surfing.**

The Stud The Stud, which has been around for almost 40 years, is one of the most successful gay establishments in town. The interior has an antiques-shop look. Music is a balanced mix of old and new, and nights vary from cabaret to oldies to discopunk. Check their website in advance for the evening's offerings. Drink prices range from $3.25 to $8. Happy hour runs Monday through Saturday 5 to 9pm with $1 off well drinks. 399 Ninth St. (at Harrison St.). © **415/863-6623** or 415/252-STUD (252-7883) for event info. www.studsf.com. Cover free–$10.

Twin Peaks Tavern FREE Right at the intersection of Castro, 17th, and Market streets is one of the Castro's most famous (at 35 years old) gay hangouts. It caters to an older crowd but often has a mixture of patrons and claims to be the first gay bar in America. Because of its relatively small size and desirable location, the place becomes fairly crowded and convivial by 8pm, earlier than many neighboring bars. 401 Castro St. (at 17th and Market sts.). © **415/864-9470.**

14 Arcades

Musée Mécanique Open daily, this fun arcade has penny arcade machines, fortunetellers, games of skill, and beautifully restored antique mechanical musical instruments. Pier 45 (at Taylor St.). © **415/386-1170.** www.museemechanique.org.

Portal One Arcade Located on the second floor of Metreon, this arcade has a pub inside where you can relax while your teenagers play hyperbowl, retro, sports, and virtual reality video games. This place might be too overwhelming for the preschool and younger set. 101 4th St. (at Mission St.). ✆ **415/369-6013.** www.portal1arcade.com.

Riptide Arcade With 100-plus video games, virtual reality units, and even a shooting gallery on offer, you run the risk of losing your hearing and a lot of quarters in this loud, dark room. PIER 39. ✆ **415/981-6300.** www.riptidearcade.com.

FREE Nerd Alert: Free PlayStation

If you're in the mood to play some free video games, head over to the **Westfield Metreon** entertainment center at the corner of Fourth and Mission in the SoMa district. This 350,000-square-foot high-tech complex houses the only store in the country devoted to PlayStation, with several gaming consoles set up with the latest game releases. Open daily from 10am to 10pm, it's also a good place to kill time before the movies.

Small, free and cheap things that make daily life more comfortable, fun and healing, are the focus of this chapter.

6 FREE & DIRT-CHEAP LIVING

Comparing rent checks with friends and family in other parts of the country can be a cringe-inducing experience for a San Franciscan, but then again, do their own Main Streets play home to such postcard-picturesque views? As you sign your check with too many zeros and hand it off to the landlord, you may not be thinking about it, but there's something priceless about living in an urban landscape just a bridge hop away from some of the most beautiful drives and hikes in the country. And then there's the wide breadth of cultural and social services at our feet. It's not to say that living in the city is easy, but we just need to know where to look to get a break.

SAN FRANCISCO LIVING

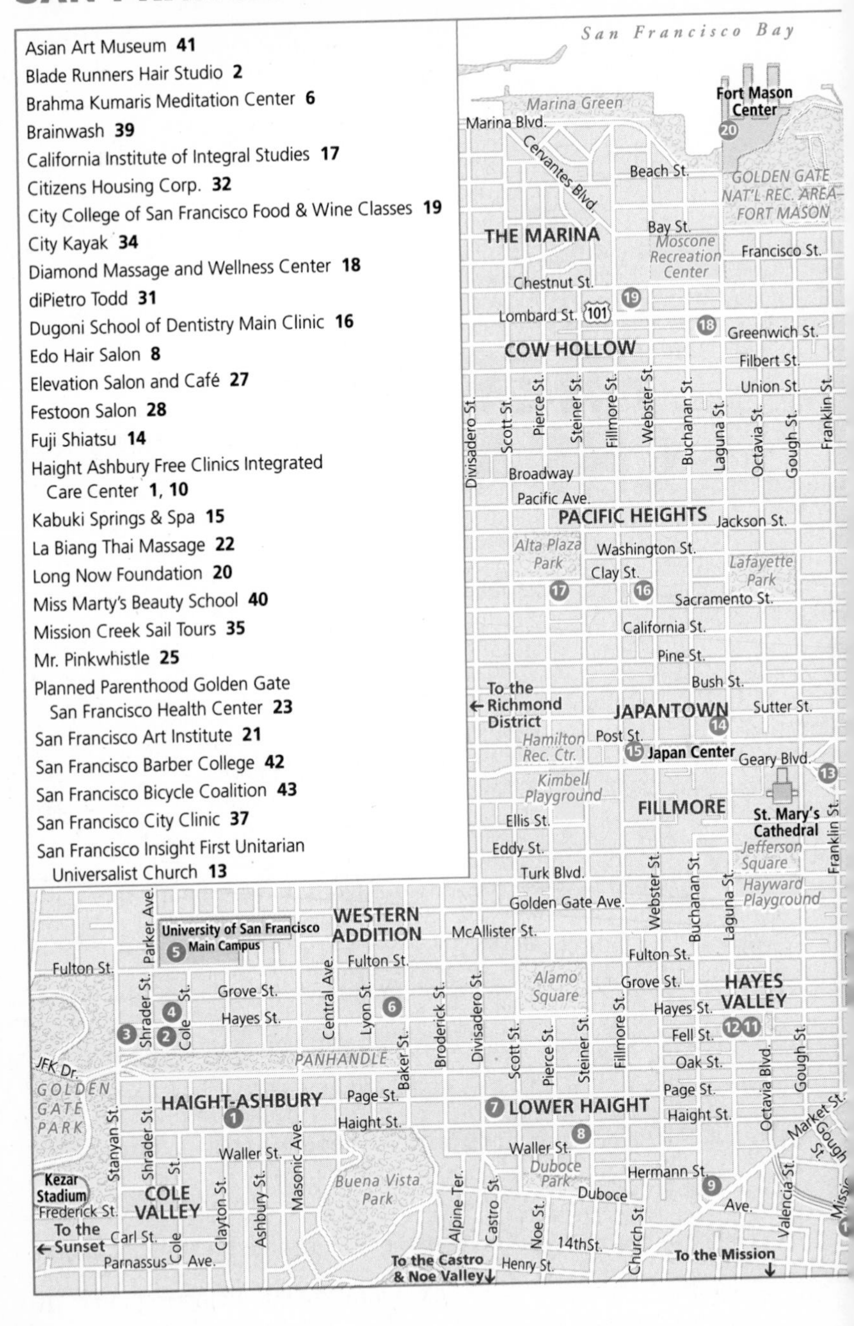

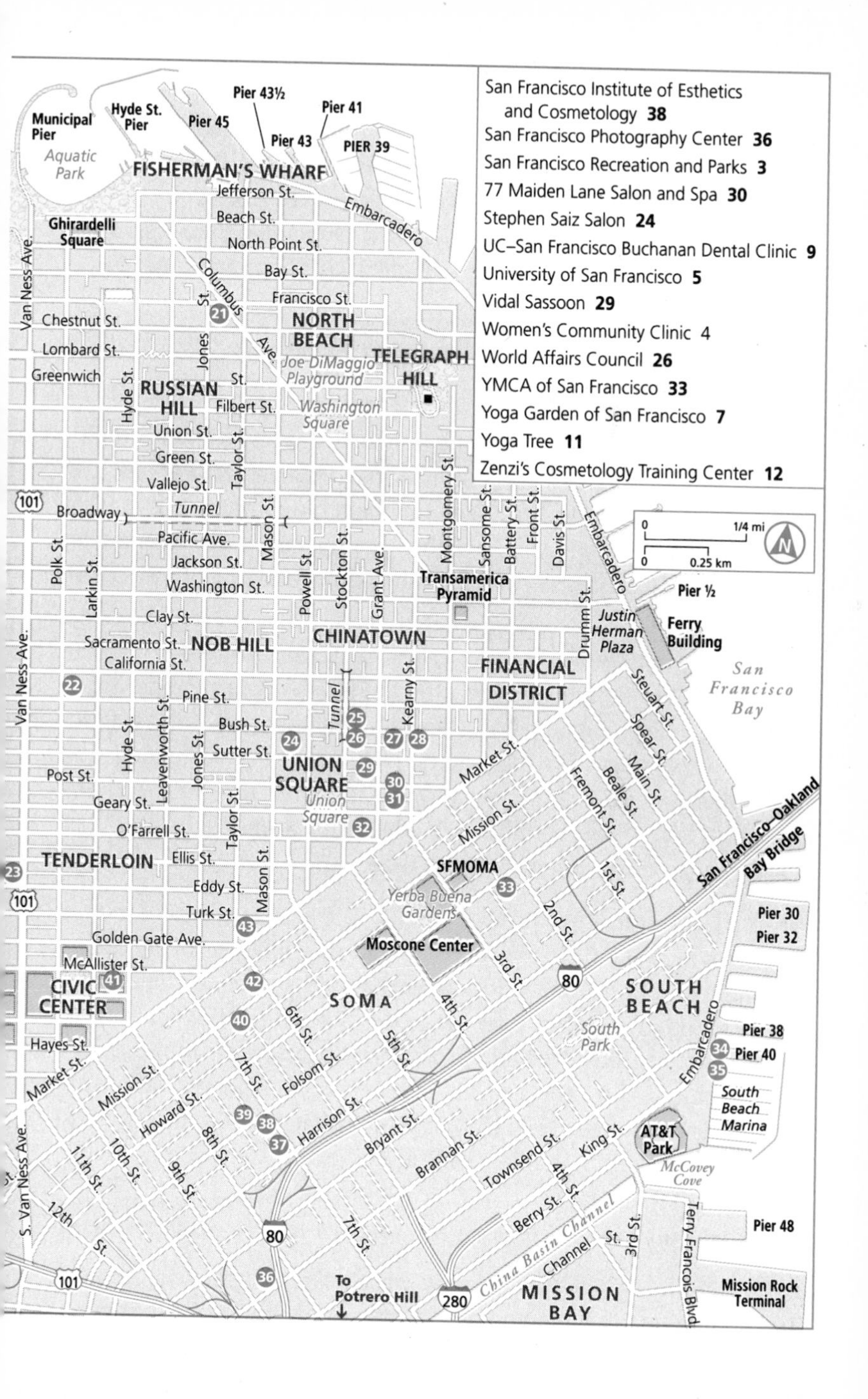
San Francisco Institute of Esthetics and Cosmetology 38
San Francisco Photography Center 36
San Francisco Recreation and Parks 3
77 Maiden Lane Salon and Spa 30
Stephen Saiz Salon 24
UC–San Francisco Buchanan Dental Clinic 9
University of San Francisco 5
Vidal Sassoon 29
Women's Community Clinic 4
World Affairs Council 26
YMCA of San Francisco 33
Yoga Garden of San Francisco 7
Yoga Tree 11
Zenzi's Cosmetology Training Center 12
0 1/4 mi
0 0.25 km
N
Municipal Pier
Hyde St. Pier
Pier 45
Pier 43½
Pier 43
Pier 41
PIER 39
Aquatic Park
FISHERMAN'S WHARF
Jefferson St.
Beach St.
North Point St.
Bay St.
Francisco St.
Embarcadero
Ghirardelli Square
Van Ness Ave.
Columbus Ave.
Chestnut St.
Lombard St.
Greenwich
Jones St.
NORTH BEACH
TELEGRAPH HILL
Joe DiMaggio Playground
Washington Square
RUSSIAN HILL
Hyde St.
Filbert St.
Union St.
Green St.
Vallejo St.
Taylor St.
Broadway
Tunnel
Pacific Ave.
Jackson St.
Washington St.
Clay St.
Sacramento St.
California St.
NOB HILL
CHINATOWN
FINANCIAL DISTRICT
Polk St.
Larkin St.
Mason St.
Powell St.
Stockton St.
Grant Ave.
Montgomery St.
Sansome St.
Battery St.
Front St.
Davis St.
Drumm St.
Transamerica Pyramid
Pier ½
Justin Herman Plaza
Ferry Building
San Francisco Bay
Pine St.
Bush St.
Sutter St.
Post St.
Geary St.
O'Farrell St.
Ellis St.
Eddy St.
Turk St.
Golden Gate Ave.
McAllister St.
Hayes St.
Leavenworth St.
Kearny St.
UNION SQUARE
Union Square
TENDERLOIN
CIVIC CENTER
Market St.
Mission St.
Steuart St.
Spear St.
Main St.
Beale St.
Fremont St.
1st St.
2nd St.
3rd St.
4th St.
5th St.
6th St.
7th St.
8th St.
9th St.
10th St.
11th St.
12th St.
SFMOMA
Yerba Buena Gardens
Moscone Center
San Francisco–Oakland Bay Bridge
Pier 30
Pier 32
SOMA
SOUTH BEACH
South Park
Pier 38
Pier 40
South Beach Marina
Folsom St.
Howard St.
Harrison St.
Bryant St.
Brannan St.
Townsend St.
King St.
AT&T Park
McCovey Cove
Berry St.
China Basin Channel
Channel St.
Terry Francois Blvd.
Pier 48
S. Van Ness Ave.
To Potrero Hill
MISSION BAY
Mission Rock Terminal
101
80
280
21
22
23
24
25
26
27
28
29
30
31
32
33
34
35
36
37
38
39
40
41
42
43

This is a chapter for San Francisco residents who might not know about these cool free and cheap programs that can be a lifesaver in times of need (or sudden need of an apartment!); for people who are considering a move here and wondering how they can swing the expense; and for visitors, who might be in need of some lifestyle necessities: from good cheap highlights, to an acupuncture session, to a massage, to a dentist who can cement a lost filling back in.

1 Free & Cheap Classes & Talks

LECTURES & SEMINARS

One of the best things about living in a city is access to free and dirt-cheap readings, lectures, and seminars. San Francisco's museums and institutes of higher learning offer innumerable ways to add a little extra knowledge to your life, whether that means sitting in on a tête-à-tête with Toni Morrison or leaving the office for a lunchtime lecture on nuclear arms.

Asian Art Museum Together with the Society for Asian Art, the museum delves far and wide to offer the public lectures and symposiums that reflect contemporary Asian cultural topics as well as explorations into the past. FINE PRINT Some lectures are free with admission to the museum ($12 during the day, $5 after 5pm on Thurs, and free every first Sun of the month) while others cost a small fee.

200 Larkin St. ✆ 415/581-3500. www.asianart.org.

California Academy of Sciences The academy has a lot to brag about with its new Golden Gate Park digs, which house an aquarium, a planetarium, a natural history museum, and a rainforest under one roof. Among the lectures offered are the ones in the Benjamin Dean series, featuring distinguished professors on the topics of astronomy and astrobiology. A variety of lectures are free with general admission to the museum. FINE PRINT Lectures in the Benjamin Dean series cost $5 and take place in Kanbar Hall at the Jewish Community Center, 3200 California St.

Golden Gate Park, 55 Music Concourse Dr. ✆ 415/379-8000. www.calacademy.org.

City Arts & Lectures, Inc. A great reference point for lectures and performances, the organization hosts conversations with some of the most luminous names in literature, music, and politics. At about

$20 apiece, it isn't necessarily dirt cheap, but to sit in front of the likes of such guests as Eve Ensler, Annie Leibovitz, and Quincy Jones for a splurge if you're a fanboy or gurl, it's certainly worth it. **FREE ALERT:** Also, if there's someone you're dying to hear but can't afford it, all programs can be heard in edited and delayed broadcasts on KQED-FM (88.5).

www.cityarts.net.

City College of San Francisco Food & Wine Classes Cooking workshops and wine-tasting sessions are on the menu at this school, where prices come cheaper if you register early. Three-hour classes aren't supercheap, but at about $15 per hour, they're significantly less than at private cooking schools. Visit the department's website for the most current offerings. Classes in the past have included everything from sushi making to "Cooking with Artichokes."

Marina Middle School, 3500 Fillmore St. (at Chestnut St.). ✆ 415/561-1860. www.ccsf.com.

The Long Now Foundation Seminars about long-term thinking are the thing at this foundation, which was established to promote the anti-here and now. A $10 donation is welcomed for attendance at sessions such as a "Synthetic Biology Debate" and "Bot-mediated Reality," but no one will be turned away.

Fort Mason Center. ✆ 415/561-6582. www.thelongnow.com.

Read All About It!

From regular local reading series in bookstores and bars to the latest hot author on a national bookstore, you can get an excellent comprehensive listing of what's up (both free and admission-charging events) at the San Francisco *Chronicle*'s excellent SFGate.com. Surf over to **www.sfgate.com/eguide/books/events** and put in your parameters (neighborhood, date, and so on).

San Francisco Art Institute The Art Institute offers public programs throughout the year in a mission to provide direct access to the major practitioners and theorists of the contemporary global art and culture scene. Film screenings, a visiting artists and scholars lecture series, and panel discussions are among the many free and cheap options.

800 Chestnut St. ✆ 415/749-4563. www.sfai.edu.

Readings & Clean Clothes!

You can do your laundry, listen to live music or a poetry reading, dine, and check your stock portfolio online for free at SoMa's **Brainwash,** the hippest laundromat on the planet. It's open Monday through Thursday from 7am to 11pm, Friday and Saturday from 7am to midnight, and Sunday from 8am to 11pm; rates are $3 for 20 minutes. 1122 Folsom St., between Seventh and Eighth streets (✆ **415/861-FOOD** [861-3663]; www.brainwash.com).

★ **San Francisco City College** In addition to a full roster of continuing education courses, lectures, and seminars, City College offers working adults courses for just $20 per unit, plus an $11-per-semester health fee. So a three-course load (nine units) per semester would total just $191. Financial aid is also available to those who qualify. Visit the school's website for more.

50 Phelan Ave. ✆ **415/561-1860.** www.ccsf.edu.

San Francisco Photography Center Photography doesn't tend to be the cheapest of hobbies, with the costs of equipment and developing (or printing, if you're doing it digitally) running toward the high end. Classes aren't usually dirt cheap, but at this city-funded center, affordable learning time can be had. A basic 6-week class will set you back $165, with darkroom access available between classes at no cost.

Somarts Cultural Bldg., 934 Brannan St. ✆ **415/205-4914.** www.sfphotocenter.com.

★ **San Francisco Public Library** Class offerings through the city's library system are vast, and those that teach basic computer skills predominate, including sessions on Internet usage, and how to type and use e-mail. Library-goers though will also find the more esoteric, such as a class on harps. Yes, harps. To see the latest offerings, visit **http://sfpl.lib.ca.us**.

Sharon Art Studio This studio is the city's largest public community art center, and you can dip your hands into everything from ceramics and glasswork to drawing, painting, and jewelry making. An 8- to 10-week class ranges in price from $85 to $150.

Golden Gate Park (by Bowling Green Dr. btw Kennedy and King sts.). ✆ **415/753-7004.** www.sharonartstudio.org.

University of San Francisco The university offers a wide variety of free lectures and seminars, with everything from a look at Afghan arts and artifacts to a physics and astronomy colloquium series. Check out the online calendar for lectures and dates.

2130 Fulton St. ✆ **415/422-5555.** www.usfca.edu/calendar.

World Affairs Council If you're a political junkie or just want to hear some talk on current events, check out one of the World Affairs Council's public programs, where policymakers, business execs, and academics discuss and debate foreign policy and global affairs. Topics run a wide gamut, from a noontime lecture on global climate change to a discussion on India's place among the global elite.

312 Sutter St. ✆ **415/982-5028.** www.itsyourworld.org.

CUTTING A RUG CHEAPLY

City College of San Francisco Dance The department offers both free and low-cost dance events ($5–$10 admission when it's not free), with tango parties, swing lessons, and folk dance among the choices. Live music and special guests sometimes infuse the events with a little something extra. Visit the dance department's website for the latest schedule.

www.ccsf.edu/cgi-bin/htsearch.pl.

Lindy in the Park FREE Spend a part of your weekend spinning around in Golden Gate Park, where there's a free swing dance party every Sunday, from 11am to 2pm. If you're a novice, take advantage of a free lesson between noon and 12:30pm.

JFK Dr. (btw 8th and 10th aves.). www.lindyinthepark.com.

Queer Jitterbugs The jitterbugs take their name from swing, and from their focus on teaching dance to same-sex couples, but when it comes to cutting a rug, all are welcome, partner or not, male or female. In addition to a variety of free dance events, the jitterbugs host weekly classes in swing, salsa, and ballroom. FINE PRINT While their dances are free, you do have to pay to take a class.

✆ **415/305-8242.** www.queerjitterbugs.com.

Rhythm and Motion The center's namesake classes fuse dance with a high-energy workout, and additional offerings include everything from jazz to salsa to ballet. After purchasing a first single class (to the tune of $12), new students will receive their second class for free, plus $10 off an eight-class pass and a coupon to bring a friend for free.

351 Shotwell St. ✆ 415/863-9830. www.rhythmandmotion.com.

San Francisco Caper Cutters Of course you can do some square dancing in San Francisco; you can do anything here. The Caper Cutters offer Monday-evening dance sessions at St. Paul's Presbyterian Church. Watching is free, but dancing will cost you $5 as a guest, $45 per quarter as a member. The latter will grant you free access to all weekly dances.

1399 43rd Ave. (at Judah St.). ✆ 415/753-5013. www.sfsquaredancing.org.

2 Cheap(er) Health & Wellness

It's a sad fact that health insurance has become something of a luxury these days, and many of us live hoping not to get sick, or injured. There's no need to go without care completely, as a variety of clinics and community organizations offer sliding-scale fees, so you can get treatment for everything from a simple cold to a chronic illness. In 2007, the city also launched a groundbreaking program, **Healthy San Francisco** (www.healthysanfrancisco.org), to help provide basic and ongoing medical care to city residents, regardless of their ability to pay.

ACUPUNCTURE

American College of Traditional Chinese Medicine FREE Taking a holistic approach to illnesses, especially those of the chronic sort, has gained a lot of ground in recent years, and acupuncture is among the most well known of options. At this college, the best deal is one that'll go straight to your head: acupuncture for the ears. FINE PRINT The treatment is free, but donations are welcomed.

450 Connecticut St. (btw 19th and 20th sts.). ✆ 415/282-9603. www.actcm.edu.

Quan Yin Healing Arts Center Readjust your body's Qi, or vital energy, with an acupuncture session at this center, where fees come in tiers based on gross monthly income.

455 Valencia St. (btw 15th and 16th sts.). ✆ 415/861-4964. www.quanyinhealingarts.com.

Insuring Yourself

For freelance writers, actors, and those in the entertainment field, a lack of insurance is often par for the course. But a number of industry organizations look out for their own. **The Actor's Fund** (www.actorsfund.org), for example, provides a Health Insurance Resource Center with extensive listings, and a city guide for San Francisco can be downloaded online. The **Freelancers Union** is working on rolling out group-rate health-insurance coverage nationwide. Right now, they're partnered with UnitedHealthcare's Golden Rule Insurance Co. to provide coverage in various states, including California.

For those who don't fall into the writing or entertainment fields, the **San Francisco Health Plan** (www.sfhp.org) is a managed care plan that provides affordable medical, dental, and visual insurance. Qualification varies by program, so it's best to contact the enrollment team (✆ **888/558-5858**). In general, a single adult qualifies if his or her monthly income is up to $2,600 or annual income is up to $31,200.

COMMUNITY MEDICAL CLINICS

Haight Ashbury Free Clinics Services at the clinics are available to all, though the focus is on the uninsured and underinsured. Continuity care is available to those living with chronic illnesses, including HIV, diabetes, and asthma, and urgent-care services are available too.

Integrated Care Center, 1735 Mission St. (at 13th St.). ✆ **415/746-1940.** Also at Haight Clinic, 558 Clayton St. (at Haight St.). ✆ **415/746-1950.** www.hafci.org.

Magnet FREE This Castro-based men's health outreach center offers HIV testing and other sexual health services for gay men and by gay men. Services are free of charge, and the center also hosts cultural events and art shows.

4122 18th St. ✆ **415/581-1600.** www.magnetsf.org.

Planned Parenthood Golden Gate Reproductive health services for both men and women can be found at the San Francisco branch of this national organization. Emergency contraception, HIV testing, and routine gynecological exams are just a few of the organization's offerings. Drop-ins are taken first-come, first-serve, but it's best to make an appointment.

San Francisco Health Center, 815 Eddy St. ✆ **800/967-PLAN** (967-7526). www.ppgg.org.

San Francisco City Clinic The clinic's specialty is in diagnosing and treating STDs, and it provides confidential, low-cost drop-in services for anyone over the age of 12. Because no appointments are made, waits can be long. It's best to show up earlier in the day. A $10 donation is requested, but no one will be turned away if he or she can't pay. The clinic opens at 8am on Monday, Wednesday, and Friday, and at 1pm on Tuesday and Thursday.

356 7th St. (btw Folsom and Harrison sts.). ✆ **415/487-5500.** www.sfcityclinic.org.

San Francisco Free Clinic FREE There's no fee for medical services here, as donations of funds, medications, and physician time form the basis of the clinic. Patients are seen by appointment only, and appointments can be made between the hours of 1 and 4:30pm, Monday through Friday. Preventive care, cancer screening, STD diagnosis and treatment, and vaccinations are among the offerings.

4900 California St. (at 11th Ave.). ✆ **415/750-1966.** www.sffc.org.

Women's Community Clinic FREE Reproductive-oriented services are the focus at this clinic, which serves women and girls age 12 and older who live below the federal poverty line, and who have no health insurance or have inadequate insurance. All services are free, and the center also provides complimentary acupuncture for those suffering from a variety of women's health issues.

2166 Hayes St. (btw Cole and Shrader sts.), Ste. 104. ✆ **415/379-7800.** www.womenscommunityclinic.org.

COUNSELING

Counseling Centers of California Institute of Integral Studies Found throughout the city, the centers are staffed by grad students and postgrad interns who are trained in a variety of therapeutic modes, including conventional psychotherapy. Session costs are based on a sliding scale, and appointments can be made during the day, in the evening, or on weekends.

Center for Somatic Psychotherapy, ✆ **415/558-0880**; Golden Gate Integral Counseling Center, ✆ 415/561-0880; Integral Counseling Center, ✆ 415/776-3109;

Integral Counseling Center, ✆ 415/648-2644; Psychological Services Center, ✆ 415/575-6200, www.ciis.edu/counseling.

San Francisco Psychotherapy Research Group Clinic and Training Center If you want to discuss stress or anxiety, have a family problem, or are battling an addiction, the clinic's staff of post-doc fellows, predoc interns, and supervising clinicians and faculty can help. Anyone looking for therapy and unable to afford private fees is welcome. An initial consultation will cost $50 and further fees are determined on an income-based sliding scale. Fees top out at $85 per session.

9 Funston Ave. ✆ **415/561-6771.** http://sfprg.org.

DENTAL CARE

Dugoni School of Dentistry Getting a cavity filled here may not be dirt cheap, but dental care is about 30% to 40% less than at a typical private dentist in the area. New patients are welcomed on a first-come, first-served basis between 8:30 and 9:30am or between 12:30 and 1:30pm Monday through Friday. All return visits are by appointment.

Main Clinic, 2155 Webster St., Level C. ✆ **415/929-6501.** www.dental.pacific.edu.

UC-San Francisco Buchanan Dental Clinic Prices at the clinic are generally 10% to 15% cheaper than what you'd find at a private dentist's office. The first appointment is an exam and X-ray, which will set you back $150. A cleaning is $70.

100 Buchanan St. ✆ **415/476-5608.**

3 Cheap Housing Resources

Housing prices are down across the country, even in San Francisco, and buying has surged in the city's lower-priced communities as those who have some extra dough to spare take advantage of the times. But for us apartment dwellers, we almost don't know the difference; it's just high rents as usual. For a dash of recourse, taking a look at a few resources before you start your hunt might help you keep some cash in your pocket.

NO-FEE RENTALS

Gearing up to put a deposit on an apartment can be daunting, what with first and last month's rent and a deposit the usual protocol. To add to that, having to set down a broker's fee—typically a month's rent or a 10% to 15% surcharge—is an extra punch to the gut. To avoid one, go straight to the source, and speak directly with the landlord if you know what building you're interested in. If you don't, a few websites can help you sift through the offerings.

ApartmentSource You can search for plenty of no-fee rentals on this site, and also have potential matches e-mailed to you. Many of the listings provide contact info for the buildings' leasing offices.

www.apartmentsource.com.

★ **Craigslist** The San Francisco-born list remains a top source for apartment searching, as you can often bypass the brokers and go directly to the owners themselves.

www.craigslist.com.

Oodle Oodle combs through millions of listings from all over the Web so that you don't have to. Its "smarter classifieds" are über user-friendly, and you can refine your search by numerous parameters, including broker fees or a lack thereof. The site will also remember your most recent searches, so after you've taken a break, you can pick up right where you left off.

www.oodle.com.

MIXED-INCOME DEVELOPMENTS

Developers and the city offer mixed-income buildings in neighborhoods throughout the city, where affordable housing can be had if you have the patience to endure the long waiting lists. For example, a new development may be required to offer a certain percentage of its units to middle or lower-income residents. Housing groups tout such developments as contributing to the diversity of urban communities, as rentals units are set aside for families, seniors, those with disabilities, and the formerly homeless.

Below are a few places where you might be able to find a lead on such vacancies (presuming your income is low enough . . . though we're not really presuming, are we?).

Citizens Housing Corp. Properties run a wide range, with everything from a reimagined, reworked Haight-Ashbury church that now holds studio and one-bedroom apartments for seniors, to a modern, award-winning development in SoMa. The website lists properties that are currently leasing, as well as projects under construction. For the latter, you can be placed on an interest list before the development is even ready for occupancy.

26 O'Farrell St., Ste. 600. ✆ 415/986-7285. www.citizenshousing.org.

Mercy Housing This not-for-profit has a wide array of housing options for qualified individuals and families all over the nation, including homes in San Francisco. Most are rental apartments, and you can search the organization's website by rent, address, and date available, among other categories. Some housing is income-restricted, meaning a prospective tenant can be eligible for housing only if his or her rent is below a particular level. Other rental rates are based on a sliding income scale, while some are a combination of both.

www.mercyhousing.org.

Mission Housing Development Corp. Securing housing can be akin to winning the lottery, literally, and this agency has one. There are continuous waiting lists for all of the corporation's properties, and it can take anywhere from 6 months to 8 years to reach the top. For information on vacancies and waiting lists, contact Caritas Management Corp., which handles the housing and application processes.

1358 Valencia St. ✆ 415/647-7191. www.missionhousing.org.

San Francisco Housing Corp. This corporation develops affordable housing projects across the Bay Area, and also provides homeownership and financial counseling. You can learn more about income requirements and search for rental apartments and town houses on the website. Homeownership opportunities for low- and median-income individuals and families are also available.

4439 3rd St. ✆ 415/822-1022. www.sfhdc.org.

4 Cheap Beauty & Bodywork

SALON STYLING

Spending top dollar doesn't always guarantee a great cut, but the stylists at top salons do generally command the big bucks for good reasons: training and seasoned expertise. San Francisco's top-notch salons offer plenty of discounted cuts and coloring services with their stylists-in-training, so if you're willing to spare a few hours as a hair model and have an open mind, you could come away with a first-rate 'do at just a fraction of what it would normally cost. Most salons will want to arrange a consultation first and then set up the actual cut or color at a later date. We list a few of the places that offer cut-rate cuts below.

Alexander G. FREE Stylists at this Outer Richmond–based salon take a "British approach to hair," with pricey rates to match. Haircuts with students, though, are free, with all-over hair coloring and highlights going for $20, and corrective coloring ringing up at $40.

3115 Clement St. (btw 32nd and 33rd aves.). ✆ **415/876-4688.** www.alexanderg.com.

Blade Runners Hair Studio Step into the Upper Haight's mod-inspired Blade Runners for an equally trendy cut. A chop session with a student in the salon's apprenticeship program will cost $15, as opposed to the salon's usual $70, and color starts at $45.

1792 Haight St. (btw Shrader and Cole sts.). ✆ **415/751-1723.** www.bladerunnerstudio.com.

diPietro Todd Stop in for a consult at diPietro Todd's Post Street outpost on Mondays between 8:30 and 9am or between 1 and 1:30pm. You'll meet with a student and discuss the options, as a wide-range of cuts and color services are available. Same-day appointments can sometimes be had, but are not guaranteed. Haircuts start at $15, with color running from $20 to $30.

177 Post St., 2nd floor (btw Grant Ave. and Kearny St.). ✆ **415/693-5549.** www.dipietrotodd.com.

Edo Hair Salon One part gallery space, one part salon, Edo is a hip Haight outpost of culture and style. Call to give your name and number, and the salon's stylists will get back to you according to the style on the lesson plan for that week—chin-length bob, long layered look, and so on. Appointments are available on Wednesday mornings at 10am. Rates for a student cut are $10, $20 for color.

601 Haight St. (at Steiner St.). ✆ 415/861-0131. www.edosalon.com.

Elevation Salon and Café At Elevation, multitasking is easy, and encouraged. Get a cut, check your e-mail, and have a coffee from the salon's in-house cafe. By acting as a model in the salon's advanced training program, the advantage is that it all doesn't have to cost so much. Appointments are available on Tuesdays; call to make one. Rates for a student cut run from $20, with color starting at $40.

451 Bush St. (btw Grant and Kearny sts.). ✆ 415/392-2969. www.elevationsalon.com.

Festoon Salon Festoon offers cheap cuts with stylists at varying skills levels. While the cheapest cuts, with beginning students, are offered at Festoon's Berkeley salon, appointments with more advanced students can be had at the salon's downtown Claude Lane location. Call to make an appointment for any day of the week except for Monday. Expect to shell out $25 for cuts and $33 to $60 for coloring. Pencil in 2 to 3 hours for cuts and 2 to 4 for color.

9 Claude Lane (btw Bush and Sutter sts.). ✆ 888/35SALON. www.festoonsalon.com.

Mr. Pinkwhistle Sit back in your chair, relax, and take in the contemporary art while smiling over the fact that as a hair model you're getting a $20 cut at a salon that would normally set you back $75 under a junior stylist and $160 under the expertise of a "master craftsman." Color for hair models runs between $20 and $40. Call or stop by during regular business hours for a consultation.

580 Bush St. (btw Stockton St. and Grant Ave.). ✆ 415/989-7465. www.mrpinkwhistle.com.

77 Maiden Lane Salon and Spa Hover above the shopping madness of the Union Square district and set up an appointment to model for one of 77 Maiden Lane's Monday classes, with haircuts for $10, tints for $25, and highlights for $40.

77 Maiden Lane (btw Grant Ave. and Kearny St.). ✆ 415/391-7777. www.77maidenlane.com.

Stephen Saiz Salon FREE Model cuts are free at Stephen Saiz, and color ranges from $10 to $15. Appointments vary according to the salon's training needs, so it's best to call and see what's on the lesson plan for the week.

560 Sutter St., #200 (btw Powell and Mason sts.). ✆ 415/398-2345. www.stephensaizsalon.com.

Vidal Sassoon The world-renowned salon asks potential models to be open to cut and/or color. You'll be supervised by a Sassoon instructor, but be prepared to hang out for up to 3 hours for a cut and 5 hours for color. Call to see what the salon's needs are.

359 Sutter St. (btw Stockton St. and Grant Ave.). ✆ **415/397-5105.** www.sassoon.com.

BARBER COLLEGES

Barber colleges and cosmetology schools offer a wide array of services, with everything from barber cuts for men to waxing and manicures on the menus.

Bayview Barber College Haircuts are $8 and senior cuts are $6. Experience among students varies.

4912 3rd St. (btw Quesada and Palou aves.). ✆ **415/822-3300.** www.bayviewbarbercollege.com.

Miss Marty's Beauty School Basic haircuts at Miss Marty's will set you back $10, with cut and styling going for $20. All students working on clients are in their senior phase of their program and a licensed instructor will monitor all work.

1087 Mission St. (btw 6th and 7th sts.). ✆ **415/227-4240.** www.missmartys.com.

San Francisco Barber College Cuts with students at this barber college are $8, and men and women are welcome. Shaves run $8.

64 6th St. (btw Jessie and Mission sts.). ✆ **415/621-6802.**

San Francisco Institute of Esthetics and Cosmetology Cut and styling starts at $15, with everything from up-dos to a "Bling Bling Blonde" (from $55) color treatment and "Guy Lights" (from $30) available too.

1067 Folsom St., Ste. 200 (btw 7th and Sherman sts.). ✆ **866/355-1SFI** (355-1734). www.sanfranciscoinstitute.com.

Womack's Salon Academy FREE Free cuts are offered on Tuesdays with students in Womack's apprenticeship program. All students are working stylists and are in the process of getting their licenses in the state of California, so experience varies widely, with some counting years of salon time under their belts.

598 Silver Ave. (at Madison St.). ✆ **415/334-7774.** www.womacksalonacademy.com.

Zenzi's Cosmetology Training Center This Hayes Valley beauty school offers $7.50 trims, $50 facials, and everything in between—

deep-conditioning hair treatments, makeup application, bikini waxing, you name it.

551 Hayes St. (btw Laguna St. and Octavia Blvd.). ✆ 415/575-3540. www.zenzis.org.

MASSAGE

★ Diamond Massage and Wellness Center As part of its mission of giving back to the San Francisco community, the center offers a free massage program to specific sponsored groups each month of the year. Those working in the art, music, or film industries, for example, might receive a free massage in June, while government, state, and city workers receive free massages the next month. Check out the center's website to see the types of groups qualified as well as the offered dates. Also, look out for the 15-minute "De-Stressor" at $18 a pop, 10% discount for teachers, and free massage for referring a friend.

1841 Lombard St. (btw Buchanan and Laguna sts.). ✆ 415/921-1290. www.diamondwellness.com.

Fuji Shiatsu The Japanese art of shiatsu is the massage style of choice at this Japantown *maison*. Before noon, all hour-long morning appointments ring up at $45.

1721 Buchanan St. (btw Sutter and Post sts.). ✆ 415/346-2167. www.fujishiatsusf.com.

Bargain Bathing of the Mind & Body

Kabuki Springs & Spa, at 1750 Geary Blvd. at Fillmore Street (✆ **415/922-6000;** www.kabukisprings.com), is the Japan Center's most famous tenant and was once an authentic, traditional Japanese bathhouse. Now it's more of an upscale pan-Asian spa charging up to $130 per treatment, but access to their deluxe deep ceramic communal tubs, sauna, and steam room costs only $20 per person all day ($25 Sat–Sun) from 10am to 10pm (Tues is the only clothing-required coed day—other days of the week switch between men-only and women-only). The price includes use of the bath salts and chilled cucumber face cloths, as well as complimentary tea. If you want to splurge on your body, the spa offers an array of massages (the shiatsu is incredible) and ayurvedic treatments, body scrubs, wraps, and facials, which start at about $65. ***Note:*** A photo ID is required.

La Biang Thai Massage If you prefer the athletics of a Thai massage to the zone-out time that is a Swedish massage, visit La Biang, where a 30-minute session will set you back just $30 and a 60-minute appointment is $55.

1339 Polk St. (btw Austin and Pine sts.). ✆ **415/931-7692.**

Stacy Simone, Certified Massage Therapist Based in the Mission District, Simone specializes in integrated sessions of Swedish, Deep Tissue, Trigger Point, Thai, Reflexology, and/or CranioSacral therapies. In addition to her full treatments, which come at full prices, Simone offers low-cost, hour-long massage sessions. The sessions are available on a sliding scale between $40 and $70. Appointment times are limited; call to schedule one and mention the special rate.

✆ **415/254-4763.** www.littleepiphany.com/massage.htm.

World School of Massage and Holistic Healing Arts Bay Area residents can support the World School by offering up their bodies for students practicing various therapies, including Swedish Massage, Vibrational Healing Massage, and Cranial Sacral Balancing, among other mind-numbingly relaxing services. Hour-long appointments are available for just $40 per hour.

401 32nd Ave. (at Clement St.). ✆ **415/221-2533.**www.worldschoolmassage.com.

5 Free & Cheap Sports & Recreation

BIKERS' TOWN

Touting a bike-friendly transportation system and miles of dedicated bike lanes, San Francisco is a city for riders, and there are plenty of resources to match.

Critical Mass One of the most well-known organized rides, Critical Mass was born in San Francisco in the early '90s and continues to this day, with riders taking over the streets on the last Friday of every month. While there are no official organizers, the ride is loosely coordinated, and riders begin meeting around 5:30pm at Justin Herman Plaza.

Justin Herman Plaza, Market St. at the Embarcadero.

Different Spokes San Francisco A bicycling club for the LGBT community and its friends, Different Spokes hosts a slew of rides throughout the year, all over the Bay Area and beyond. It's not necessary to become a member to join in on the rides, but $10 membership does allow one to post rides to the club's calendar, and offers access to discounts on cycling accessories, parts, and service.

P.O. Box 14711. www.dssf.org.

★ **San Francisco Bicycle Coalition** The coalition is one of the oldest bicycle advocacy organizations in the country, and its programs and services are vast. Register for a free urban bike ed class, where you can take a classroom street-skills course and practice on the road. The coalition also sponsors rides, family biking events, and free maintenance clinics throughout the year.

995 Market St., #1550 (btw 5th and 6th sts.). ✆ **415/431-BIKE** (431-2453). www.sfbike.org.

FREE Lawn Bowling Lessons

Hey, you never know—you might really like lawn bowling. Free lessons of this easy-to-learn sport are offered every Wednesday at noon by the **San Francisco Lawn Bowling Club** (SFLBC to us locals) at the Golden Gate Park Bowling Green, located just south of the tennis courts on Bowling Green Drive (duh) between Middle Drive East and MLK Jr. Drive near Sharon Meadow and the Carousel. In the late spring and summer, additional lessons are given during the evenings; call to confirm (✆ **415/487-8787**).

HITTING THE GYM

While nothing can quite compare to a cost-free run in the sun or bike ride by the Bay, when fickle winter comes around, it sometimes pays to high-tail it to the gym.

Live Fit Gym This Mission District gym isn't fancy, but at $37 for the basic gym membership, it is something of a steal. If you enjoy circuit training and the ability to get in and out after 30 minutes, this place is for you. Additional offerings include massages, yoga, and fitness classes, all at additional pricing, of course.

969 Valencia St. (btw 20th and 21st sts.). ✆ **415/641-4288.** www.livefitgym.com.

★ **San Francisco Recreation and Parks** Among the most affordable options in the city are classes offered through San Francisco Recreation and Parks. The department maintains more than 200 parks, playgrounds, and open spaces throughout the city, and the system also includes 15 full-complex recreation centers. In addition to weight rooms, dance studios, and indoor basketball courts, you'll find a full range of exercise and fitness courses at can't-be-beat prices. An aerobics course, for example, costs as little as $1.50 an hour. The city also offers assistance to low-income families through a Recreation Scholarship Fund.

501 Stanyan St. ✆ 415/831-2700. www.parks.sfgov.org.

24 Hour Fitness Branches of this national chain can be found all over the city, with membership to one specific club costing about $37, plus a $40 initiation fee. It might be worth it to drop an extra three bucks though, which gets you access to all clubs in the "active" or basic category. At the "Superclubs," you'll find pools, saunas, volleyball and tennis courts, but also higher pricing.

✆ 800/204-2400. www.24hourfitness.com.

YMCA of San Francisco The YMCA has 10 branches with fitness facilities. Offerings vary from site to site, but most feature weight rooms and group fitness classes. The Stonestown, Presidio, Embarcadero, and Shih Yu-Lang Central branches all have pools, which might make their fees more pricey. At the Embarcadero site, for example, which offers a five-lane pool and a cardio room with great views of the Bay, there's a $25 initiation fee and $49 monthly fee for young adults, $65 monthly fee for adults. At the Richmond site, which has no pool, young adults pay $39 per month, while adults pay $55. Financial assistance is available for those who qualify.

631 Howard St., Ste. 500. ✆ 415/777-9622. www.ymcasf.org.

M-M-M-MEDITATION

A little peace of mind is priceless, and in the city, there are a number of centers to help you achieve it.

★ **Brahma Kumaris Meditation Center** FREE Spend your lunch hour destressing at the Brahma Kumaris center, where all sessions, including lunchtime meditation, are offered free of charge. Seminars and workshops are cost-free too, with offerings including stress-management and self-empowerment classes.

401 Baker St. (at Hayes St.). ✆ 415/563-4459. www.bksanfrancisco.com.

Makom Shalom FREE For those looking for an alternative meditative brand to the city's many Buddhist centers, Makom Shalom, a program of the San Francisco Jewish Conservative Synagogue, is an option. The program is intended to promote and sponsor Jewish study, prayer, and ritual within a meditative environment, and its sessions are open to all, regardless of spiritual background or experience, for free.

301 14th Ave. (at Clement St.). ✆ 415/221-8736. www.bethshalomsf.org.

San Francisco Insight This meditation community offers classes, retreats, and other community events in the Buddhist practice. Weekly sessions held on Sunday begin with a 45-minute meditation, followed by a talk and discussion. Five-week introductory courses, which include one daylong retreat, cost $50.

First Unitarian Universalist Church, Starr King Rm., 1187 Franklin St. at Geary. www.sfinsight.org.

San Francisco Meditation Group FREE Based in the Ingleside District, the group offers a variety of services throughout the week, with meditation services generally consisting of a period of chanting, followed by silent meditation, free to all.

385 Ashton Ave. ✆ 415/584-8270. www.srf-sanfrancisco.org.

San Francisco Shambhala Meditation Center This Tibetan Buddhist group is one in a network of urban meditation and rural retreat centers. Those new to the process of getting their Zen on should check out the center's free instructional sessions, offered on Tuesday, Wednesday, and Sunday.

1630 Taraval St. ✆ 415/731-4426. www.sf.shambhala.org.

SWIMMING POOLS

The city runs nine **swimming pools,** all of them indoors, except for the Mission Pool, which is open only during the summer. "Scrip booklets," packs of 10 adult swim tickets, can be purchased for $36, or $3.60 per swim. You can tack on a lesson for just $1. For more information, call ✆ **415/831-2747,** or visit www.sfgov.org/site/recpark.

One of our favorites is the **North Beach Pool** at 661 Lombard St. (✆ 415/391-0407), the recent beneficiary of a multimillion-dollar renovation. The natatorium boasts two parallel 90-foot pools, one warm and one cold, plus a retractable ceiling and floor-to-ceiling windows.

YMCA of San Francisco See "Hit the Gym" for info on YMCA memberships, which can offer access to member pools, including those at the Stonestown, Presidio, Embarcadero, and Shih Yu-Lang Central branches. One of the cheapest options might be getting your swim time in during "Community Swim." At the Central branch, for example, the aquatic facilities are open to families within the community three times a week, at $1 per person. Space is limited.

631 Howard St., Ste. 500. ✆ 415/777-9622. www.ymcasf.org.

WATERSPORTS

It's not easy to forget we live in the City by the Bay, what with amazing views around every corner. But it can be tougher to actually get out on the water, as sports like sailing aren't known for being dirt cheap.

City Kayak It may go by quickly, but to get a taste of paddling out on the Bay, you can take a **free** kayaking lesson on Sundays at 12:30pm. The entire class will take half an hour, with 15 minutes on the water. Limited seats are available, so get to class on time.

South Beach Harbor, Embarcadero at Townsend St. ✆ 415/357-1010. www.citykayak.com.

Mission Creek Sail Tours Mission Creek offers discounted tours each month for about $50 per person. The "Attitude Adjustment" or "Full Moon Specials," as they're called, offer a great way to get out on the water, especially compared to the usual hourly rates of $130 during the weekdays and $165 on weekends; think of it as a "cheap splurge." Visit the website or call to find out about upcoming tours.

Tours launch from South Beach Harbor near Pier 40 on the Embarcadero. ✆ 408/910-0095. www.sfsailtours.com.

Swim Art If you're brave, you might want to check out Swim Art, which offers open-water group swimming sessions in the Bay. Group swims are $10, with sessions offered during both summer and winter. Just don't forget your wet suit.

✆ 415/299-9098. http://swim-art.com.

YOGA AND TAI CHI

Taking time to destress and improve your health? Sounds like a winning combination. Yoga and tai chi promote both, with yoga the more aerobic option and tai chi focusing on gentle, flowing movements.

Mission Yoga If you're ready to feel the heat, Mission Yoga is the place to be, with Bikram yoga courses offered up to six times a day. New-student specials are offered at the can't-be-beat price of $30 for

30 days, and donation-based classes in the studio's sunroom are also available. Just drop in and pay what you can.

2390 Mission St. (at 20th St.). ✆ **415/401-YOGA** (401-9642). www.bikramyoga mission.com.

★ **Purusha Yoga** FREE How typically San Francisco does yoga in the park sound? Free yoga classes are offered in Golden Gate Park on Saturday mornings. Class begins at 11am and students meet at the park's Botanical Gardens entrance.

Near 9th Ave. and Lincoln Way. ✆ **617/359-3404.** www.purushayoga.com.

Sivananda Yoga Vedanta Center FREE The center provides free meditation classes every day, and open house events featuring a 90-minute yoga class are held about once a month.

1200 Arguelle Blvd. ✆ **415/681-2731.** www.sfsivananda.org.

Free Classes in the (Sports) Basement

It's possible to do a lot more at the Sports Basement than pick up a new pair of running shoes. The sports equipment retailer offers a number of community services, including **free yoga classes** on Sundays at 9am. Call the number below for the latest schedule. It's at 610 Old Mason St. in the Presidio. ✆ **415/437-0100.** www.sports basement.com.

★ **Tai Chi in the Parks** FREE Tai chi classes sponsored by the Mayor's Office of Criminal Justice are offered free of charge throughout the week in a number of the city's parks. Locations include the Golden Gate Park Senior Center and Spreckels Lake, Pilgrim Community Center, West Portal Playground, and Brooks Park. There's no need to register; just show up and dress comfortably. Call or visit the website below for schedules.

✆ **415/584-8366.** www.sfnpc.org/taichi.

Yoga Garden of San Francisco FREE The Yoga Garden offers a free introduction to yoga workshop every few months. Classes are small and advanced registration is required. Just bring yourself, in comfortable clothing, and everything else will be provided.

286 Divisadero St. ✆ **415/552-9644.** http://yogagardensf.com.

Tee Time on the Cheap

In San Francisco, golfing isn't merely the domain of the privileged. The city and county count six municipal golf courses under the jurisdiction of the Recreation and Parks departments (though Sharp Park Golf Course is farther south in Pacifica), and residents—and their pocketbooks—can benefit from using city greens. To qualify as a resident, players will need to obtain golf resident cards. Benefits include advanced reservations and discounts.

Gleneagles Golf Course

Located in McLaren Park at the far southern part of the city, the par-36 course is a challenging one, with moderate to heavy forestation and rolling, sometimes steep, hills. A 9-hole game during the week runs for $15, and 18 holes is $23. On weekends (Fri–Sun), the prices rise to $19 and $31, respectively. 2100 Sunnydale Ave. (btw Brookedale and Persia sts.). ✆ **415/587-2425.** www.gleneaglesgolfsf.com.

Golden Gate Park Golf Course

Playing a 9-hole game right in the park will set you back just $10 on the weekdays if you're a resident and $12 on the weekends. A twilight game's even cheaper, at $7 during the week and $10 on weekends. Near 47th Avenue and Fulton Street. ✆ **415/751-8987.** www.goldengateparkgolf.com.

Harding Park and Fleming Golf Courses

San Francisco residents can play an 18-hole game at Harding, on the border of Lake Merced, for $46 during the week, with weekend tee time coming in at $59. The 9-hole Fleming course is $20 for residents during the week and $22 on the weekends. Skyline Boulevard and Harding Road. ✆ **415/664-4690.** www.harding-park.com.

Lincoln Park Golf Course

Weekdays for residents at 18-hole Lincoln Park cost $21, and weekends are $26. Players won't be able to miss the great views of the city and Golden Gate Bridge. 34th Avenue and Clement Street. ✆ **415/221-9911.** www.lincolnparkgc.com.

Yoga Tree Beginners can get an introduction and seasoned yoga practitioners can refresh their skills through a 2-hour Yoga 101 Workshop, priced at $35. At the conclusion of the workshop, students will receive a free week of unlimited classes at all of Yoga Tree's four locations.

519 Hayes St. (btw Octavia and Laguna sts.). ✆ **415/626-9707.** Also at 780 Stanyan St. (btw Waller and Beulah sts.), ✆ 415/387-4707; 1234 Valencia St. (btw 23rd and 24th sts.), ✆ 415/647-9707; and 97 Collingwood St. (at 18th St.), ✆ 415/701-YOGA (701-9642). www.yogatreesf.com.

From the hip to the absurd to the erotic, you'll find all kinds of fun bargains in San Francisco's shops, galleries and malls.

7 SHOPPING

For some people bargain hunting is a way of life. Just the thought of paying full price gives them the heebie-jeebies. It's the thrill of the chase they seek, such as unearthing a perfectly fitting pair of Jimmy Choos from the depths of the Neiman Marcus bargain box. "Victory is mine!" she shouts as she floats past the other suckers paying retail.

If you're this person (and you know you are), then you'll love bargain hunting in San Francisco, where the shopping scene is incredibly diverse. Every style, era, fetish, and financial status is represented here—not in big, homogenous shopping malls, but in hundreds of

10 Souvenirs under $15 (Some under $10!)

- $6 Golden Gate Bridge playing cards, mug, or kitchen towel at the Golden Gate Bridge Gift Shop (south end of GGB; ✆ 415/923-2333).
- $5 limited-edition souvenir cable car tickets (collect all four!) at the Powell Street or Hyde Street cable car ticket booths.
- $13 Ghirardelli Cable Car Tin containing 17 individually wrapped assorted-flavor chocolates at Ghirardelli Square (p. 88).
- $11 giant fortune cookie at Mee Mee Bakery, 1328 Stockton St., between Broadway and Vallejo streets in Chinatown (✆ 415/362-3253).
- $8 black-and-white posters of Jack Kerouac and Neal Cassady (looking rather James Deanish) at City Lights bookstore in North Beach (p. 214).
- $12 1-pound bag of Sumatra beans from Peet's Coffee & Tea, way better than anything Starbucks ever sold.
- $8.75 Tin Toy Cable Car with Ringing Bell at the Cable Car Museum gift shop (p. 81).
- $6 Barry Bonds 700 Home Run Commemorative Cap (was $20!) at the Giant Dugout store, 24 Willie Mays Plaza (✆ 415/972-2000).
- $10 Chinese Baoding Balls (aka exercise balls, meditation balls, medicine balls, health balls) or various other related trinkets in Chinatown.

boutiques and secondhand stores scattered throughout the city. Whether it's a Chanel knockoff or Chinese herbal medicine you're looking for, San Francisco's got it.

San Francisco is also loaded with thrift stores and secondhand clothing stores, a prime source of cool couture for local hipsters (though prices on hip quasi-vintage clothing can be steep). Haight, Valencia, and Mission streets are the best spots for super scores. For discounts on all kinds of new merchandise, there are several factory outlets South of Market (see Dirt-Cheap Shopping Zones below), though it's not what it used to be since all those condo towers were built and filled with Gucci-toting DINKS.

Whatever. Just pick a shopping neighborhood, give yourself a spending budget, and you're sure to end up with at least a few affordable take-home treasures.

1 Dirt-Cheap Shopping Zones

San Francisco has many shopping areas, but the following places are where you'll find the best deals.

UNION SQUARE & ENVIRONS If you have to ask, you can't afford it. Keep walking.

CHINATOWN Chinatown is one of the most popular neighborhoods among tourists, though the bounty to be found here is often of dubious value—souvenirs made in Taiwan, jade jewelry at a discount, or XXX-rated fortune cookies. Hand-painted signs swear that everybody is going out of business and must sell everything at incredibly low prices right now. Sidewalk stalls are stuffed with every plastic and rubber item ever sold for less than $5. Herbalists sell dragon's blood and other exotic ingredients next to vegetable stands, jewelry stores, banks, and dim sum parlors. There are some fun bazaars, though, and the smells alone are worth the visit. Grant Avenue is the area's main thoroughfare, and the side streets between Bush Street and Columbus Avenue are full of restaurants, markets, and eclectic shops. Stockton Street is best for grocery shopping (including live fowl and fish). Walking is best, since traffic through this area is slow at best and parking is next to impossible. Most stores in Chinatown are open daily from 10am to 10pm. Take bus no. 1, 9X, 15, 30, 41, or 45.

UNION STREET Oh-so-prettified Union Street (btw Van Ness Ave. and Fillmore St.) has become rather old hat and overpriced, a favorite haunt of well-heeled tourists and visiting suburbanites. Union Street's shops seem to sell stuff from everywhere but San Francisco—New York bagels, Seattle coffee, European clothes. It's also a great place to find top-quality children's clothing and toys or just watch the beautiful people parade by. Take bus no. 22, 41, 45, 47, 49, or 76.

CHESTNUT STREET Parallel and a few blocks north, Chestnut is a younger version of Union Street. It holds endless shopping and dining choices, and an ever-tanned, superfit population of postgraduate singles who hang around cafes and scope each other out. Take bus no. 22, 28, 30, 43, or 76.

FILLMORE STREET Fillmore Street (btw Sutter and Jackson sts.) is the nouveau-chic area that's on the verge of becoming the next Union Street. A few short years ago, when there were just a handful of interesting shops and cafes—and D & M Wine and Liquor Co., the best wine store in the city—some of the merchants tried to establish this small patch of real estate as part of wealthy Pacific Heights rather than the notoriously slummy Fillmore District. They succeeded. Now you have to wait in line to get a cup of coffee on a Sunday morning, the bars are jammed with GQ-model look-alikes, and the sidewalks are congested with yuppie baby strollers. Still, some of the best looky-loo shopping in town is packed into 5 blocks of Fillmore Street. Most of the wares for sale ain't cheap, but a girl can dream, can't she? Take bus no. 1, 2, 3, 4, 12, 22, or 24.

HAIGHT STREET Haight Street ain't what it used to be, but it's still quasi-psychedelic and filled with people and things you certainly won't see in Kansas. Vintage clothing stores are a big thing, but the value ranges from great deals on retro fashions to ridiculously overpriced castoffs. Don't get caught paying $75 for a used Levi's jacket just because some guy with a mohawk cut the sleeves off it. If you're looking for avant-garde new clothing and shoes, this is the place. And if you're a man looking for a pair of shimmering red cha-cha heels in a perfect size 12, this may be the only place. Most of the shops are between Central and Stanyan streets. Bus nos. 6, 7, 66, and 71 run the length of Haight Street, and nos. 33 and 43 run through upper Haight Street. The Muni streetcar N line stops at Waller Street and Cole Street.

SOMA Although this area isn't suitable for strolling, you'll find almost all the discount shopping in warehouse spaces south of Market: Jeremys, Burlington Coat Factory, Loehmann's, and so on. This is the district to go to if you really need to get stuff done discount-shopping-wise.

HAYES VALLEY The Hayes Valley (Hayes St. btw Franklin and Buchanan sts.) is a happy byproduct of the 1989 earthquake, which brought down a nearby freeway and let the sunshine in. It's fun, hip, eclectic, friendly, and not yet full of itself, mainly because it's not the prettiest area in town, with some of the shadier housing projects a few blocks away. But while most neighborhoods cater to more conservative or trendy shoppers, lower Hayes Street, between Octavia and Gough, celebrates anything vintage, artistic, or downright funky. Still in its developmental stage, it's definitely the most interesting new shopping area in town, with furniture and glass stores, thrift shops, trendy shoe stores, and men's and women's clothiers. You can find lots of great antiques shops south on Octavia and on nearby Market Street. Take bus no. 16AX, 16BX, or 21.

FISHERMAN'S WHARF & ENVIRONS The tourist-oriented malls along Jefferson Street include hundreds of shops selling your typical tourist schlock. Oddly enough, I found a camera shop here selling Nikons at dirt-cheap prices, so there are deals to be found here.

Just the Facts: Hours, Taxes & Shipping

Store hours are generally Monday through Saturday from 10am to 6pm and Sunday from noon to 5pm. Most department stores stay open later, as do shops around Fisherman's Wharf, the most heavily visited area (by tourists). Sales tax in San Francisco is 8.5%, which is added on at the register for all goods and services purchased. If you live out of state and buy an expensive item, you might want to have the store ship it home for you. You'll have to pay for shipping, but you'll escape paying the sales tax. Most of the city's shops can wrap your purchase and ship it anywhere in the world. If they can't, you can send it yourself, through UPS (✆ 800/742-5877), FedEx (✆ 800/463-3339), or the U.S. Postal Service.

THE MISSION DISTRICT The Mission District (btw 16th and 24th sts.) is a weird and wonderful place to shop, if you can handle being on two planets at once. Mission Street has the tightest cocktail dresses and shiniest spiked-heel shoes in town, alongside pure white confirmation and wedding dresses. Valencia Street sells used books and new vibrators, candles for Catholic and other rituals, expensive clothes that look like they've already been through the wringer, antiques, and thrift shop treasures.

NORTH BEACH North Beach will never leave you bored, with everything from beatnik bookstores and hippie poster shops to tattoo parlors and record stores. You can buy postcards, wigs, shoestrings, old clothes, new clothes, incense, bells, beads, crystals, jewelry, pasta machines, furniture, focaccia, and anything else you can imagine—even a new set of boccie balls.

THE RICHMOND/SUNSET Much of the shopping in these districts is largely residential enclaves. Sunset's shopping zone is concentrated around 9th Avenue and Irving Street. The N-Judah streetcar travels right to this corner. The magic shop **Misdirections** (p. 225) is the single best reason to head out this way (when's the last time you were in a magic shop?). On the Richmond side of the park, Clement Street is the prime retail area, starting at Arguello Street and heading south. This area is similar to Chinatown, only less crowded and more eclectic. The mix of stores includes terrific used bookstores and eclectic Chinese shops selling cheap knickknacks. Parking is metered and easiest to find before 10:30am. The no. 38-Geary bus stops 1 block to the south.

2 Bargain Shopping from A to Z

ART

★ Catharine Clark Gallery Catharine Clark's is a different kind of gallery experience. Although many galleries focus on established artists and out-of-this-world prices, Catharine's exhibits works by up-and-coming contemporary as well as established artists (mainly from California). It nurtures beginning collectors by offering a purchasing plan that's almost unheard of in the art business. You can buy a piece on layaway and take up to a year to pay for it—interest free! Prices here make art a realistic purchase for almost everyone for a change, but serious collectors also frequent the shows because Clark has such a keen eye for talent. Shows change every 6 weeks. Open Tuesday through Friday 10:30am to 5:30pm and Saturday 11am to 5:30pm. Closed Sunday and Monday. 150 Minna St., ground floor (btw Third and New Montgomery sts.). ✆ **415/399-1439.** www.cclarkgallery.com.

★ Hang Check out this amazingly affordable gallery for attractive pieces by yet-to-be-discovered Bay Area artists. The staff is friendly and helpful, and the gallery is designed to cater to new and seasoned collectors who appreciate original art at down-to-earth prices. 556 Sutter St. ✆ **415/434-4264.** www.hangart.com.

ART & CRAFT SUPPLIES

★ **Cliff's Variety** This store is loaded with amusing, useful, necessary, or just plain fun items, among them art supplies. The store is half a block from the Castro Street Muni Station. 479 Castro St. (btw 17th and 18th sts.). ✆ **415/431-5365.** www.cliffsvariety.com.

Discount Fabrics In addition to pretty good deals on dressmaking and upholstery fabric, these stores stock notions and craft supplies. 525 4th St. ✆ **415/495-4201.** Other locations are at 1432 Haight St., ✆ 415/621-5584; 2315 Irving St., ✆ 415/564-7333; and 525 4th St., ✆ 415/495-4201.

Flax If you go into an art store for a special pencil and come out $300 later, don't go near this shop. Flax has everything you can think of in art and design supplies, an amazing collection of blank bound books, children's art supplies, frames, calendars—you name it. You could lose yourself here just looking at all the pens, not to mention the papers, and ribbons. There's a gift for every type of person here at every price range. 1699 Market St. (at Valencia and Gough sts.). ✆ **415/552-2355.** www.flaxart.com.

Mendel's Art Supplies & Far Out Fabrics Providing exactly what the name says, this is a fun place to shop because it's packed with cool merchandise, from hemp twine to fake fur and a crazy array of fabrics. If you're looking to create your own costume from scratch, this is the place to go. 1556 Haight St. (btw Ashbury and Clayton sts.). ✆ **415/621-1287.** www.mendels.com.

★ **SCRAP** A beloved resource for teachers, artists, and creative locals, SCRAP (Scroungers' Center for Reusable Art Parts) is a center for recycled fabric, wood, paper, and other bits and bobs usable for various creations. Prices are very low. Closed Monday, Friday, and Sunday. 801 Toland St. (btw McKinnon and Newcomb aves.). ✆ **415/647-1746.** www.scrap-sf.org.

BOOKS

In addition to the listings below, there's a **Barnes & Noble** superstore at 2550 Taylor St., between Bay and North Point streets, near Fisherman's Wharf (✆ **415/292-6762**); and a four-storied **Borders** at 400 Post St., at Union Square (✆ **415/399-1633**).

Book Passage If you're moseying through the Ferry Building Marketplace, drop into this cozy independent that emphasizes (for tourists and locals alike) local travel, boating on the Bay, food, cooking, sustainable agriculture and ecology, fiction, culinary and regional history and literature, and photo and gift books about the Bay Area. The store also hosts lots of author events; check their website for details. Ferry Building Marketplace (at the Embarcadero and Market St.). ✆ **415/835-1020.** www.bookpassage.com.

The Booksmith Haight Street's best selection of new books is in this large, well-maintained shop. It carries all the top titles, along with works from smaller presses, and more than 1,000 different magazines. 1644 Haight St. (btw Clayton and Cole sts.). ✆ **800/493-7323** or 415/863-8688.

★ **City Lights Booksellers & Publishers** Brooding literary types browse this famous bookstore owned by Lawrence Ferlinghetti, the renowned Beat Generation poet. The three-level bookshop prides itself on a comprehensive collection of art, poetry, and political paperbacks, as well as more mainstream books. The first all-paperback bookstore in San Francisco, this city institution dates to 1953. At the time, most people thought hardcover books were superior to paperbacks in terms of both the quality of the content and the quality of the paper. Ferlinghetti challenged this attitude and made great literature available to everyone by stocking his bookstore with less-costly paperback editions. The San Francisco Board of Supervisors recently designated the store a cultural and architectural landmark, assuring a long and happy life for the building. Ferlinghetti's brainchild is also on its way to becoming a national historic site. Open daily from 10am to midnight. 261 Columbus Ave. (at Broadway). ✆ **415/362-8193.** www.citylights.com.

Comic Outpost Comic books, sports and fantasy cards, and models are the draw to get you out into this Sunset District shop. 2381 Ocean Ave. (btw Paloma Ave. and San Fernando Way). ✆ **415/337-6754.** www.comicoutpost.net.

Cover to Cover Booksellers This little bookstore sold so many copies of the first two Harry Potter books that J. K. Rowling did a book signing and reading here, much to the delight of every child in Noe Valley. 1307 Castro St. (at 24th St.). ✆ **415/282-8080.** www.covertocoversf.com.

★ **Green Apple Books** The local favorite for used books, Green Apple is crammed with titles—more than 60,000 new and 100,000 used books and DVDs. Its extended sections in psychology, cooking, art, and history; collection of modern first editions; and rare graphic comics are superseded only by the staff's superlative service. 506 Clement St. (at Sixth Ave.). ✆ **415/387-2272.** www.greenapplebooks.com.

Isotope Comics Popular with collectors of Silver Age comics, the store also carries Japanese Manga and animation video, action figures, and accessories. 326 Fell St. (at Gough St.). ✆ **415/621-6543.** www.isotopecomics.com.

Modern Times Bookstore This collectively owned progressive bookstore in the Mission stocks fiction and nonfiction for adults and children, plus an extensive collection of books in Spanish. 888 Valencia St. ✆ **415/282-9246.** www.mtbs.com.

CONSIGNMENT STORES

★ **GoodByes** One of the best new- and used-clothes stores in San Francisco, GoodByes carries only high-quality clothing and accessories, including an exceptional selection of men's fashions at unbelievably low prices (for example, $350 preowned shoes for $35). Women's wear is in a separate boutique across the street. 3464 Sacramento St. and 3483 Sacramento St. (btw Laurel and Walnut sts.). ✆ **415/346-6388.** www.goodbyessf.com.

★ **The Next-to-New Shop & Consignment Boutique** Everything from grandma's Tiffany china and Chanel jewelry to Jimmy Choo shoes and Ferragamo flats is sold at bargain prices at the boutique consignment store that uses the proceeds to benefit community programs. It's a great place to stylishly supplement your work wardrobe or spiffy up your apartment. Furniture and household items are sold as well, but it's mostly about the clothes. 2226 Fillmore St. (btw Sacramento and Clay sts.). ✆ **415/567-1627.**

Repeat Performance Everything sold at the consignment boutique benefits the San Francisco Symphony. The books, clothing, home accessories, jewelry, furniture, china, strollers, shoes, and such sold here are of higher quality (and price) than the thrift stores, particularly the formalwear. 2436 Fillmore St. (btw Jackson and Washington sts). ✆ **415/563-3123.**

COSTUMES

Costumes on Haight This is a must-stop for anyone caught short without a Paris Hilton mask or fright wig. With more than 1,000 costumes and accessories galore, it's a hoot to look around. 735 Haight St. ✆ **415/621-1356.**

DISCOUNT CLOTHING

Burlington Coat Factory Warehouse As its name hints, you'll find hundreds of coats—from cheapies to designer—as well as men's and women's clothing, shoes, and accessories. But the best deal is the home section, where designer bedding, bath accessories, and housewares go for a fraction of their normal retail prices. 899 Howard St. (at Fifth St.). ✆ **415/495-7234.** www.coat.com.

Isda & Co. Outlet The discount manufacturers based South of Market have made bargain shopping in San Francisco a popular pursuit. This store in South Park, a little subneighborhood south of Market, carries fashionable women's wear suitable for the office and after-hours at outlet prices. 21 S. Park (at 2nd St.). ✆ **415/512-1610.** www.isda-and-co.com.

Jeremys This boutique is a serious mecca for fashion hounds thanks to the wide array of top designer fashions, from shoes to suits, at rock-bottom prices. There are no cheap knockoffs here, just good men's and women's clothes and accessories that the owner scoops up from major retailers who are either updating merchandise or discarding returns. 2 S. Park (btw Bryant and Brannan sts. at Second St.). ✆ **415/882-4929.** www.jeremys.com.

Loehmann's San Francisco's branch of Loehmann's—the nation's only upscale off-price specialty retailer—caters to a sophisticated white-collar crowd, offering professional clothing, shoes, and accessories at bargain prices. Be sure to check out the Back Room, where designer clothes are sold for 30% to 65% less than the Union Square department stores. 222 Sutter St. (btw Kearny St. and Grant Ave.). ✆ **415/982-3215.** www.loehmanns.com.

★ **Nordstrom Rack** Okay, I'm letting you in on my sorta-secret place to buy high-quality clothes at steep discounts. Nordstrom Rack, the off-price division of Nordstrom, Inc., first opened in the basement of a downtown Seattle store in 1975 as a clearance department, and since then it's become so popular it's grown into its own division. The

Rack carries merchandise from Nordstrom stores and Nordstrom.com at 50% to 60% off original Nordstrom prices—brand-name apparel, accessories, shoes, accessories, bath and beauty products, home accents, and so on. Heck, they even offer in-store alterations and tailoring at a competitive cost. 555 9th St. (btw Brannan and Bryant sts.). ✆ **415/934-1211.** www.store.nordstrom.com.

Rolo Garage The sign out front always says that everything in the entire store is 50% off and they're not kidding. You'll find deep discounts on Rolo's line of urban street wear and accessories. Still, $50 for a $100 pair of designer jeans seems pretty steep. 1301 Howard St. (at Ninth St.). ✆ **415/861-1999.** www.rolo.com.

FASHION

American Rag Cie Fashionistas flock to this find, on an unlikely stretch of busy Van Ness, for vintage and new duds sure to make you look street-swank. Check it out for everything from Juicy Couture to Paul & Joe and from European vintage to modern masters such as Diesel. If you're looking to find a hip T-shirt (an Obama Hope shirt, for instance) to go with your overpriced Lucky jeans, this is the place. 1305 Van Ness Ave. (at Sutter St.). ✆ **415/474-5214.**

★ **H & M** This ever-trendy and cheap Swedish clothing chain opened in Union Square at the end of 2004, and had lines out the door all through the holiday season—and not just for their collection by Stella McCartney. Drop in anytime for trendy cuts and styles sure to satisfy the hip him and her along on the trip. 150 Powell St. (btw Ellis and O'Farrell sts.). ✆ **415/986-4215.**

★ **RAG** If you want to add some truly unique San Francisco designs to your closet, head to RAG, or Residents Apparel Gallery, a co-op shop where around 55 local emerging designers showcase their latest

XOX-Rated Truffles

If you're anywhere near North Beach, you really should treat yourself to a truffle. **XOX Truffles** (754 Columbus Ave.; ✆ **415/421-4814**) is a tiny store devoted to nickel-sized truffles in a huge assortment of flavors. These bites of bliss are all handmade under the direction of a French chef, who removed himself from the rigors of the restaurant world to bring pleasure to us chocoholics. It's open Monday through Saturday from 9am to 6pm.

creations. Prices are great; fashions are forward, young, and hip; and if you grab a few pieces, no one at home's going to be able to copy your look. 541 Octavia St. (at Hayes St.). © **415/621-7718.** www.ragsf.com.

Zara Think Banana Republic at a much better price. It's hard to resist the designer knockoffs at this ultracool retailer selling affordable designer fashions from Spain. Service sucks though. 250 Post St. © **415/399-6930.** A 2nd location is at Westfield San Francisco Centre, 865 Market St. © 415/817-5021.

FLEA MARKET

Alemany Flea Market Get an early start on Sunday mornings for the one local, regularly scheduled flea market within city limits. Sellers take up position in a giant parking lot off I-280, at the southern edge of Bernal Heights (below the Mission District). There's a hodgepodge of junk including furniture and tools. The same site hosts the Alemany Farmers' Market, a smaller counterpart to the one at the Ferry Building, on Saturdays from 6am to 5pm. 100 Alemany Blvd., at the Hwy. 101/I-280 Interchange. © **415/647-2043.**

FOOD

Boulangerie A bit of Paris on Pine Street, this true-blue bakery sells authentically French creations, from delicious and slightly sour French country wheat bread to rustic-style desserts, including the locally famous *cannelés de Bordeaux,* custard baked in a copper mold. And if you're looking for a place to eat Boulangerie bread and pastries, visit their cafes—**Boulange de Polk,** at 2310 Polk St. near Green Street (© **415/345-1107**), or **Boulange de Cole,** at 1000 Cole St. at Parnassus Street (© **415/242-2442**). Closed Monday. 2325 Pine St. (at Fillmore St.). © **415/440-0356,** ext. 204. www.baybread.com.

★ **Cowgirl Creamery Cheese Shop** San Francisco is fanatical about cheese, and much of the local enthusiasm can be attributed to the two women who created the small-production Cowgirl Creamery, located in the Ferry Building Marketplace but still imparting the simple neighborhood shop feel. Here's how you do it: Sample, then buy a hefty slice of your favorite cheese, then enjoy it on the waterfront with some crusty Acme Bread and a piece of fruit from Capay Farms (all within the same building). Ferry Building Marketplace, no. 17. © **415/362-9354.** www.cowgirlcreamery.com.

★ **Ferry Building Marketplace** A one-stop shop for some of the city's finest edibles, the renovated historic Ferry Building is home to the revered Acme Bread Company, Scharffen Berger Chocolate, the Imperial Tea Court, Peet's Coffee, Cowgirl Creamery Cheese Shop (see above), Recchiuti Confections, and more. There's no better place to load up on the Bay Area's outstanding bounty. Ferry Building Plaza (at the foot of Market St. at the Embarcadero). ✆ **415/693-0996.** www.ferrybuildingmarketplace.com.

Golden Gate Fortune Cookies Co. This tiny, touristy factory sells fortune cookies hot off the press. You can purchase them in small bags or in bulk, and you can even bring your own messages and watch them being folded into fresh cookies before your eyes. Even if you're not buying, stop in to see how these sugary treats are made (although the staff can get pushy for you to buy). Open daily until 8:30pm. 56 Ross Alley (btw Washington and Jackson sts.). ✆ **415/781-3956.**

★ **Joseph Schmidt Confections** Here, chocolate takes the shape of exquisite sculptural masterpieces—such as long-stemmed tulips and heart-shaped boxes—that are so beautiful, you'll be hesitant to bite the head off your adorable panda bear. Once you do, however, you'll know why this is the most popular—and reasonably priced—chocolatier in town. 3489 16th St. (at Sanchez St.). ✆ **800/861-8682** or 415/861-8682. www.josephschmidtconfections.com.

Ten Ren Tea Co., Ltd. At the Ten Ren Tea Co. shop, you will be offered a steaming cup of tea when you walk in the door. In addition to a selection of almost 50 traditional and herbal teas, the company stocks a collection of cold tea drinks and tea-related paraphernalia, such as pots, cups, and infusers. If you can't make up your mind, take home a mail-order form. The shop is open daily from 9am to 9pm. 949 Grant Ave. (btw Washington and Jackson sts.). ✆ **415/362-0656.** www.tentea.com.

GAMES

GameScape This great store features specialty games and is run by folks who take their games seriously. There are so many games packed into this store that it's a bit overwhelming if you don't know exactly what you're looking for. 333 Divisadero St. (at Fell St.). ✆ **415/621-4263.**

Amazing Grazing

There's no better way to spend a sunny Saturday morning in San Francisco than to stroll the Ferry Building Marketplace and Farmers' Market, snacking your way through some of America's finest organic produce—it's one of the most highly acclaimed farmers' markets in the United States. While foraging among the dozens of stalls crammed with Northern California fruit, vegetables, bread, shellfish, and dairy items, you're bound to bump elbows with the dozens of Bay Area chefs (such as Alice Waters) who do their shopping here. The enthusiastic vendors are always willing to educate visitors about the pleasures of organic produce, and often provide free samples. It's a unique opportunity for city dwellers to buy freshly picked organic produce directly from small family-operated farms.

On Saturday mornings the market is in its full glory. Nearly the entire building is enrobed with local meat ranchers, artisan cheese makers, bread bakers, specialty food purveyors, and farmers. On Saturdays make sure you arrive by 10:30am to watch "Meet The Farmer," a half-hour interview with one of the farmers, food artisans, or other purveyors who give the audience in-depth information about how and where their food is produced. Then, at 11am, Bay Area chefs give cooking demonstrations using ingredients purchased that morning from the market (you get to taste their creations and then leave with the recipe in hand). Several local restaurants also have food stalls selling their cuisine—including breakfast items—so don't eat before you arrive. You can also pick up locally made vinegars, preserves, herbs, and oils, which make wonderful gifts.

If you decide you want a local foodie to lead you on a culinary excursion of the Marketplace and Farmers' Market, my friend Lisa

GIFTS

★ **The Canton Bazaar** Amid a wide variety of handicrafts, here you'll find an excellent selection of inexpensive silk items—lanterns, kimonos, blouses, handbags—from mainland China. Everything sold

Rogovin, an "Epicurean Concierge" and founder of "In the Kitchen with Lisa," offers guided culinary excursions. Some of Lisa's top noshing tips include these:

- Mortgage Lifter heirloom tomatoes dipped in special Rosemary Salt from Eatwell Farm.
- Creamy and sweet Barhi dates from Flying Disk Ranch, spread on an épi baguette from Acme Bread Company with a touch of fresh Panir cheese from Cowgirl Creamery.
- Whatever's in season at Hamada Farms, such as their Tahitian pomelos and Oro Blanco grapefruits.
- Fleur de Sel chocolates at Recchiuti Confections.
- Scharffen Berger's Bittersweet Mocha chocolate bars made with ground Sumatra coffee beans from Peet's Coffee & Tea.
- Warm liquid Valrhona chocolate at Boulette's Larder (nirvana, she says).
- For more information about Lisa's guided culinary tours, log onto her website at www.inthekitchenwithlisa.com, or call her at ✆ **415/806-5970**.

The Ferry Building Marketplace is open Monday through Friday from 10am to 6pm, Saturday from 9am to 6pm, and Sunday from 11am to 5pm. The Farmers' Market takes place year-round, rain or shine, every Tuesday and Saturday from 10am to 2pm. From spring to fall it also runs on Thursdays from 4 to 8pm and Sundays from 10am to 2pm. The Ferry Building is located on the Embarcadero at the foot of Market Street (about a 15-min. walk from Fisherman's Wharf). Call ✆ **415/693-0996** for more information or log onto www.ferryplazafarmersmarket.com or www.ferrybuildingmarketplace.com.

here is great for gifts because they'll assume you spent way more than you did. Open daily until 10pm. 616 Grant Ave. (btw Sacramento and California sts.). ✆ **415/362-5750.** www.cantonbazaar.com.

Chong Imports This basement-level treasure-trove of assorted crap . . . er . . . imported items is one of the best places in Chinatown to find inexpensive gifts and housewares. 838 Grant Ave. (btw Clay and Washington sts.). ✆ **415/982-1432.**

Cost Plus World Market At the Fisherman's Wharf cable car turntable, Cost Plus is a vast warehouse crammed to the rafters with Chinese baskets, Indian camel bells, Malaysian batik scarves, and innumerable other inexpensive items from Algeria to Zanzibar. More than 20,000 items from 50 nations, imported directly from their countries of origin, pack this warehouse. There's also a decent discount wine shop here. It's open Monday through Saturday from 9am to 9pm and Sunday from 10am to 8pm. 2552 Taylor St. (btw N. Point and Bay sts.). ✆ **415/928-6200.**

★ **Dandelion** Tucked in an out-of-the-way location in SoMa is the most wonderful collection of gifts, collectibles, and furnishings. There's something for every taste and budget here, from an excellent collection of teapots, decorative dishes, and gourmet foods to silver, books, cards, and picture frames. Don't miss the Zen-like second floor, with its peaceful furnishings in Indian, Japanese, and Western styles. The store is closed Sunday and Monday except during November and December, when it's open daily. Hours are 10am to 6pm. 55 Potrero Ave. (at Alameda St.). ✆ **415/436-9500.** www.dandelionsf.com.

Distractions This is the best of the Haight Street shops selling underground-rave wear, street fashion, and electronica CDs. You'll find pipes, toys, and stickers liberally mixed with lots of cool stuff to look at. 1552 Haight St. (btw Ashbury and Clayton sts.). ✆ **415/252-8751.**

Good Vibrations Don't be afraid to ask when you're at Good Vibrations, an airy, comfortable bookstore/sex-toy shop owned and run by women. Their mail-order business is one of the most successful in the country, but this flagship store in the Mission District is still small,

An Unusual Museum

The **Good Vibrations** sex-toy shop (603 Valencia St. at 17th St., ✆ **415/522-5460**; www.goodvibes.com) is worth visiting just to see their vibrator museum.

personal, and as far from sleazy as you could possibly get. The clientele is primarily women, but the books and toys are for both sexes. 603 Valencia St. (at 17th St.). ✆ **415/522-5460** or 800/BUY-VIBE (289-8423) (for mail order). www.goodvibes.com. A 2nd location is at 1620 Polk St. (at Sacramento St.). ✆ 415/345-0400.

Just for Fun & Scribbledoodles Stationery, cards, frames, board games, *Mad Lib* books, elegant journals, and other gift items are what you'll find at this popular Noe Valley store. 3982 24th St. (btw Noe and Sanchez sts.). ✆ **415/285-4068.** www.justforfun.invitations.com.

Kárikter Comics for adults are a booming business, and San Francisco sells more than its share. Union Square's Kárikter offers a complete library of beautifully illustrated books about the popular European comic book adventurers Tin Tin and Asterix; it's the only official Tin Tin store in the United States. Kárikter stocks the books in a variety of languages—*The Little Prince* in French, for example—along with watches, luggage, clocks, and other collectibles. The store's staff is helpful and friendly, and there are even beanbag chairs up front to curl up in as you read. 418 Sutter St. (at Stockton St.). ✆ **415/434-1120.** www.karikter.com.

Kati Koos Need a little humor in your life? Previously called Smile, this store specializes in whimsical art, furniture, clothing, jewelry, and American crafts guaranteed to make you grin. It's a great source for inexpensive gifts. Closed Sunday. 500 Sutter St. (btw Powell and Mason sts.). ✆ **415/362-3437.** www.katikoos.com.

★ **Soko Hardware** You'd never guess it from the name, but this Japantown store is the Wal-Mart of Japanese housewares, selling a dizzying array of ceramic plates, tea sets, sake cups, as so on—all of which make terrific gifts (well, it was *meant* to be a gift, but it's mine now!). 1698 Post St. (btw Buchanan and Laguna sts.). ✆ **415/931-5510.**

Tai Yick Trading Company This is a real find for tiny china tea sets, miniature Chinese bowls, and all kinds of porcelain and pottery. It's a good Chinatown store for cheap household goods. 1400 Powell St. (at Broadway St.). ✆ **415/986-0961.** www.taiyick.com.

HOUSEWARES/FURNISHINGS

Alessi Italian designer Alberto Alessi, who's known for his whimsical and colorful kitchen-utensil designs, such as his ever-popular spider-like lemon squeezer, opened a flagship store here. Drop by to drool over the $500 gorgeous stainless-steel double boilers and head home with a nifty $10 salt-and-pepper set or designer fly swatter (for reals!). 424 Sutter St. (at Stockton St.). © **415/434-0403.** www.alessi.com.

Big Pagoda Company When I need to buy a stylish friend a gift, I head to this downtown Asian-influenced design shop for cool, unique, and contemporary finds. Within the bi-level boutique, East meets West and old meets new in the form of anything from an antique Chinese scholar's chair to a new wave table that hints at Ming or Mondrian. Its furniture and glass art are hardly cheap (an antique Tibetan dragon head goes for $30,000), but you can get fabulous designer martini glasses at $15 a pop. Open Monday through Saturday 10am to 6pm. 310 Sutter St. (at Grant St.). © **415/296-8881.** www.bigpagoda.com.

★ **Propeller** This airy skylight-lit shop is a must-stop for lovers of the latest in übermodern furniture and home accessories. Owner/designer Lorn Dittfeld handpicks pieces done by emerging designers from as far away as Sweden, Italy, and Canada, as well as a plethora of national newbies. Drop in to lounge on the hippest sofas and browse the table filled with pretty and practical gifts like ultracool magnetic spice racks (and tell Lorn that Matt Poole says hello). 555 Hayes St. (btw Laguna and Octavia sts.). © **415/701-7767.** www.propellermodern.com.

The Wok Shop This shop has every conceivable implement for Chinese cooking, including woks, brushes, cleavers, circular chopping blocks, dishes, oyster knives, bamboo steamers, and strainers. It also sells a wide range of kitchen utensils, baskets, handmade linens, and aprons from China—all at sweatshop prices. 718 Grant Ave. (at Clay St.). © **415/989-3797** or 888/780-7171 for mail order. www.wokshop.com.

Zinc Details This is one of those kinds of stores that you want to check out even if you can't afford anything it sells. Zinc, a contemporary furniture and knickknack shop, has received accolades everywhere from *Elle Decor Japan* to *Metropolitan Home* to *InStyle* for its amazing collection of glass vases, pendant lights, ceramics from all over the world, and furniture from local craftspeople. A portion of these true works of art is made specifically for the store. While you're in the 'hood, check out their sister store around the corner at 2410 California St. (✆ **415/776-9002**), which showcases contemporary designer furniture. 1905 Fillmore St. (btw Bush and Pine sts.). ✆ **415/776-2100.** www.zincdetails.com.

MAGIC SHOPS

House of Magic Plenty of gag gifts and sleight-of-hand tricks are on hand to wow your friends and work mates. Rubber masks, wigs, and very real-looking spiders are stocked as well. 2025 Chestnut St. ✆ **415/346-2218.**

Misdirections All the rubber masks, tasteless jokes, novelties, and magic books a country magician needs in order to survive. Closed Mondays. 1236 9th Ave. ✆ **415/566-2180.**

MUSEUM STORES

Asian Art Museum Store You'll find a small selection of inexpensive Sino souvenirs here, from books and posters to occasional origami kits or other exhibition-related items. 200 Larkin St. ✆ **415/581-3600.**

de Young Museum Store Downstairs, this creative museum shop carries inspired art books, posters, and postcards, as well as exotic instruments from around the world (all certified as "fairly traded" to boot). Upstairs, sleek housewares like Scandinavian cutting boards or Japanese bowls tempt bargain shoppers. Golden Gate Park, 50 Hagiwara Tea Garden Dr. ✆ **415/863-3330.**

★ **Exploratorium** The shop inside this science center is well stocked with brainy games, toys, books, and crafts, with curb appeal for kids of all ages. In fact, you'll likely be as tempted by the offerings as the kids. 3601 Lyon St. (at Marina Blvd.). ✆ **415/397-5673.** www.exploratorium.edu.

Museum of the African Diaspora MoAD's gift shop is petite, but includes some interesting books on Africa and African Americans and a collection of adorable beaded African dolls. 685 Mission St. ✆ **415/358-7200.**

★ **SFMOMA MuseumStore** With an array of artistic cards, books, jewelry, housewares, furniture, knickknacks, and creative tokens of San Francisco, it's virtually impossible not to find something here you'll consider a must-have gift or souvenir (check out the San Francisco FogDome, a clever take on the snow globe!). Aside from being one of the locals' favorite shops, it offers far more tasteful mementos than most Fisherman's Wharf schlock. FYI, their satellite shop at SFO's International terminal is a great place to kill time. Open late (until 9:30pm) on Thursday nights. 151 Third St. (2 blocks south of Market St., across from Yerba Buena Gardens). ✆ **415/357-4035.** www.sfmoma.org.

MUSIC

Amoeba Records Don't be scared off by the tattooed, pierced, and fierce-looking employees in this beloved new and used record store highlighting indie labels. They're actually more than happy to recommend some great music to you. If you're looking for the latest from Britney, this might not be the store for you (though they *do* have everything), but if you're into interesting music that's not necessarily on every station all the time, check this place out. You can buy, sell, and trade in this cavernous, loud Haight Street hot spot. 1855 Haight St. (btw Shrader and Stanyan sts.). ✆ **415/831-1200.**

I Play a Mean *Guzheng*

The **Clarion Music Center** in Chinatown offers $15 group classes on how to play the Chinese *erhu* (two-string fiddle), *guzheng* (zither), and *w* (flute). The classes are held every Saturday from 5 to 6:30pm and beginners are welcome. For more information call ✆ **415/391-1317** or log onto www.clarionmusic.com. Better yet, just show up at 816 Sacramento St. (btw Grant Ave. and Waverly Place) on Saturday evening with $15 in cash.

★ **Recycled Records** Easily one of the best used-record stores in the city, this loud shop in the Haight has cases of used "classic" rock LPs, sheet music, and tour programs. It's open from 10am to 8pm daily. 1377 Haight St. (btw Central and Masonic sts.). ✆ **415/626-4075.** www.recycledrecords.com.

Streetlight Records Overstuffed with used music in all three formats, this place is best known for its records and excellent CD collection. It also carries new and used DVDs and computer games. Rock music is cheap, and the money-back guarantee guards against defects. 3979 24th St. (btw Noe and Sanchez sts.). ✆ **415/282-3550.** www.streetlightrecords.com. A 2nd location is at 2350 Market St. (btw Castro and Noe sts.). ✆ 415/282-8000.

Virgin Megastore With thousands of CDs, including an impressive collection of imports, videos, DVDs, a multimedia department, a cafe, and related books, this enormous Union Square store can make any music lover blow his or her entire vacation fund. It's open Sunday through Thursday from 10am to 11pm and Friday and Saturday from 10am to midnight. 2 Stockton St. (at Market St.). ✆ **415/397-4525.**

MUSICAL INSTRUMENTS

★ **Clarion Music Center** This fascinating Chinatown store/museum stocks dozens of unusual instruments, including didgeridoos, taiko drums, flutes, and shakers from every culture. It's also great for CDs and unique knickknacks/gifts like Chinese lion dance masks. 816 Sacramento St. (btw Grant Ave. and Waverly Place). ✆ **415/391-1317.** www.clarionmusic.com.

SHOES

DSW Shoe Warehouse This big Union Square discount emporium can be a hit-or-miss shopping experience. The best deals are down in the clearance basement, where prices are reduced another 30%. Both men's and women's brand-name shoes ranging from sneakers to pumps and dress shoes are sold. 111 Powell St. (btw Ellis and O'Farrell sts.). ✆ **415/445-9511.** www.dswshoe.com.

Skechers USA I'll save you the trouble of searching for a cheap shoe store in SF. Head straight for the sale rack at this Mission District outlet and complete your wardrobe for under $20 (for shoes usually going for $80 or more). And these aren't just urban sneakers, mind you, but also quality leather dress shoes, platform sandals, flats, and boots that I've seen for sale at Macy's for five times the price. And that "half off second pair" deal always suckers me in. 2600 Mission St. ✆ **415/401-6211.** A 2nd location is at 770 Market St. ✆ **415/781-8703.**

SPORTS STORES

Hi's Tackle Box This all-purpose supplier of fishing gear draws enthusiasts from around the Bay Area. I get most of my best free fishing tips from this place. 3141 Clement St. ✆ **415/221-3825.**

Purple Skunk *The* hot spot for longboards, skateboards, and snowboards, with a hip, helpful staff. 5820 Geary Blvd. (btw 22nd and 23rd aves.). ✆ **415/668-7905.** www.purpleskunk.com.

REI This San Francisco branch of this preeminent sporting goods/outdoor adventure store always has a few bargains, but you really need to shop around. I always spend more than I can afford here but dammit I need those crampons. 840 Brannan St. ✆ **415/934-1938.**

Skates on Haight The premier place for skates, skateboards, and skate rentals. 1818 Haight St. ✆ **415/752-8375.**

★ **Sports Basement** Never mind that signs on the walls still read FROZEN FOODS and BAKERY at this former military PX in the Presidio. This place now stocks the best-priced selection of sporting goods in town and has a huge free parking lot to boot. 1590 Bryant St. (at 15th St.). ✆ **415/575-3000.** A 2nd location is in Potrero Hill, 610 Old Mason St. (at the Marina Green). ✆ 415/437-0100. www.sportsbasement.com.

THRIFT STORES

Clothes Contact This Mission District thrift shop sells most of its used clothing by the pound ($10 per), which sounds terrific until you put an old leather bomber jacket on the scale and see how much it weighs. They specialize in themed dress-up stuff—Laverne and Shirley, '70s prom, naughty nurse—and it's the go-to place when you're looking for Halloween get-ups, theme parties, or something weird to wear at Bay to Breakers. 473 Valencia St. (at 16th St.). ✆ **415/621-3212.**

Community Thrift Store This massive Mission District thrift store relies entirely on donations to stock its shelves. It's sort of junky (I wouldn't suggest trying on the clothes), but there's a great book and record section here along with the occasional choice piece of vintage furniture or light fixture. 623 Valencia St. (btw 17th and 18th sts.). ✆ **415/861-4910.** www.communitythriftsf.org.

Goodwill Stores You already know how this one works: hit-or-miss secondhand shopping, but when you score a hit, the price is definitely right. There are eight Goodwill Stores scattered through the city. 820 Clement St.; 3801 Third St.; 1700 Fillmore St.; 1580 Mission St.; 2279 Mission St.; 822 Geary Blvd.; 1700 Haight St.; 61 W. Portal. © **415/575-2101.** www.goodwill.org.

Thrift Town The unique thing about this Mission District thrift store is its grab bag section in the rear, with items stuffed into sealed plastic bags to be sold for a dollar or two. It's also the place to go if you're looking to furnish your apartment as cheaply as possible. 2101 Mission St. (at 17th St.). © **415/861-1132.** www.thrifttown.com.

TOYS

★ **Ambassador Toys** Classic European dolls, wonderful wooden toys and puzzles, and clever games and books are among the great playthings at this fantastic toy store. The clerks are happy to wrap gifts as well. 186 W. Portal Ave. (at 14th Ave.). © **415/759-8697.** A 2nd location is at 2 Embarcadero Center (at Market St.). © 415/345-8697. www.ambassadortoys.com.

The Chinatown Kite Shop This shop's playful assortment of flying objects includes attractive fish kites, windsocks, hand-painted Chinese paper kites, wood-and-paper biplanes, pentagonal kites, and do-it-yourself kite kits, all of which make great souvenirs or decorations. Prices range from $8 for a 60-inch handmade Tiger Kite to $300 for a gnarly computer-designed Powerfoil. Open daily from 10am to 8pm. 717 Grant Ave. (btw Clay and Sacramento sts.). © **415/391-8217.** www.chinatownkite.com.

Puppets on the Pier I actually go to this PIER 39 store to find gifts for my niece and nephew. From kittens, bunnies, and puppies to whales, dragons, and even cockroaches, the collection of puppets is amazing. PIER 39, Beach at Embarcadero. © **415/781-4435.**

VINTAGE CLOTHING

Aardvark's One of San Francisco's largest secondhand clothing dealers, Aardvark's has seemingly endless racks of shirts, pants, dresses, skirts, and hats from the past 30 years. It's open daily from 11am to 7pm. 1501 Haight St. (at Ashbury St.). © **415/621-3141.**

Buffalo Exchange This large and newly expanded storefront on upper Haight Street is crammed with racks of antique and new fashions from the 1960s, 1970s, and 1980s. It stocks everything from suits and dresses to neckties, hats, handbags, and jewelry. Buffalo Exchange anticipates some of the hottest new street fashions. 1555 Haight St. (btw Clayton and Ashbury sts.). ✆ **415/431-7733.** A 2nd shop is at 1210 Valencia St., at 24th St. ✆ 415/647-8332. www.buffaloexchange.com.

Crossroads Trading Co. Unlike other thrift stores, Crossroads gets some of its merchandise from wholesalers, so you'll also find new items in various sizes. There are four locations in the city, but the best selection is in the Haight. You can sell or trade your clothes here as well, but you'll only get about 35% of what they'll sell it for. 1519 Haight St. (at Ashbury St.). ✆ **415/355-0555.** Other locations are at 2123 Market St., ✆ 415/552-8740; 1901 Fillmore St., ✆ 415/775-8885; 555 Irving St., ✆ 415/681-0100. www.crossroadstrading.com.

La Rosa On a street packed with vintage-clothing shops, this is one of the more upscale options. Since 1978, it has featured a selection of high-quality, dry-cleaned secondhand goods. Formal suits and dresses are its specialty, but you'll also find sport coats, slacks, and shoes. The more moderately priced sister store, **Held Over,** is located at 1543 Haight St., near Ashbury (✆ **415/864-0818**); and their discount store, **Clothes Contact,** is located at 473 Valencia St., at 16th Street (✆ **415/621-3212**). 1711 Haight St. (at Cole St.). ✆ **415/668-3744.**

Wasteland The tatted staff here is choosy about what used clothes it'll take in, so clothing and accessories here are hip and retro at the same time. Not everything on the rack is a bargain, however. 1660 Haight St. (btw Belvedere and Cole sts.). ✆ **415/863-3150.** www.thewasteland.com.

WINE & SAKE

True Sake Amid woven sea grass flooring, colorful back-lit displays, and a so-hip Hayes Valley location are more than 140 varieties of Japanese-produced sake ranging from an $8 300ml bottle of Ohyama to a $180 720ml bottle of Kotsuzumi Rojohanaari—which, incidentally, owner Beau Timken (who is on hand to describe each wine) says is available at no other retail store in the U.S. 560 Hayes St. (btw Laguna and Octavia sts.). ✆ **415/355-9555.** www.truesake.com.

Wine Club San Francisco The Wine Club is a discount warehouse that offers bargains on more than 1,200 domestic and foreign wines. Bottles cost between $4 and $1,100. 953 Harrison St. (btw Fifth and Sixth sts.). ✆ **415/512-9086.**

Why not climb some of the city's hills on one of our itineraries designed to show you several different sides of San Francisco?

ITINERARIES FOR THE INDIGENT (OR THRIFTY)

There are some cities that are best seen on foot, and San Francisco is one of them. Unlike sprawling metropolises such as Los Angeles or Dallas, whose seemingly boundless boundaries blur the line between city and suburbia, San Francisco is constrained by bay and sea to a mere 47 square miles of increasingly coveted real estate.

And yes, you'll have to walk up and down a few hills, but don't let that deter you from one of San Francisco's greatest free pleasures—leisurely strolling around the neighborhoods and soaking in the sights and sounds. Listed below are three of my favorite neighborhoods for touring in bipedal fashion, plus a bonus tour of the best bike ride of your life.

Right, then: Let's get started.

1 Getting to Know North Beach

Start:	Intersection of Montgomery Street, Columbus Avenue, and Washington Street.
Finish:	Washington Square.
Time:	Three hours, including a stop for lunch.
Best Times:	Monday through Saturday between 11am and 4pm.
Worst Times:	Sunday, when shops are closed.
Hills That Could Kill:	The Montgomery Street hill from Broadway to Vallejo Street; otherwise, this is an easy walk.

Along with Chinatown, North Beach is one of the city's oldest neighborhoods. Originally the Latin Quarter, it became the city's Italian district when Italian immigrants moved "uphill" in the early 1870s, crossing Broadway from the Jackson Square area and settling in. They quickly established restaurants, cafes, bakeries, and other businesses familiar to them from their homeland. The "Beat Generation" helped put North Beach on the map, with the likes of Jack Kerouac and Allen Ginsberg holding court in the area's cafes during the 1950s. Although most of the original Beat poets are gone, their spirit lives on in North Beach, which is still a haven for bohemian artists and writers. The neighborhood, thankfully, retains its Italian village feel; it's a place where residents from all walks of life enjoy taking time for conversation over pastries and frothy cappuccinos.

1 Transamerica Pyramid
If there's one landmark you can't miss, it's the familiar building on the corner of Montgomery Street and Columbus Avenue, the Transamerica Pyramid (take bus no. 15, 30X, or 41 to get there). Noted for its spire (which rises 212 ft. above the top floor) and its "wings" (which begin at the 29th floor and stop at the spire), this pyramid is San Francisco's tallest

ITINERARY 1: NORTH BEACH

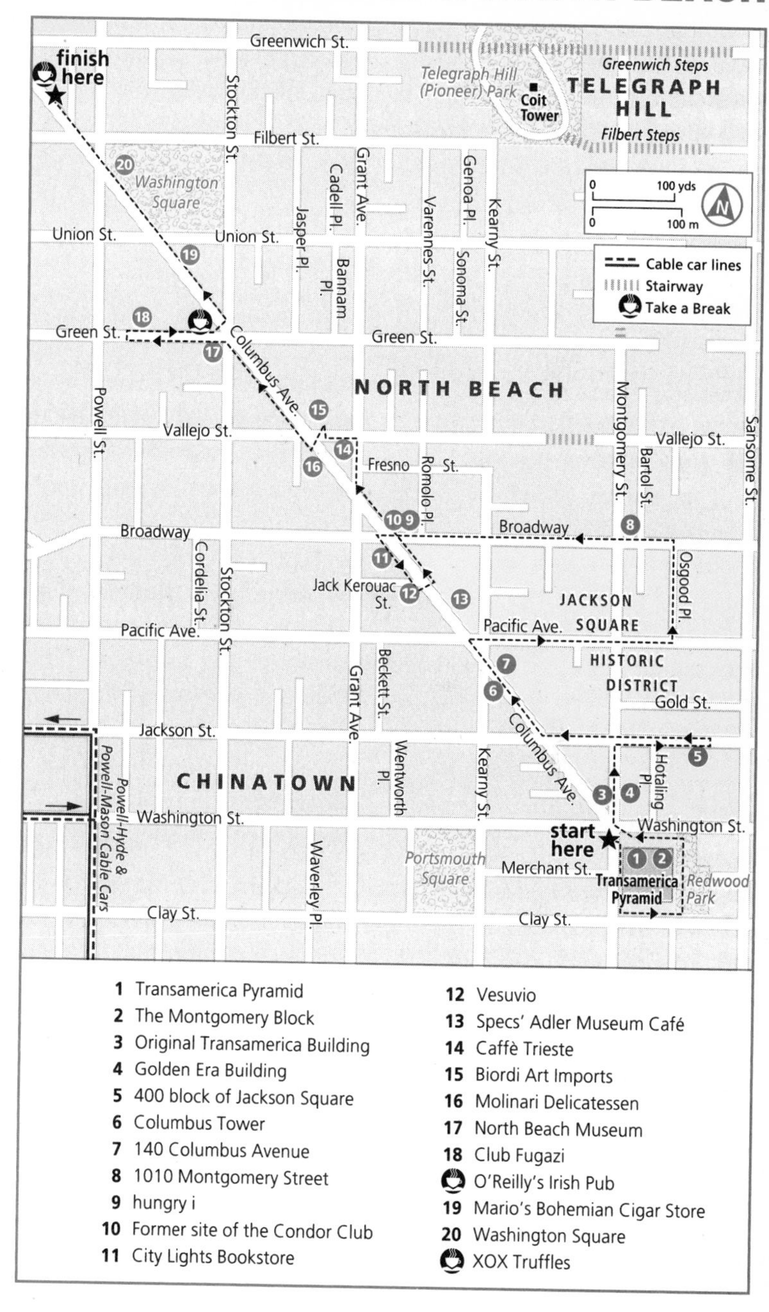

building and a hallmark of the skyline. You might want to take a peek at one of the rotating art exhibits in the lobby or go around to the right and into ½-acre Redwood Park, which is part of the Transamerica Center. The Transamerica Pyramid occupies part of the 600 block of Montgomery Street, which once held a historic building called the Montgomery Block.

2 The Montgomery Block

Originally four stories high, the Montgomery Block was the tallest building in the West when it was built in 1853. San Franciscans called it "Halleck's Folly" because it was built on a raft of redwood logs that had been bolted together and floated at the edge of the ocean (which was right at Montgomery St. at that time). The building was demolished in 1959 but is fondly remembered for its historical importance as the power center of the city. Its tenants included artists and writers of all kinds, among them Jack London, George Sterling, Ambrose Bierce, Bret Harte, and Mark Twain. This is a picturesque area, but there's no particular spot to direct you to. It's worth looking around, however, if only for the block's historical importance. From the southeast corner of Montgomery and Washington streets, look across Washington to the corner of Columbus Avenue, and you'll see the original Transamerica Building, located at 4 Columbus Ave.

3 Original Transamerica Building

The original Transamerica Building is a Beaux Arts flatiron-shaped building covered in terra cotta; it was also the home of Sanwa Bank and Fugazi Bank. Built for the Banco Populare Italiano Operaia Fugazi in 1909, it was originally a two-story building and gained a third floor in 1916. In 1928, Fugazi merged his bank with the Bank of America, which was started by A. P. Giannini, who also created the Transamerica Corporation. The building now houses a Church of Scientology. Cross Washington Street and continue north on Montgomery Street to no. 730, the Golden Era Building.

4 Golden Era Building

Erected around 1852, this San Francisco historic landmark building is named after the literary magazine *The Golden Era,* which was published here. Some of the young writers who worked on the magazine were known as "The Bohemians"; they included Samuel Clemens (also known as Mark Twain) and Bret Harte (who began as a typesetter here). Backtrack a few dozen feet and stop for a minute to admire the exterior of the annex, at no. 722, which, after years of neglect and lawsuits, has finally been stabilized and is going to be developed. The Belli Annex, as it is currently known, is registered as a historic landmark. Continue north on Washington Street, and take the first right onto Jackson Street. Continue until you hit the 400 block of Jackson Square.

5 400 Block of Jackson Square

Here's where you'll find some of the only commercial buildings to survive the 1906 earthquake and fire. The building at no. 415 Jackson (ca. 1853) served as headquarters for the Ghirardelli Chocolate Company from 1855 to 1894. The Hotaling Building (no. 451) was built in 1866 and features pediments and quoins of cast iron applied over the brick walls. At no. 441 is another of the buildings that survived the disaster of 1906. Constructed between 1850 and 1852 with ship masts for interior supporting columns, it served as the French Consulate from 1865 to 1876. Cross the street, and backtrack on Jackson Street. Continue toward the intersection of Columbus Avenue and Jackson Street. Turn right on Columbus and look across the street for the small triangular building at the junction of Kearny Street and Columbus Avenue, Columbus Tower (also known as the Sentinel Building).

6 Columbus Tower

If you walk a little farther, and then turn around and look back down Columbus, you'll be able to get a better look at Columbus Tower. The flatiron beauty, a building shaped to a triangular site, went up between 1905 and 1907. Movie director and producer Francis Ford Coppola bought and restored it in the mid-1970s; it is now home to his film production company, American Zoetrope Studios. The building's cafe showcases all things Rubicon (Coppola's winery)—including olive oil, Parmesan cheese, and wine. It's a great place to stop for a glass of wine, an espresso, or a thin-crusted pizza snack. Across the street from Columbus Tower on Columbus Avenue is 140 Columbus Ave.

7 140 Columbus Ave.

Although it was closed for a few years, the **Purple Onion** (© **415/956-1653**), famous for its many renowned headliners who often played here before they became famous, is again host to an eclectic mix of music and comedy. Let's hope the next Phyllis Diller, who's now so big that she's famous for something as simple as her laugh—and who was still struggling when she played a

2-week engagement here in the late 1950s—will catch her big break here, too. Continue north on Columbus, and then turn right on Pacific Avenue. After you cross Montgomery Street, you'll find brick-lined **Osgood Place** on the left. A registered historic landmark, it is one of the few quiet—and car-free—little alleyways left in the city. Stroll up Osgood and go left on Broadway to 1010 Montgomery St. (at Broadway).

8 1010 Montgomery St.

This is where Allen Ginsberg lived when he wrote his legendary poem, "Howl," first performed on October 13, 1955, in a converted auto-repair shop at the corner of Fillmore and Union streets. By the time Ginsberg finished reading, he was crying and the audience was going wild. Jack Kerouac proclaimed, "Ginsberg, this poem will make you famous in San Francisco." Continue along Broadway toward Columbus Avenue. This stretch of Broadway is San Francisco's answer to New York's Times Square, complete with strip clubs and peep shows that are being pushed aside by restaurants, clubs, and an endless crowd of visitors. It's among the most sought-after locations in the city as more and more profitable restaurants and clubs spring up. Keep walking west on Broadway, and on the right side of the street, you'll come to **Black Oak Books,** 540 Broadway. It sells new and used discount books and is worth a quick trip inside for a good, cheap read. A few dozen yards farther up Broadway is the current location of the hungry i.

9 hungry i

Now a seedy strip club (at 546 Broadway), the original hungry i (at 599 Jackson St., which is under construction for senior housing) was owned and operated by the vociferous "Big Daddy" Nordstrom. If you had been here while Enrico Banducci was in charge, you would have found only a plain room with an exposed brick wall and director's chairs around small tables. A Who's Who of nightclub entertainers fortified their careers at the original hungry i, including Lenny Bruce, Billie Holiday (who first sang "Strange Fruit" there), Bill Cosby, Richard Pryor, Woody Allen, and Barbra Streisand. At the corner of Broadway and Columbus Avenue, you will see the former site of the Condor Club.

10 Former Site of the Condor Club

The Condor Club was located at 300 Columbus Ave.; this is where Carol Doda scandalously bared her breasts and danced topless for the first time in 1964. Note the bronze plaque claiming the Condor Club as BIRTHPLACE OF THE WORLD'S FIRST TOPLESS & BOTTOMLESS ENTERTAINMENT. Go inside what is now the Condor Sports Bar and have a look at the framed newspaper clippings that hang around the dining room. From the elevated back room, you can see Doda's old dressing room and, on the floor below, an outline of the piano that would descend from the second floor with her atop it. When you leave the Condor Sports Bar, cross to the south side of Broadway. Note the mural of jazz musicians painted on the entire side of the building directly across Columbus Avenue. Diagonally across the intersection from the Condor Sports Bar is the City Lights bookstore.

11 City Lights Booksellers & Publishers

Founded in 1953 and owned by one of the first Beat poets to arrive in San Francisco, Lawrence Ferlinghetti, City Lights is now a city landmark and literary mecca. Located at 261 Columbus Ave., it's one of the last of the Beat-era hangouts in operation. An active participant in the Beat movement, Ferlinghetti established his shop as a meeting place where writers and bibliophiles could (and still do) attend poetry readings and other events. A vibrant part of the literary scene, the well-stocked bookshop prides itself on its collection of art, poetry, and political paperbacks. Upon exiting City Lights bookstore, turn right, cross aptly named Jack Kerouac Street, and stop by Vesuvio, the bar on your right.

12 Vesuvio

Because of its proximity to City Lights bookstore, Vesuvio became a favorite hangout of the Beats. Dylan Thomas used to drink here, as did Jack Kerouac, Ferlinghetti, and Ginsberg. Even today, Vesuvio, which opened in 1949, maintains its original bohemian atmosphere. The bar is located at 255 Columbus Ave. (at Jack Kerouac St.) and dates from 1913. It is an excellent example of pressed-tin architecture. Facing Vesuvio across Columbus Avenue is another favorite spot of the Beat Generation:

13 Spec's Adler Museum Café

Located at 12 Saroyan Place, this is one of the city's funkiest bars, a small, dimly lit watering hole with ceiling-hung maritime flags and exposed brick walls crammed with memorabilia. Within the bar is a minimuseum that consists of a few glass cases filled with mementos brought by seamen who frequented the pub from the '40s and onward. From here, walk back up Columbus across Broadway to

Grant Avenue. Turn right on Grant, and continue until you come to Vallejo Street. At 601 Vallejo St. (at Grant Ave.) is Caffè Trieste.

14 Caffè Trieste

Yet another favorite spot of the Beats and founded by Gianni Giotta in 1956, Caffè Trieste is still run by family members. The quintessential San Francisco coffeehouse, Trieste features opera on the jukebox, and the real thing, performed by the Giottas, on Saturday afternoons. Any day of the week is a good one to stop in for a cappuccino or an espresso—the beans are roasted right next door. Go left out of Caffè Trieste onto Vallejo Street, turn right on Columbus Avenue, and bump into the loveliest shop in all of North Beach, Biordi Art Imports, located at 412 Columbus Ave.

15 Biordi Art Imports

This store has carried imported hand-painted majolica pottery from the hill towns of central Italy for more than 50 years. Some of the colorful patterns date from the 14th century. Biordi handpicks its artisans, and its catalog includes biographies of those who are currently represented. Across Columbus Avenue, at the corner of Vallejo Street, is the Molinari Delicatessen.

16 Molinari Delicatessen

This deli, located at 373 Columbus Ave., has been selling its pungent, air-dried salamis since 1896. Ravioli and tortellini are made in the back of the shop, but it's the mouthwatering selection of cold salads, cheeses, and marinades up front that captures the attention of most folks. Each Italian sub is big enough for two hearty appetites. Walk north to the lively intersection of Columbus, Green, and Stockton streets, and look for the U.S. Bank at 1435 Stockton St. On the second floor of the bank, you'll find the North Beach Museum.

17 North Beach Museum

The North Beach Museum displays historical artifacts that tell the story of North Beach, Chinatown, and Fisherman's Wharf. Just before you enter the museum, you'll find a framed, handwritten poem by Lawrence Ferlinghetti that captures his impressions of this primarily Italian neighborhood. After passing through the glass doors, visitors see many photographs of some of the first Chinese and Italian immigrants, as well as pictures of San Francisco after the 1906 earthquake. You can visit the museum any time the bank is open (unfortunately, it's closed on weekends), and admission is free. Now backtrack toward Columbus Avenue and go left on Green Street to Club Fugazi, at 678 Green St.

18 Club Fugazi

It doesn't look like much from the outside, but Fugazi Hall was donated to the city (and more important, the North Beach area) by John Fugazi, the founder of the Italian bank that was taken over by A. P. Giannini and turned into the original Transamerica Corporation. For many years, Fugazi Hall has been staging the zany and whimsical musical revue *Beach Blanket Babylon*. The show evolved from Steve Silver's Rent-a-Freak service, which consisted of a group of partygoers who would attend parties dressed as any number of characters in outrageous costumes. The fun caught on and soon became *Beach Blanket Babylon*.

If you love comedy, you'll love this show. We don't want to spoil it for you by telling you what it's about, but if you get tickets and they're in an unreserved-seat section, you should arrive fairly early because you'll be seated around small cocktail tables on a first-come, first-served basis. (Two sections have reserved seating, four don't, and all of them frequently sell out weeks in advance; however, sometimes it is possible to get tickets at the last minute on weekdays.) You'll want to be as close to the stage as possible. This supercharged show (www.beachblanketbabylon.com) is definitely worth the price of admission, which ranges from $25 to $78, depending on the day of the week and your seat. As you come out of O'Reilly's, turn left, cross Columbus Avenue, and then take a left onto Columbus. Proceed 1 block northwest to Mario's Bohemian Cigar Store.

Take a Guinness Break!

Head back the way you came on Green Street. Before you get to Columbus Avenue, you'll see O'Reilly's Irish Pub (622 Green St.), a homey watering hole that dishes out good, hearty Irish food and a fine selection of beers.

19 Mario's Bohemian Cigar Store

Located at 566 Columbus Ave., across the street from Washington Square, this is one of North Beach's most popular neighborhood hangouts. No, it does not sell cigars, but the cramped and casual space overlooking Washington Square does sell killer focaccia sandwiches, coffee drinks, beer, and wine. Our next stop, directly across Union Street, is Washington Square.

20 Washington Square

This is one of the oldest parks in the city. The land was designated a public park in 1847 and has undergone many changes since then. Its current landscaping dates from 1955. You'll notice **Saints Peter and Paul Church** (the religious center for the neighborhood's Italian community) on the northwest end. Take a few moments to go inside and check out the traditional Italian interior. Note that this is the church in which baseball great Joe DiMaggio married his first wife, Dorothy Arnold. He wasn't allowed to marry Marilyn Monroe here because he had been divorced. He married Monroe at City Hall and came here for publicity photos.

Today the park is a pleasant place in which to soak up the sun, read a book, or chat with a retired Italian octogenarian who has seen the city grow and change.

From here, you can see the famous Coit Tower at the top of Telegraph Hill to the northwest. If you'd like to get back to your starting point at Columbus and Montgomery streets, walk south (away from the water) on Columbus.

. . . Now a Chocolate Break!

Celebrate such a wonderful walking tour with a chocolate treat at **XOX Truffles** (754 Columbus Ave., btw Filbert and Greenwich), home of the finest handmade chocolate truffles in San Francisco.

2 A Bayside Stroll Along the Embarcadero

Start:	AT&T Park.
Finish:	Aquatic Park.
Time:	Half a day.
Best Time:	Any warm weekday.
Worst Time:	Any summer Saturday when PIER 39 is packed with tourists.
Hills That Could Kill:	None.

If you've had it with the all those hills, you'll appreciate this easy and quite flat 3-mile stroll along the Embarcadero, heading northwest through Fisherman's Wharf and culminating at the base of a steep little

ITINERARY 2: THE EMBARCADERO & FISHERMAN'S WHARF

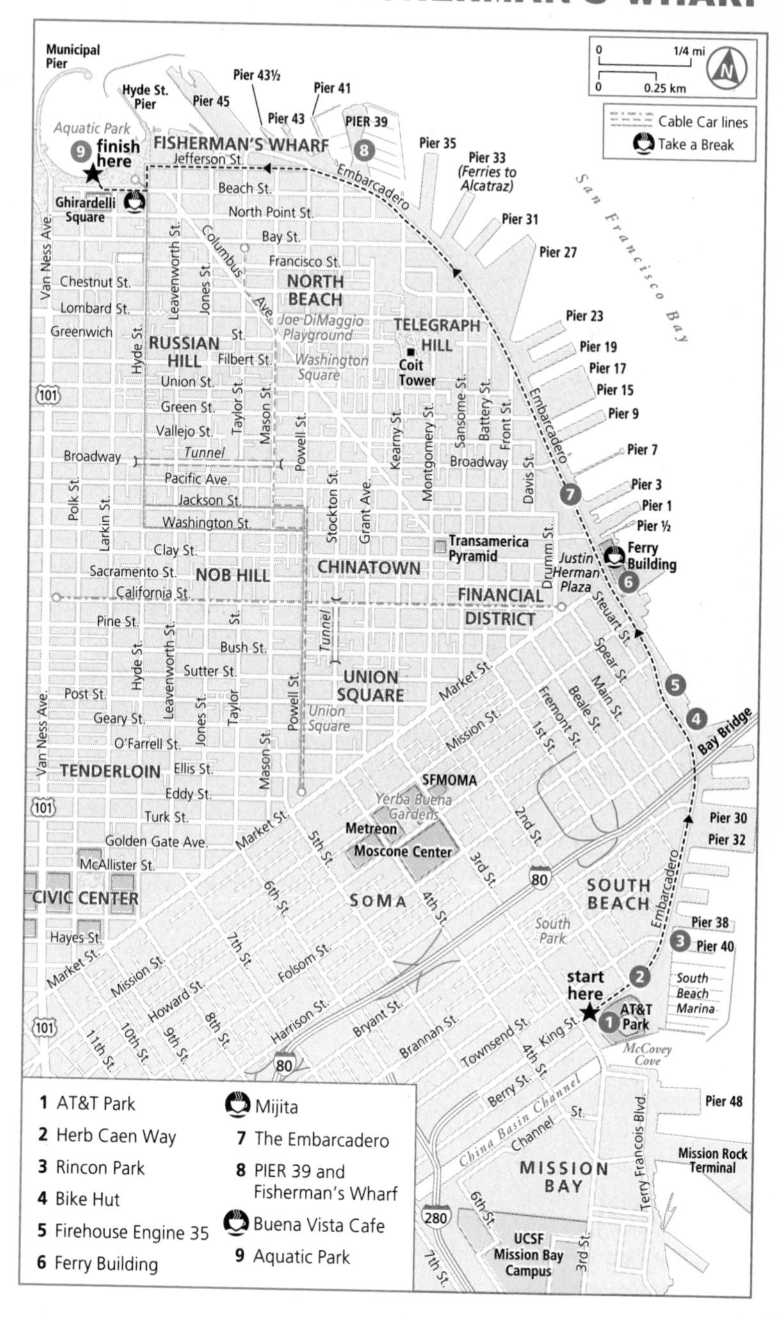

hill that you can give the finger to. With stops to eat and drink, it should take you about half a day, and there's even a little reward at the end: a visit to the Buena Vista Café for the perfect pick-me-up—an eye-opening Irish Coffee topped with fresh whipped cream.

1 AT&T Park

To get to AT&T Park, take the closest Muni streetcar. All the underground streetcars, except certain N-Judah trains, end at the Embarcadero Station. If you are not already on an N-Judah that goes to the Mission Bay/Cal Train Station, cross to the other side of the platform at the Embarcadero Station and board one. As you come out from below ground, look for the large brick Hills Plaza, at 345 Spear St., constructed in 1925. Just south of this national landmark building is AT&T Park, home of the heartbreaking San Francisco Giants baseball team, located at 2nd and King streets, was the first privately financed major-league baseball park since Dodger Stadium in 1962. From the stadium, walk north on:

2 Herb Caen Way

This section of the Embarcadero honors the departed newspaper columnist Herb Caen, who reported on the city's movers and shakers and wrote about San Francisco with humor and passion for 50 years. Next you'll come to:

3 Rincon Park

This park contains a giant bow-and-arrow sculpture by internationally renowned artists Claes Oldenburg and Coosje van Bruggen called Cupid's Span. At 60 feet tall and 140 feet wide, it's hard to miss. The sculpture was commissioned by Donald and Doris Fisher, founders of Gap Inc., who donated it to the City of San Francisco. Continuing along the Embarcadero, the next landmark you come to on Pier 40 is the:

4 Bike Hut

The owner of this not-for-profit shop hires and trains at-risk youth to repair bikes, and he's a bit of a character in his own right. If you decide to abandon your walk in favor of a bike ride, you can rent a bike for $5 an hour or $20 per day. Fees include a lock and helmet. Open daily 10am to 6pm (✆ **415/543-4335;** www.thebikehut.com). Continue down the Embarcadero toward the Bay Bridge. On your right is Pier 24, the home of:

5 Firehouse Engine 75

Peek through the fence to see Fireboat 1. If you've ever wondered what happens if a ship catches fire in the bay, now you know. The view opens up as you pass the bridge. Sailboats ply the water, bicyclists and skaters zip by, and coming into view is the:

6 Ferry Building

Built in 1898, this building was once the city's transportation hub. Today, the elegantly refurbished building houses some of the best gourmet food stores in the city. Before 2pm on Tuesdays, Saturdays, and spring and fall Sundays, you'll find a terrific farmers' market here (also on Thurs evenings in spring and fall). Saturdays are the big day, with musicians strumming in the back area while you enjoy free samples of ripe fruits, roasted nuts, and local cheeses.

Taco or Burrito Break!

On Saturdays, buy breakfast from one of the restaurant carts behind the Ferry Building. Grab a bench and enjoy a mouth-watering meal as you watch the ferries come and go. At other times, one of the best bargains in the Ferry Building is **Mijita,** with its inexpensive but top-quality Mexican specialties such as fresh fish tacos and hearty burritos, all enjoyed with a view of the bay.

7 The Embarcadero

Continue northwest, along the Embarcadero. The entire stretch of oceanfront walkway between the Ferry Building and Fisherman's Wharf is a magnet for pedestrians, cyclists, and runners. What you will find along this stretch of city, in addition to views of the bay and urban skyline, are several 13-foot-tall metal pylons and bronze plaques embedded in the sidewalk. The pylons and plaques are imprinted with photographs, drawings, poetry, and historical facts about the waterfront. Continue along the water until you get to:

8 PIER 39 & Fisherman's Wharf

The distance from Pier 7 to PIER 39 is less than a mile, but as you approach Fisherman's Wharf the activity level rises dramatically. The number of people waiting for ferries to Alcatraz or Sausalito, combined with tourists milling around the boardwalk, gives a carnival-like feel to the atmosphere. Once you pass the masses on Jefferson Street, the crowd thins and the city begins to feel like it's yours again by the time you reach the end of this stroll at:

9 Aquatic Park

Just past Hyde Street Pier is Aquatic Park, where you'll see a grassy area, a long curved pier, some cement bleachers, and a small strip of man-made beach. It's here that, every morning, hearty members of the Dolphin Club brave the beach's frigid waters, where temperatures usually linger in the low 50s (10°–12°C), rarely cresting 60°F (16°C). Walk out on the pier for great views, then head over to the Buena Vista Café for a well-earned refreshment (see box).

Irish Coffee Break!

Celebrate your stroll along the bay with an Irish Coffee at the venerable **Buena Vista Cafe** (2765 Hyde St. at Beach St.), a National Historic Landmark where the first Irish coffee in America was served in 1952.

3 A Wild Ride on the City's Glass Elevators

Start:	Union Square.
Finish:	Westin St. Francis Hotel.
Time:	Ninety minutes.
Best Time:	Sundays or any day at dusk.
Worst Time:	Check-in and checkout times at the hotels (9-11am and 3-4pm).
Hills That Could Kill:	California Street from Montgomery to Mason streets, but you can cheat and take the cable car.

This tour takes you up, down, and around Downtown and Union Square as you hunt out the most exciting of the city's glass elevators within San Francisco's skyscraper hotels. Like Jimmy Stewart in the Hitchcock film *Vertigo*, your sphincter factor might go to 11 as you race skyward at 1,000 feet per minute on a Willy Wonka–style tour of San Francisco. Best of all, these thrill rides are open 24/7 and are totally free.

From Union Square, walk east on Post Street toward Market Street. At Kearny Street, turn right and walk to Market Street. Check out **Lotta's Fountain,** an important icon of the 1906 earthquake (painted gold, it's hard to miss). Continue walking toward the bay down Market Street. Turn left on Drumm Street to the:

1 Hyatt Regency Hotel

Inside the atrium lobby, look for the bank of five glass elevators. One was used in the Mel Brooks movie *High Anxiety*. There may be a line of people waiting to ride the 20 stories up to the Equinox Restaurant, which revolves and provides a fabulous 360-degree view of the city but only mediocre

ITINERARY 3: THE CHEAP THRILLS TOUR

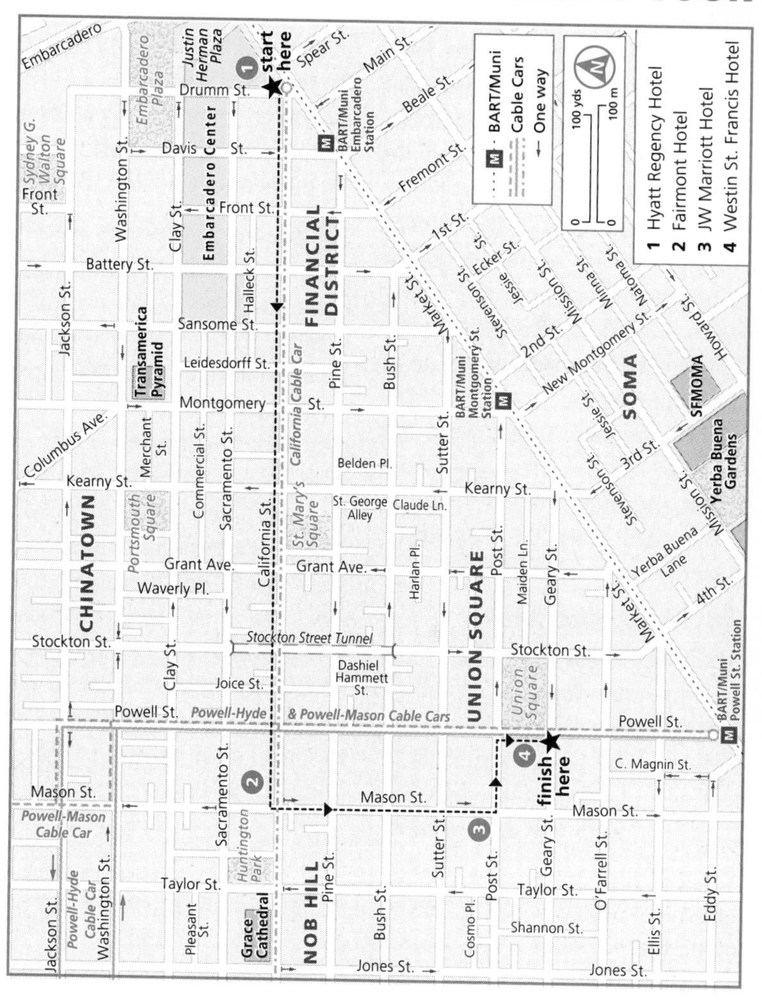

food and overpriced drinks. The mostly interior view from the elevators is grand; the lobby of the Hyatt, with its sculpture, greenery, and terraces, is a spectacular sight. When you are finished with the Hyatt, stop by the **Ferry Building** across the Embarcadero to admire the restored atrium and glass skylights. Then board a California Street cable car (½ block from the Hyatt) and get off at Mason Street, which will put you right in front of the:

2 Fairmont Hotel

You'll find the Fairmont's glass elevator at the east end of the hotel. Running at 500 feet per minute, it won't take long to ascend the 24 stories to the Fairmont Crown. You'll see Coit Tower to the left, Chinatown straight ahead, and SoMa and the South Bay to the right. Beware of wedding parties in the elevators—they can seriously cramp your view. Back on the lobby level, walk down the hall on the California Street side of the hotel and out the back to the Fairmont's garden. When you are ready to resume, cross California Street and head downhill (south) on Mason Street. At Post Street, turn right and walk into the:

3 JW Marriott Hotel

If it looks vaguely familiar, that's because its designer, John C. Portman, also designed the Hyatt Regency. The hotel's atrium is 17 stories and, again, the brass- and glass-enclosed elevator, moving at a dramatic 750 feet per minute, offers an exhilarating interior view. From the Pan Pacific, walk east 1 block to Powell Street and turn right. At the corner of Powell and Geary streets is our final stop, the:

4 Westin St. Francis Hotel

Last but definitely not least, the five outside glass elevators at the Westin St. Francis are so awesome that school groups sometimes come by on field trips. The elevators are located at the 32-story Tower Building. Push "32" and prepare for a 30-second, 1,000-foot-per-minute rush to the top—the fastest elevators in the city. The views of Downtown, Coit Tower, and the Bay Area are absolutely beautiful on a clear day. In fact, you may have to give this ride another go at night for comparison's sake.

4 Bikes, Bridges, Bay Views & Cold Beers

Start:	Hyde Street, between Beach and North Point streets near Ghirardelli Square.
Finish:	Fisherman's Wharf.
Time:	All day.
Best Time:	The earlier the better, starting at least by noon.
Worst Time:	Late afternoon—you don't want to be riding toward Tiburon in the dark.
Hills That Could Kill:	The hill from Crissy Field up to the Golden Gate Bridge.

This is one of my all-time favorite things to do on my day off—ride a bike from Fisherman's Wharf to Sam's Anchor Cafe in Tiburon (that small peninsula just north of Alcatraz Island). The beautiful and exhilarating ride takes you over the Golden Gate Bridge, through the heart of Sausalito, and along the scenic North Bay bike path, ending with a well-earned mai tai and lunch at the best outdoor cafe in the Bay Area. And here's the best part: You don't have to bike back. After lunch, you can take the passenger ferry across the bay to Fisherman's Wharf—right to your starting point. Brilliant.

1 Rent a Bicycle

Walk, take a bus, or ride the Powell–Hyde cable car (which goes right by it) to **Blazing Saddles** bicycle rental shop at 2715 Hyde St., between Beach and North Point streets near Ghirardelli Square (✆ **415/202-8888**). Rent a single or tandem bike for a full day (about $30), and be sure to ask for (1) a free map pointing out the route to Sam's in Tiburon, (2) ferry tickets, (3) a bicycle lock, and (4) a bottle of water. Bring your own sunscreen, a hat (for the deck at Sam's), and a light jacket—no matter how warm it is right now, the weather can change in minutes. Each bike has a small pouch hooked to the handlebars where you can stuff your stuff.

The Warming Hut

Start pedaling along the map route to Golden Gate Bridge. You'll encounter one short, steep hill right from the start at Aquatic Park, but it's okay to walk your bike (hey, you haven't had your coffee fix yet). Keeping riding westward through Fort Point and the Marina Green to Crissy Field. At the west end of Crissy Field, alongside the bike path, is the Warming Hut, a white, barnlike building where you can fuel up with a light snack and coffee drinks. (Don't eat too much.) Several picnic tables nearby offer beautiful views of the bay.

2 Biking the Golden Gate

After your break, there's one more steep hill up to the bridge. Follow the bike path to the west side of the bridge (pedestrians must stay on the east side), cross the bridge, and take the road to your left heading downhill and crossing underneath Highway 101. Coast all the way to Sausalito.

3 Exploring Sausalito

You'll love Sausalito. Coasting your bike onto Bridgeway is like being transported to one of those seaside towns on the French

ITINERARY 4: BIKING FROM THE CITY TO SAM'S

Bloody Mary Time!

If you're thirsty, ask for a table on the bayside deck at Horizons (558 Bridgeway; ✆ 415/331-3232) and order a Bloody Mary, but don't eat yet.

Riviera. Lock the bikes and mosey around on foot for a while.

4 North Bay Tour

Back on the bike, head north again on the bike path as it winds along the bay. When you reach the Mill Valley Car Wash at the end of the bike path, turn right onto East Blithedale Avenue, which will cross Highway 101 and turn into Tiburon Boulevard. (This is the only sucky part of the ride where you'll encounter traffic.) About a mile past Highway 101, you'll enter a small park called Blackie's Pasture. (Look for the life-size bronze statue erected in 1995 to honor Tiburon's

Lunch at Sam's Anchor Cafe

Ride your bike all the way to the south end of Tiburon and lock it at the bike rack near the ferry dock. Walk over to the ferry loading dock and check the ferry departure schedule for "Tiburon to Pier 39/Fisherman's Wharf." Then walk over to **Sam's Anchor Cafe** (27 Main St.; ✆ **415/435-4527;**), request a table on the back patio overlooking the harbor, and relax with a cool drink—you've earned it.

beloved "mascot" Blackie.) Now it's an easy cruise on the bike path all the way to Sam's.

5 Ferry Ride Back to San Francisco

When it's time to leave, board the ferry with your bike (bike riders board first, so don't stand in line) and enjoy the ride from Tiburon to San Francisco, with a short stop at Angel Island State Park. From Pier 39 it's a short ride back to the rental shop.

A Little Irish in Your Coffee?

After all this adventuring, it's time to reenergize your body and soul with an Irish coffee at the **Buena Vista Cafe** (2765 Hyde St.; ✆ **415/474-5044,** across from the cable car turnaround), a short walk from the bike-rental shop. After libations, take the cable car back to your hotel for some rest and a shower, and then spend the rest of the evening enjoying dinner.

If this isn't one of the best days you've had on your vacation, send me this book and I'll eat it.

Here are the fast facts about getting into town, getting around town, and resources for planning your time while you're here.

9 SAN FRANCISCO BASICS FROM A TO Z

1 Getting into SF & Getting Around

Airports Two major airports serve the city—**San Francisco International Airport** (SFO; ✆ **650/821-8211;** www.flysfo.com) and **Oakland International Airport** (OAK; ✆ **510/563-3300;** www.oaklandairport.com). Most travelers use SFO, which is 14 miles south of downtown San Francisco (via Hwy. 101 or 280). Fares to either airport are usually comparable, so if a flight to SFO is sold out, there may still be available seats on flights to the lesser-known OAK, which is only a few minutes from the Coliseum BART stop (four stops from San Francisco's Financial District). Keep in mind, however, that public transportation from SFO is less expensive and far more accessible.

GETTING INTO THE CITY

Public transport is available from the San Francisco airport to downtown via **BART** (Bay Area Rapid Transit; ✆ **510/464-6000;** www.bart.gov), which runs daily from SFO to downtown San Francisco. This route avoids traffic on the way and cost substantially less—about $6 one-way—than shuttles or taxis. Just jump on a free airport shuttle bus to the International terminal, enter the BART station in the International terminal, and you're on your way. A **taxi** ride to the city center costs about $30 to $35 plus tip and usually takes about 20 to 30 minutes, depending on traffic. The taxis are located on the airport's lower level between terminals (during busy periods a uniformed taxi dispatcher will hail a cab for you). We don't recommend you start your trip on such an expensive note. Shuttle **vans** that carry up to six passengers offer door-to-door service for around $17 to most hotels and take 20 to 30 minutes; they're easy to catch at the airport, but reservations are required for your return trip from the city to the airport. Some of the most popular shuttles are **Bay Shuttle** (✆ **415/564-3400**); **Door-to-Door Airport Express** (✆ **415/775-5121**); **Lorrie's Airport Shuttle** (✆ **415/334-9000**); **Quake City Shuttle** (✆ **415/255-4899**); **Super Shuttle** (✆ **415/558-8500;** www.supershuttle.com); and **Yellow Airport Shuttle** (✆ **415/282-7433**). The **SFO Airporter** (✆ **650/246-8942;** www.sfoairporter.com) is an express bus that offers door-to-door service to most major hotels for $15; no reservations are required.

The airport offers a toll-free **hotline** (✆ **415/817-1717**) for information on ground transportation. It's available weekdays from 7:30am to 5pm local time. During operating hours, a real person answers the line and gives you a rundown of all your options for getting into the city from the airport. If you're coming into Oakland, the **Bayporter Express** (✆ **877/467-1800** in the Bay Area, or **415/467-1800** elsewhere; www.bayporter.com) is a popular Oakland Airport shuttle service that charges $26 to downtown San Francisco. You can also take the BART from Oakland's airport into San Francisco for $3.

GETTING AROUND SAN FRANCISCO

BART Bay Area Rapid Transit (BART) is essentially a commuter railway that links neighboring communities with San Francisco. There are eight stations in the city itself, but they're not terribly useful for getting around the city (take the bus—it's faster). Fares depend on the distance of the ride, but for a special excursion fare, you can ride the entire system as far as you want, in any direction you want, as long as you exit the system at the same station you entered. All tickets are dispensed from machines at the stations. Contact its website at www.bart.gov or call ✆ **510/464-6000.**

A Desire for Streetcars

San Francisco's famous cable cars aren't the only rolling blast from the past. One of Muni's Metro streetcar lines, the F-Market line, consists of several beautifully restored and beloved 1930s streetcars, from cities all across the country. The colorful, eye-catching line runs along Market Street from Castro to the Downtown district and is a quick and charming way to tour the city (that, and the streetcars make great photo ops).

Buses San Francisco Municipal Railway (Muni) buses are marked on the front, side, and back with the number of the line and the destination. Fare is $1.50. To find out which bus to take to get where you want to go, call ✆ **415/673-MUNI** (6864) (www.sfmuni.com). Route maps are usually posted at the bus-stop shelters as well. Official Muni route maps are available throughout the city at newsstands and many other stores for $2.

Cable Cars There are three cable car routes: The Powell–Hyde line begins at Powell and Market streets and ends at Victorian Park near the Maritime Museum and Aquatic Park; the Powell–Mason line also begins at Powell and Market streets, but it ends at Bay and Taylor streets near Fisherman's Wharf; and the boring California Street line starts at California and Market streets and ends at Van Ness Avenue. Fare is $5 per ride.

Muni Metro Streetcars Five of Muni's six streetcar lines, designated J, K, L, M, and N, run underground downtown and on the streets in the outer neighborhoods. The sleek rail cars make the same stops as BART (see above) along Market Street, including Embarcadero Station (in the Financial District), Montgomery and Powell streets (both near Union Square), and the Civic Center (near City Hall). Past the Civic Center, the routes branch off: The J line takes you to Mission Dolores; the K, L, and M lines run to Castro Street; and the N line parallels Golden Gate Park and extends all the way to the Embarcadero and AT&T Park. Streetcars run about every 15 minutes, more frequently

Muni Discount Passes

Muni discount passes, called **Passports,** entitle holders to unlimited rides on buses, streetcars, and cable cars. It's a good deal (and very convenient) if you plan on taking the bus to get around the city. A Passport costs $11 for 1 day, $18 for 3 days, and $24 for 7 consecutive days. Another option is buying a CityPass, which entitles you to unlimited Muni rides for 7 days, plus admission to the numerous attractions. Passports are also sold every day from 8am to midnight at the information booths in the baggage-claim areas at San Francisco International Airport. You can also buy a Passport or CityPass at the San Francisco Visitor Information Center, Powell/Market cable car booth, Holiday Inn Civic Center, and TIX Bay Area booth at Union Square, among other outlets.

during rush hours. They operate Monday through Friday from 5am to 12:15am, Saturday from 6am to approximately 12:15am, and Sunday from approximately 8am to 12:20am. The L and N lines operate 24 hours a day, 7 days a week, but late at night, regular buses trace the L and N routes, which are normally underground, from atop the city streets. Because the operation is part of Muni, the fares are the same as for buses, and passes are accepted.

Taxis This isn't New York, so don't expect a taxi to appear whenever you need one—if at all. If you're downtown during rush hour or leaving a major hotel, it won't be hard to hail a cab; just look for the lighted sign on the roof that indicates the vehicle is free. Otherwise, it's a good idea to call one of the following companies to arrange a ride; even then, there's been more than one time when the cab never came for me. What to do? Call back if your cab is late and insist on attention, but don't expect prompt results on weekends, no matter how nicely you ask. The companies are **Veteran's Cab** (© **415/552-1300**), **Luxor Cabs** (© **415/282-4141**), **De Soto Cab** (© **415/970-1300**), and **Yellow Cab** (© **415/626-2345**). Rates are approximately $2.85 for the first mile and 45¢ each fifth of a mile thereafter.

Driving Around You don't need a car to explore downtown San Francisco—in fact, driving a car in the city can be a nightmare. If you drive yourself, or rent a car, you're likely to end up stuck in traffic with lots of aggressive and frustrated drivers, pay upward of $30 a day to park, and spend a good portion of your visit looking for a parking space. The city is compact but can be very confusing with all the one-way streets, so if you're going to drive, be sure to get a map.

Remember, San Francisco is a city of hills (43, to be exact), and since you probably don't want your car to roll down one while you're not in it, there's only one sure bet: Curb your wheels. Turn the front tires toward the street when you're parked facing uphill and toward the curb when you're parked facing downhill. This is not just a good idea, it's the law in San Francisco. Know what the curb colors mean: Red means no stopping or parking; yellow means all commercial vehicles may stop for up to a half-hour; yellow-and-black means only commercial trucks during business hours; green-yellow-and-black is a taxi zone; blue is for cars with California disabled placards; green means all vehicles may stop for up to 10 minutes; white means all vehicles are limited to a 5-minute stop while the adjacent business is still open. Also keep an eye out for those sneaky street-cleaning signs.

Parking Garages Some of the reasons we urge you not to drive in the city is the maddening dearth of parking spaces, wickedly efficient parking enforcement personnel, and absurdly expensive parking lots. Yes, San Francisco does have relatively inexpensive parking lots, but there are only 10 of them; and unless you know where to go (or get lucky), you won't find them. In Chinatown, try the Portsmouth Square Garage, with an entrance on Kearny between Washington and Clay (504 spaces), or the Golden Gateway Garage, with an entrance on both Washington and Clay streets between Battery and Davis (1,095 spaces). In the Nob Hill/Union Square area, there's St. Mary's Square Garage, with entrances on Pine, Kearny, and California, bordered by Grant (828 spaces), or the Sutter-Stockton Garage, with entrances on Stockton and Bush, bordered by Grant and Sutter (1,865 spaces). Right in Union Square, try the Union Square Garage, with an entrance on Geary Street, bordered by Powell, Post, and Stockton (1,030 spaces), or the Ellis-O'Farrell Garage, with entrances on O'Farrell and Ellis, bordered by Powell and Stockton (925 spaces). If you're hanging out in SoMa or near the MOMA, we recommend the Fifth & Mission Garage, with entrances on Mission or Minna, bordering Fourth and Fifth streets (2,622 spaces), and the Moscone Center Garage, with an entrance on Third Street, between Howard and

Surfing Around SF: The Best City Sites

In one of the most tech-friendly cities in the country, it's only right that there be a whole lot of websites to make living a little easier.

- **511.org.** Type in a starting point and a destination in the Bay Area, and 511's **TripPlanner** will give you a few different itineraries, listing how long each portion of the trip will take, and what time you need to catch a bus, the Muni train, or whatever mode of transport comes next. The site also provides rideshare and traffic info, as well as a mapper for bikes, the aptly named BikeMapper.
- **Craigslist.org.** What can you not find on this site? A San Francisco Bay brainchild, Craigslist plays host to job postings, apartment listings, personals, and almost anything you can think of. For the Bay area, you can refine your search by region, from the city itself, to the East Bay to the entire peninsula.
- **Fecalface.com.** Yes, the site may be unfortunately named, but it does an amazing job of supporting contemporary artists in the San Francisco area and beyond. In addition to plenty of eye candy, visitors will find a gallery guide and calendar that lists free art shows and openings.
- **Flavorpill.com.** Flavorpill's editors comb through the week's cultural happenings so that you don't have to. Events are packaged in a nice little e-mail, an easy pill to swallow. Among the listings are art exhibits, book readings, and music festivals.

Folsom (732 spaces). Finally, two cheap garages near the Civic Center and Hayes Valley are the Civic Center Garage, with an entrance on McAllister between Polk and Larkin (840 spaces), and the Performing Arts Garage, with an entrance on Grove between Gough and Franklin (612 spaces).

Towaway Zones Nobody loves to tow cars more than San Francisco's Finest. It's big money for the city (almost 30% of all parking

- **Funcheapsf.com.** A great guide to free and dirt-cheap events in the Bay Area, the site is updated often and you can find something to do on any given day of the week, without spending a dime. You can also sign up for a weekly mailing list, which will give you 20 to 50 things to mark on your calendar.
- **Goldstar.com.** This events newsletter provides e-mail updates on music and sporting events, movies, and comedy shows, with tickets available at half-price or better. You can customize your newsletter so you receive only events you're interested in. Signing up is free.
- **Laughingsquid.com.** The site's Squid List is a curated compilation of art, cultural, and technological events taking place in the Bay Area. You can visit the site or sign up for an e-mail newsletter.
- **Myopenbar.com.** A drink can be the perfect end to a tough day, but a free one makes it even better. The San Francisco edition of this site will give you the inside scoop on where to get your booze free or cheap. While some events are 1-night-only affairs, some listings are for bars that do a weekly special, like $1 Pabst Blue Ribbons every Wednesday.
- **Yelp.com.** I can't remember how I made choices before Yelp. Search for services such as haircuts or auto repairs, find a doctor or restaurant, and read reviews by fellow city dwellers before you step out the door. When your friends aren't close by to give recommendations, it's the best substitute around.

tickets issued in the state are issued in San Francisco), and the odds are always against you if you park illegally. You'll shell out a minimum of $35 for the most minor parking violation, plus another $100 or more for towing, plus storage fees. If you park in a disabled zone, the violation alone will cost $250 to $275, not to mention the towing fees and hassle of getting the car back.

2 Visitor Resources

Events Hotline Call the **Visitor Information Center** (✆ **415/391-2000;** www.sfvisitor.org) 24 hours a day for a recorded message listing San Francisco's events and activities in five different languages.

GLBT Resources The lesbian and gay communities in the Bay Area are very well organized and have countless resources at their disposal. The ***Bay Area Reporter*** (www.ebar.com) is the best-known gay publication, with complete listings of organizations and events. It's distributed at bars, bookstores, cafes, and stores around the city.

Newspapers The city's main daily is the San Francisco *Chronicle,* distributed throughout the city and Northern California. The massive Sunday edition includes a "Datebook" section—an excellent preview of the week's upcoming events. The free weekly *San Francisco Bay Guardian* and *San Francisco Weekly,* tabloids of news and listings, are indispensable for nightlife information; they're widely distributed through street-corner kiosks and at city cafes and restaurants. Of the many free tourist-oriented publications, the most widely read are *Where San Francisco* and *San Francisco Guide.* Both handbook-size weeklies contain maps and information on current events. You can find them in most hotels, shops, and restaurants in the major tourist areas.

Visitor Information Center The San Francisco Visitor Information Center, on the lower level of Hallidie Plaza, 900 Market St., at Powell Street (✆ **415/391-2000;** www.onlyinsanfrancisco.com), is the best source of specialized information about the city. Even if you don't have a specific question, you might want to request the free Visitors Planning Guide and the San Francisco Visitors kit. The kit includes a 6-month calendar of events; a city history; shopping and dining information; and several good, clear maps; plus lodging information. The bureau highlights only its members' establishments, so if it doesn't have what you're looking for, that doesn't mean it's nonexistent.

3 Health, Safety & Local Laws & Customs

All-night Pharmacies Forgot your pills, eh? Not to worry. *Walgreens* 24-Hour Prescription Service (498 Castro St., ✆ **415/861-3136;** 3201 Divisadero St., ✆ 415/931-6415) to the rescue.

Climate Mark Twain supposedly said the coldest winter he ever spent was summer in San Francisco. It's true that July can be downright chilly, but the truth is that the city is rarely—if ever—what a New England Yankee would call cold, or what a Georgia belle would call hot. In fact, the weather is predictably unpredictable. A sunny morning can turn into a chilly afternoon, just as a thick morning fog often gives way to a gorgeous sun-drenched day (or, as I'm fond of saying, "If you don't like the weather, wait five minutes"). The standard pitch is that temperatures don't drop below 40°F (4°C) or rise above 70°F (21°C), but don't believe it. Every year there are many 80°F (27°C) days that are sworn to be the exception; there's no predicting when they might occur. In general, September and October are the warmest months, and May through September months are the driest. No matter when you visit, be sure to pack warm clothing and dress in layers.

When You've Got to Go . . .

Those weird, oval-shaped, olive-green kiosks on the sidewalks throughout San Francisco are high-tech self-cleaning public toilets. They've been placed on high-volume streets to provide relief for pedestrians. French potty-maker JCDecaux gave them to the city for free—advertising covers the cost. It costs 25¢ to enter, with no time limit, but I don't recommend using the ones in the sketchier neighborhoods such as the Mission because they're mostly used by crackheads and prostitutes. Toilets can also be found in hotel lobbies, bars, restaurants, museums, department stores, railway and bus stations, and service stations. Large hotels and fast-food restaurants are often the best bet for clean facilities. Restaurants and bars in resorts or heavily visited areas may reserve their restrooms for patrons.

Doctors If you have a serious emergency, you should go directly to a hospital emergency room, but for other medical needs, **Saint Francis Memorial Hospital,** 900 Hyde St., between Bush and Pine streets on Nob Hill (✆ **415/353-6000**), provides emergency service 24 hours a day; no appointment is necessary. The hospital also operates a **physician-referral service** (✆ **800/333-1355** or 415/353-6566). In an emergency dial 911 from any phone, including pay phones. For more information on

FREE Free 411

It's bound to happen: The day you leave this guidebook back at your crash pad for an unencumbered stroll through Pacific Heights, you'll forget the address of the great happy hour spot you had earmarked. If you're traveling with a mobile device, call © GOOG-411 (466-4411), a free voice-activated service where you say where or what you're looking for, and it will (sometimes) connect you with the business you're looking for. If you're calling from a mobile device, GOOG-411 can even send you a text message with more details and a map: Just say "text message" or "map it." Cool, eh?

You can also send a text message to © 46645 (GOOGL) for a lightning-fast response. For instance, type "sam wo san francisco" and within 10 seconds you'll receive a text message with the address and phone number. This nifty trick works in a range of search categories: Look up weather ("weather philadelphia"), language translations ("translate goodbye in spanish"), currency conversions ("10 usd in pounds"), movie times ("harry potter 60605"), and more.

lower-cost medical care, see chapter 6, "Free & Dirt-Cheap Living."

Emergencies Like anywhere else, call **911,** but don't be surprised if you get put on hold. Other emergency/information numbers: Ambulance (© 415/931-3900); Poison Control Center (© 800/876-4766); and Suicide Prevention (© 415/781-0500).

Liquor Laws Packaged alcoholic beverages are sold at liquor, grocery, and some drugstores 6am to 2am daily. Most bars and restaurants are licensed to sell all alcoholic beverages during those same hours, but some have only beer-and-wine licenses. No alcohol may be sold from 2am to 6am. Legal drinking age is 21; proof of age is required.

Phone Facts The area code for San Francisco is **415.** As is the case with most big metropolitan areas, though, the number of area codes in San Francisco is expanding with the population and use of the Internet and other digital services. For now, dial 1-510 before numbers in Berkeley, Oakland, Richmond, and most of Alameda County; dial 1-925 for numbers in Walnut Creek, Concord, and most of Contra Costa County; dial 1-650 for numbers on the Peninsula; and dial 1-408 for numbers in San Jose and

Santa Cruz. When in doubt, dial the operator. Local calls are free on private phones, 50¢ in a pay phone. For directory assistance, dial 411.

Safety San Francisco, like any other large city, has its fair share of crime, but most folks don't have firsthand horror stories. In some areas, you need to exercise extra caution, particularly at night—notably the Tenderloin, the Western Addition (south of Japantown), the Mission District (especially around 16th and Mission sts.), the lower Fillmore area (also south of Japantown), around lower Haight Street, and around the Civic Center. In addition, there are a substantial number of homeless people throughout the city with concentrations in and around Union Square, the Theater District (3 blocks west of Union Sq.), the Tenderloin, and Haight Street, so don't be alarmed if you're approached for spare change. Basically, just use common sense. For additional crime-prevention information, phone **San Francisco SAFE** (✆ **415/553-1984**).

Smoking Laws If San Francisco is California's most European city in looks and style, the comparison stops when it comes to smoking in public. Each year, smoking laws become stricter. Since 1998, smoking has been prohibited in restaurants and bars. Although there have been arguments against it, so far the law has been enforced in most establishments. Hotels are also offering more nonsmoking rooms, which often leaves those who like to puff out in the cold—sometimes literally.

Free Earthquake Advice

Earthquakes are fairly common in California, though most are so minor you won't even notice them. However, in case of a significant shaker, there are a few basic precautionary measures to follow: If you are inside a building, do not run outside into falling debris. Seek cover—stand under a doorway or against a wall, and stay away from windows. If you exit a building after a substantial quake, use stairwells, not elevators. If you're in a car, pull over to the side of the road and stop—but not until you are away from bridges, overpasses, telephone poles, and power lines. Stay in your car. If you're out walking, stay outside and away from trees, power lines, and the sides of buildings. If you're in an area with tall buildings, find a doorway in which to stand. And if you're having cocktails find a straw.

Where to Surf (the 'net) in SF

San Francisco is totally wired. You'll find that many cafes have wireless access, as do many hotels. Check **www.wi-fihotspotlist.com**, **www.cybercaptive.com**, and **www.cybercafe.com** for a huge list of Wi-Fi hotspots, both free and those which require payment—including every Starbucks, Kinko's, or McDonald's—or stop by one of the following joints around town where you can get online access, perhaps with a sandwich and a cup o' joe.

You can do your laundry, listen to music, dine, and check your stocks online at SoMa's **Brainwash,** 1122 Folsom St., between Seventh and Eighth streets (**415/861-FOOD;** www.brainwash.com). It's open Monday through Thursday from 7am to 11pm, Friday and Saturday from 7am to midnight, and Sunday from 8am to 11pm; rates are $3 for 20 minutes.

You can't wash your clothes at **Quetzal,** 1234 Polk St., at Bush Street (**415/673-4181**), but you can get a coffee and a nosh while you're online for 16 cents a minute. They're open Monday through Saturday from 6:45am to 9pm and Sunday from 7:30am to 8pm.

For access without the ambience, try **Copy Central,** 110 Sutter St., at Montgomery Street (**415/392-6470;** www.copycentral.com), which provides access cards costing 20 cents per minute. It's open Monday through Thursday from 8am to 8pm and Friday from 8am to 7pm.

Tipping Gratuities are not included in restaurant or bar checks. Most guides suggest 15% of the total amount as a decent tip, but 20% has become more commonly accepted at restaurants. Taxi drivers should be tipped around 15%; skycaps and bellpersons should get at least $1 per bag each time they carry it.

Weather For weather information, call or surf to the National Weather Service (© **831/656-1725;** www.nws.noaa.gov).

INDEX

General Index

Accommodations

ROMMER'S® COMPLETE TRAVEL GUIDES

laska
malfi Coast
merican Southwest
msterdam
rgentina
rizona
tlanta
ustralia
ustria
ahamas
arcelona
eijing
elgium, Holland & Luxembourg
elize
ermuda
oston
razil
ritish Columbia & the Canadian Rockies
russels & Bruges
udapest & the Best of Hungary
uenos Aires
algary
alifornia
anada
ancún, Cozumel & the Yucatán
ape Cod, Nantucket & Martha's Vineyard
aribbean
aribbean Ports of Call
arolinas & Georgia
hicago
hile & Easter Island
hina
olorado
osta Rica
roatia
uba
enmark
enver, Boulder & Colorado Springs
astern Europe
cuador & the Galapagos Islands
dinburgh & Glasgow
ngland
urope
urope by Rail
Florence, Tuscany & Umbria
Florida
France
Germany
Greece
Greek Islands
Guatemala
Hawaii
Hong Kong
Honolulu, Waikiki & Oahu
India
Ireland
Israel
Italy
Jamaica
Japan
Kauai
Las Vegas
London
Los Angeles
Los Cabos & Baja
Madrid
Maine Coast
Maryland & Delaware
Maui
Mexico
Montana & Wyoming
Montréal & Québec City
Morocco
Moscow & St. Petersburg
Munich & the Bavarian Alps
Nashville & Memphis
New England
Newfoundland & Labrador
New Mexico
New Orleans
New York City
New York State
New Zealand
Northern Italy
Norway
Nova Scotia, New Brunswick & Prince Edward Island
Oregon
Paris
Peru
Philadelphia & the Amish Country
Portugal
Prague & the Best of the Czech Republic
Provence & the Riviera
Puerto Rico
Rome
San Antonio & Austin
San Diego
San Francisco
Santa Fe, Taos & Albuquerque
Scandinavia
Scotland
Seattle
Seville, Granada & the Best of Andalusia
Shanghai
Sicily
Singapore & Malaysia
South Africa
South America
South Florida
South Korea
South Pacific
Southeast Asia
Spain
Sweden
Switzerland
Tahiti & French Polynesia
Texas
Thailand
Tokyo
Toronto
Turkey
USA
Utah
Vancouver & Victoria
Vermont, New Hampshire & Maine
Vienna & the Danube Valley
Vietnam
Virgin Islands
Virginia
Walt Disney World® & Orlando
Washington, D.C.
Washington State

ROMMER'S® DAY BY DAY GUIDES

msterdam
arcelona
eijing
oston
ancun & the Yucatan
hicago
lorence & Tuscany
Hong Kong
Honolulu & Oahu
London
Maui
Montréal
Napa & Sonoma
New York City
Paris
Provence & the Riviera
Rome
San Francisco
Venice
Washington D.C.

AULINE FROMMER'S GUIDES: SEE MORE. SPEND LESS.

laska
awaii
aly
Las Vegas
London
New York City
Paris
Walt Disney World®
Washington D.C.

Frommer's® Portable Guides

Acapulco, Ixtapa & Zihuatanejo
Amsterdam
Aruba, Bonaire & Curacao
Australia's Great Barrier Reef
Bahamas
Big Island of Hawaii
Boston
California Wine Country
Cancún
Cayman Islands
Charleston
Chicago
Dominican Republic
Florence
Las Vegas
Las Vegas for Non-Gamblers
London
Maui
Nantucket & Martha's Vineyard
New Orleans
New York City
Paris
Portland
Puerto Rico
Puerto Vallarta, Manzanillo & Guadalajara
Rio de Janeiro
San Diego
San Francisco
Savannah
St. Martin, Sint Maarten, Anguila & St. Bart's
Turks & Caicos
Vancouver
Venice
Virgin Islands
Washington, D.C.
Whistler

Frommer's® Cruise Guides

Alaska Cruises & Ports of Call
Cruises & Ports of Call
European Cruises & Ports of Call

Frommer's® National Park Guides

Algonquin Provincial Park
Banff & Jasper
Grand Canyon
National Parks of the American West
Rocky Mountain
Yellowstone & Grand Teton
Yosemite and Sequoia & Kings Canyon
Zion & Bryce Canyon

Frommer's® With Kids Guides

Chicago
Hawaii
Las Vegas
London
National Parks
New York City
San Francisco
Toronto
Walt Disney World® & Orlando
Washington, D.C.

Frommer's® PhraseFinder Dictionary Guides

Chinese
French
German
Italian
Japanese
Spanish

Suzy Gershman's Born to Shop Guides

France
Hong Kong, Shanghai & Beijing
Italy
London
New York
Paris
San Francisco
Where to Buy the Best of Everything

Frommer's® Best-Loved Driving Tours

Britain
California
France
Germany
Ireland
Italy
New England
Northern Italy
Scotland
Spain
Tuscany & Umbria

The Unofficial Guides®

Adventure Travel in Alaska
Beyond Disney
California with Kids
Central Italy
Chicago
Cruises
Disneyland®
England
Hawaii
Ireland
Las Vegas
London
Maui
Mexico's Best Beach Resorts
Mini Mickey
New Orleans
New York City
Paris
San Francisco
South Florida including Miami & the Keys
Walt Disney World®
Walt Disney World® for Grown-ups
Walt Disney World® with Kids
Washington, D.C.

Special-Interest Titles

Athens Past & Present
Best Places to Raise Your Family
Cities Ranked & Rated
500 Places to Take Your Kids Before They Grow Up
Frommer's Best Day Trips from London
Frommer's Best RV & Tent Campgrounds in the U.S.A.
Frommer's Exploring America by RV
Frommer's NYC Free & Dirt Cheap
Frommer's Road Atlas Europe
Frommer's Road Atlas Ireland
Retirement Places Rated